AF564463

HISTORY OF ISLAMIC CIVILIZATION

HISTORY OF ISLAMIC CIVILIZATION

By

Ehsan Qureshi

2008

CYBER TECH PUBLICATIONS
4264/3, Ansari Road, Daryaganj, New Delhi-110002 (India)
Ph.: 011-23244078. Fax: 011-23280028
E-Mail: cyberpublicationsdelhi@yahoo.com

HISTORY OF ISLAMIC CIVILIZATION

Ehsan Qureshi

First Edition 2008

Published by :

G.S. Rawat for **Cyber Tech Publications**
4264/3, Ansari Road, Daryaganj, New Delhi-110002 (India)
Ph.: 011-23244078. Fax: 011-23280028
E-Mail: cyberpublicationsdelhi@yahoo.com

Printed at : **Amit Enterprises**, Maujpur, Delhi, (9810878184)

Preface

The external history of a religious tradition often seems divorced from the raison d'etre of faith. The spiritual quest is an interior journey; it is a psychic rather than a political drama. It is preoccupied with liturgy, doctrine, contemplative disciplines and an exploration of the heart, not with the clash of current events. Religions certainly have a life outside the soul. Their leaders have to contend with the state and affairs of the world, and often relish doing so. They fight with members of other faiths, who seem to challenge their claim to a monopoly of absolute truth; they also persecute their co-religionists for interpreting a tradition differently or for holding heterodox beliefs. Very often priests, rabbis, imams, and shamans are just as consumed by worldly ambition as regular politicians. But all this is generally seen as an abuse of a sacred ideal. These power struggles are not what religion is really about, but an unworthy distraction from the life of the spirit, which is conducted far from the madding crowd, unseen, silent, and unobtrusive. Indeed, in many faiths, monks and mystics lock themselves away from the world, since the clamour and strife of history is regarded as incompatible with a truly religious life.

Perhaps the central paradox of the religious life is that it seeks transcendence, a dimension of existence that goes beyond our mundane lives, but that human beings can only experience this transcendent reality in earthly, physical phenomena. People have sensed the divine in rocks, mountains, temple buildings, law codes, written texts, or in other men and women. We never experience transcendence directly: our ecstasy is always "earthed," enshrined in something or someone here below. Religious people are trained to look beneath the unpromising surface to find the sacred within it. They have to use their creative imaginations. Jean-Paul Sartre defined the imagination as the ability to think of what is not present. Human beings are religious creatures because they are imaginative; they are so constituted that they are compelled to search for hidden meaning and to achieve an ecstasy that makes them feel fully alive. Each tradition encourages the faithful to focus their attention on an earthly symbol that is peculiarly its own, and to teach themselves to see the divine in it.

In Islam, Muslims have looked for God in history. Their sacred scripture, the Quran, gave them a historical mission. Their chief duty was to create a just community in which all members, even the most weak and vulnerable, were treated with absolute respect. The experience of building such a society and living in it would give them intimations of the divine, because they would be living in accordance with God's will. A Muslim had to redeem history, and that meant that state affairs were not a distraction from spirituality but the stuff of religion itself. The political well-being of the Muslim community was a matter of supreme importance. Like any religious ideal, it was almost impossibly difficult to implement in the flawed and tragic conditions of history, but after each failure Muslims had to get up and begin again.

The sole purpose of bringing out this book is to make readers know about the evolution and growth of Islam.

—Author

Contents

Islam—The Straight Path

ORIGIN OF ISLAM BY MOHAMMAD (PBUH)

> *In the Name of God, the Merciful, the Compassionate Praise belongs to God, the Lord of all Being, the All-merciful, the All-compassionate, the Master of the Day of Doom. Thee only we serve; to Thee alone we pray for succour. Guide us in the straight path, the path of those whom Thou hast blessed, not of those against whom Thou art wrathful, nor of those who are astray. (The first Surah of the Quran, Arberry translation)*

The straight path of Islam requires submission to the will of God as revealed in the Quran, and recognition of Muhammad as the Messenger of God who in his daily life interpreted and exemplified that divine revelation which was given through him. The believer who follows that straight path is a Muslim.

The word *Islam* literally means "peaceful submission to the will of God—without resistance." This complete submission presupposes as an acceptable minimum a firm belief in the truth and justice of all that God has revealed in human history. In the Quran it is made clear that from most ancient times the word *Islam* has been used by all divine messengers and their followers as the name for their religion. Islam is thus the generic term applicable to every revealed religion so long as that religion is not altered by men. The Quran assures us of the intimate relation of its revelation to the previous revelations:

> *"God has ordained for you that religion which He has already commanded to Noah, Abraham, Moses, and Jesus" (Surah XLII, 13).*

Thus it is that Noah declared, "I was commanded to be among the Muslims" (Surah X, 73).

Abraham and Ishmael, (Quran), when they were constructing the Kaaba as a place of worship at Mecca, addressed God in these words: "Our Lord! Make us Muslims unto Thee and of our seed a nation of Muslims unto Thee" (Surah II, 128).

Jacob gave his sons this counsel: "... and die only as good Muslims" (Surah II, 132).

His sons reassured him with their reply, "We do worship thy Lord, the unique God, the God of thy fathers Abraham, Ishmael, Noah, and Isaac, and we are good Muslims" (Surah II, 133).

When Moses was instructing his people, he said, "Trust yourselves to God if you are true Muslims" (Surah X, 85).

The disciples of Jesus avowed, "We have believed and you can be witness that we are Muslims" (Surah V, 111).

The Quran makes it clear that Islam is the only religion acceptable to God when it says, "Lo! religion with God is Islam" (Surah III, 19).

That is, religion is submission to God's will and guidance. Again the Quran says, "And who seeketh as religion other than Islam, it will not be accepted from him" (Surah III, 85).

Thus there has been but one true religion on earth, the religion of God, to which believing men have belonged at all times and places. Each of the holy messengers of God who has taken part in revealing the nature of the religion of God has been a stone in the building of that edifice. For the Quran this unity of believing humanity is not only a fact, it is above all an essential part of religious belief.

The prophets are required to show mutual recognition and acknowledgment of each other. The believers must accept and respect all revealed books and all messengers of God without distinction between them. To show preference among the revelations of God is to be guilty of a mortal sin which destroys the very basis of our belief. "Those who wish to separate God from his envoys, those who say we believe in some and do not believe in others, those are all the true infidels, and we have prepared for the infidels a terrible torture" (Surah IV, 150-51).

Showing preference among the revelations of God is infidelity because it makes our own desire, our own passion and fanaticism, a criterion and principle of belief; because it resists the will of God which has been authenticated by the divine signs which appear with each one of His messengers.

The fundamental mission of the messengers of God has been to teach true belief about the one God and to establish justice among men. The unity of this belief springs from the one God and creates a union of the prophets and of their followers, who together form a unique spiritual nation, Islam. Thus, after enumerating the prophets from Noah to Jesus, the Quran says, "Here is your nation, one and united, and I am your Lord. Worship me, then" (Surah XXI, 92).

The belief in the divine revelation and in the spiritual peace which comes from submission to God is expressed in daily life by obeying His commandments and avoiding that which is forbidden. A humble obedience to the divine commandments is a second essential part of Islam, completing the act of faith—which is belief in God's revelation—by obeying God's commandments in practical affairs. For example, in our personal life we are commanded in the Quran to act with righteousness, to be straightforward in speech, to control our passions, and to purify our souls. In family life, we are commanded to treat women kindly, with full regard for their rights, and to be generous in our dealings with them.

In social life, God commands that all cases shall be judged with equity; justice and charity are required; no injustices shall be done to people because of hatred toward them; all life is made sacred by God and may not be ended except through justice. In spiritual life, the Muslims must have always present in their minds the idea of God and must never despair of the forgiveness of the Lord; it is in God that believers must put their trust.

"The Muslim," said Muhammad(Pbuh), "is he who spares others all his bad words and evil deeds." Thus, Islam is external peace and internal peace, peace with God and peace with all creatures, the peace which comes through submission to God. It is noteworthy, however, that historically speaking the meaning of the term *Islam* has undergone a continuous and gradual evolution in the successive divine revelations. Each new book and each new prophet constitutes a new element to be added to our creed. The most complete revelation has naturally been reserved for the latest revelation which summarizes and confirms all the others. It is thus justified to consider those who accept the last revelation as the Muslims. It is in that spirit that Quran calls them not only Muslims, but *the* Muslims.

God's latest revelation is given in the Quran; therefore, it is necessary to know the Quran in order to follow the straight path of Islam. The message of the Quran, however, is better understood by those who know the Prophet Muhammad who was the Messenger of God, the interpreter of the Quran and its living example.

MUHAMMAD (PBUH)

Muhammad(Pbuh), the son of an illustrious Arab family known for its religious accomplishments and political activities, was born in Mecca on Monday, the ninth of the month Rabi Awwal (April 20, AD 571), in the fifty-third year before the beginning of the Muslim Era. His father died before the child was born. When Muhammad lost his mother in his sixth year he was taken into the house of his grandfathers who foresaw for him a splendid future. The grandfather died two years later, leaving him to be cared for and educated by his uncle Abu Talib who had always shown a fatherly interest in him. The affectionate bond between the young lad and his uncle was so strong that he often travelled with him on caravan journeys. Tradition says that when he was twelve he accompanied his uncle on a commercial journey to Syria, where they met a Syrian monk called Bahira who recognized in the young man the characteristics of a prophet. He advised the uncle to take good care of Muhammad always, and to mistrust especially the Jews who might wish him ill if ever they learned of the prophetic mission he would be called to fulfill.

Muhammad spent his youth in humble circumstances, much of the time working as a shepherd. As he later pointed out, herding sheep was also the occupation of many other prophets, Moses and David in particular. As a young man he distinguished himself by his refined manners, his extreme shyness, his absolute chastity, and his avoidance of the easy pleasures pursued by other young men of his community. All those who knew him showed complete confidence in him for he fully deserved the name by which he was called, al-Amin, which means the true and reliable one. When he was only twenty years old he was called to sit with the most venerable shaikhs of the Fudul league, an association which cared for the weak and helpless and sought to assure peace between the tribes.

At the age of twenty-five he married the rich and virtuous Khadijah, and in his married life he revealed to his family and the community his excellent human qualities. The trade which he carried on with his wife's funds kept them in comfortable circumstances, but he used his resources only as a means of spreading happiness. For instance, in order to repay his uncle for having taken care of him in his youth, he took responsibility for the education of Abu Talib's son, Ali.

Muhammad remained a faithful, loving husband during the quarter-century of his marriage to Khadijah, and after her death he was so fond of recalling the sweet memories of their married life that he caused not a little naive jealousy in his second marriage. He was an excellent father and grandfather, showing an ideal tenderness toward his children and grandchildren. He allowed them to hang on his neck or to mount on his back, even while he was praying; he interrupted his speeches in order to greet them and made them sit with him on his chair. Some Bedouins, seeing him kiss one of his grandchildren, said, "You kiss the children? We never do that." To which the Prophet replied, "What can I do if God has deprived your hearts of all human feeling? God does not grant His mercy to those who are not merciful." (al-Bukhari, *Al Adab,* Chapter 18).

His most famous action between the time of his marriage and his prophetic calling came when he was thirty-five years old. The sacred shrine in Mecca, the Kaaba, was being rebuilt, and when the time came to place the Black Stone (the revered angular stone of the traditional monument), there was a furious competition among the Arab tribes for the honour of lifting it into position. The controversy was about to break out into a fight, with swords drawn, when Muhammad(Pbuh) was seen to enter. The crowd started shouting, "al-Amin, al-Amin!" and all submitted to the arbitration of the true and reliable one.

With his remarkable presence of mind and the impartiality which he always showed, Muhammad spread his coat on the ground, put the Black Stone on it, and asked the chiefs of the principal tribes to grasp the edges of the coat and together lift the stone to the required height. Then he took the stone and placed it with his own hands, thus resolving the dispute and restoring harmony among the tribes.

By this time Muhammad was physically, intellectually, and morally a mature person, endowed with those characteristics which made him a leader throughout the rest of his life. His figure was taller than average, solidly built, with a large chest and shoulders. He had a noble and always serene countenance, a large mouth with white, slightly separated teeth, black eyes set in a somewhat bloodshot background, a white, rosy skin, and black, wavy hair falling just below his ears. His walk was lively yet dignified. He wore simple clothes which were always clean and well-groomed.

He was very sober and normally restrained; he talked little, but always agreeably and with good humor. His sweet temperament and extreme delicacy would never allow him to force the pace of a conversation with anyone, nor would he ever show a desire to finish a discussion. He never withdrew his hand first from a handshake. While he was inflexible and impartial in applying justice to others, he was indulgent and yielding when his personal rights were involved.

When he later became sole master of the state he was not tempted by earthly wealth but remained as simple and frugal as he had always been, deliberately avoiding all luxury and pomp for his family as well as for himself. After his death his few possessions were not inherited by his relatives but were distributed among the poor. In his fortieth year he approached the decisive event which wrought a complete change in his life and in the history of mankind.

The first sign of his prophetic vocation, according to his own words, was the discovery that everything which he dreamed happened in his waking hours precisely as he had foreseen it. After a time he felt a strong inclination to seek solitude and withdrew to Mount Hira, or the Mount of Light, north of Mecca. This was a spiritual withdrawal, broken only occasionally by visits to the town for food. Muhammad(Pbuh) received his first revelation on the seventeenth day of Ramadan (February, AD 610) in the thirteenth year before the beginning of the Muslim Era. This revelation took the form of a discussion between teacher and pupil, between the Archangel Gabriel and Muhammad.

"Read!" commanded Gabriel. "I am not of those who know how to read," replied Muhammad. "Read!" Gabriel repeated. "What shall I read?" asked the astonished pupil. "Read!" insisted Gabriel. "But how shall I read?" asked the solitary hermit. The Archangel then recited the first five verses of Surah XCVI:

> *Read: In the name of thy Lord who createth, Createth man from a clot.*
>
> *Read: And thy Lord is the most Bounteous, Who teacheth by the pen,*
>
> Teacheth man that which he knew not.

This is the first fragment of the Quran. The Angel then disappeared and Muhammad, completely overcome, was starting to leave the grotto when he heard a voice calling to him. He lifted up his head and saw the Angel filling all the horizon in its immensity, and heard the Angel tell him, "O Muhammad: Really, you are the messenger of God, and I am Gabriel." After that, Muhammad saw nothing else.

When he reached home he told Khadijah of these happenings and expressed his fears. His devoted wife reassured him with wise and consoling words, "No," she said, "do not worry. God would surely not do you any harm, nor heap shame upon you, for you have never done harm. You always speak the truth, you help the feeble, you always assist those who suffer for a just cause." To comfort him further she accompanied him on a visit to her cousin, Waraqa Ibn Nawfal, who said to him, "This is good news which should fill you with rejoicing. I declare that you are the prophet announced by Jesus. Oh, that I could live until your countrymen will chase you, Muhammad, from your country." "How is it," cried Muhammad, "that they will chase me from here?" "Of course," replied Waraqa, "never has a man brought his fellow-men what you brought with you without becoming the object of persecution and hostility."

Muhammad(Pbuh) often returned to the grotto where he had received his first message to seek another revelation. He placed himself in the same condition, he walked the mountains, he turned his eyes in all directions. Days passed, weeks went by, month followed month, one year was gone, another began, and according to the account of al-Chabi even a third year came without another revelation. His only comfort was that each time when he felt himself on the brink of despair he heard, "O Muhammad, you are the messenger of God, and I am Gabriel," but without hearing the message he so ardently expected.

By this time Muhammad was forty-three years old. He continued to wake up almost every night in the hope of hearing this "heavy and grave" promised word. Each year he withdrew to Mount Hira in the month of Ramadan. Finally one day, when he had finished his retreat and was descending to the town, he heard someone calling him. He looked around, to the right, to the left, and behind him, but saw no one. Then he lifted his eyes toward heaven and recognized the Angel whom he had seen at Mount Hira. The suddenness of the apparition, the majestic immensity of the heavenly being, struck him so strongly that he could not remain standing. The sublime visitor then gave him the decree which invested him with his second responsibility: "Oh you, who cover yourself carefully, get up, and spread your announcement" (Surah LXXIV, 1-2).

Thus Muhammad must not only receive his divine knowledge, he must also transmit it to the people. To his role of Prophet was added that of Apostle. After this second message, the revelations succeeded each other without the long interruption which came between the first and second.

Muhammad's career as the Messenger of Islam lasted for twenty years, with ten years in Mecca before the Hijrah (the move from Mecca to Medina in AD 622, which is the starting date for the Muslim Era) and ten years at Medina before his death.

He began his preaching in Mecca by discreetly speaking only in his most intimate circles. Abu Bakr was the first man to be converted to Islam and Khadijah the first woman; All was the first young man. The first foreigners were Zaid Ibn Haritha, the Yemenite; Bilal Ibn Rabah, the Abyssinian; and Sohaib Ibn

Sinan, the Roman. Islam spread slowly in Mecca, privately at first, and then, in the tenth year before the Hijrah the calling to Islam became public. At first it was kind and courteous and evoked no animosity among the unbelieving. But when the message became reproachful of paganism the Arabs rose in opposition and showed their hatred.

The opposition of the Arabs was at first directed mainly toward the Prophet. It was relatively mild toward those of his believers who had a distinguished family or tribal position, but tended to be cruel toward the humble and the powerless. Therefore, in the middle of the ninth year before the Hijrah the Prophet allowed eleven men and four women to seek refuge with the King of Abyssinia, who received them well and was himself converted to Islam. By the beginning of the eighth year before the Hijrah there were scarcely forty men and about ten women who were Muslims in Mecca, and they met in secret. The conversion of such important people as Hamzah and Umar in this year gave such strong support and encouragement to the followers that they were able to say their prayers openly near the Kaaba, and the new religion began to spread more rapidly.

This new growth of Islam aroused the unbelieving to redouble their violence and persecutions and in the seventh year before the Hijrah a second contingent of refugees, eighty-three men and eighteen women, emigrated to Abyssinia. The Prophet himself became the target of a conspiracy but was protected by the two family branches most closely related to him, the Bani Hashim and the Bani al-Muttalib, who rallied around him in the Hashimid quarter. The other branches and tribes thereupon banded together in opposition and took a written oath to boycott the protecting quarters until Muhammad was handed over to them. They maintained their severe boycott for three years, abandoning it in the fourth year before the Hijrah.

The ending of the boycott would have been a great relief to the Prophet if it had not been that just at this time he suffered two cruel losses: the death of his uncle Abu Talib and shortly afterward the death of his wife Khadijah. The Prophet calls this year "the year of suffering." Having become a widower without the consoling intimacy of a wife, he married Sawdah, a courageous believer whose suffering during the persecution and emigration had just been crowned by the loss of her husband after their return from Abyssinia. Accordingly, this marriage must be considered more a compensation for her than for him.

When Muhammad lost the support which his uncle afforded him in Mecca, he left the town to look elsewhere for allies and adherents. He spent ten unsuccessful days with the tribe of Thaqif, at at-Ta'if, but he was received badly and returned disappointed to Mecca to devote his proselytizing efforts to the pilgrims' encampment at the Kaaba. Toward the end of the third year before the Hijrah he saw a faint hope in six men from Medina. These good men, who had heard the message of the Prophet during a brief encounter at Mina, responded enthusiastically to his appeal and carried the holy message to Medina where they made many converts.

Toward the end of the following year, the second before the Hijrah, five of those men from Medina with seven new converts visited the Prophet and took an oath to abstain from any polytheistic cult, from all vices, and to observe strict discipline. A year later, seventy-five men from Medina came to swear allegiance, confess their faith, and declare their submission. They also promised to defend the Prophet and their Muslim brothers if they should choose Medina as their refuge. This represents the first defense treaty in Islamic history.

Immediately after receiving this promise from the men of Medina the Prophet authorized and even obliged those men among his followers who had sufficient means to settle in Medina with their new brothers. Those who insisted upon remaining in Mecca without valid reason were to be regarded as hypocrites. But the Prophet himself did not hasten to leave his post and join the community of his faithful followers. He awaited an express authorization by revelation, an authorization which came after three months, on the day before the unfaithful had planned to carry out a plot against him.

Before the Hijrah, when Muhammad joined his followers in Medina, the Muslims did not form a nation or even a community; they did not even have a majority in Mecca. In Mecca they occupied no post of authority. They could not make a solemn call to prayer or come together for a public gathering. In Medina, however, Muslims could settle openly and Islam could develop. Communal prayer was observed solemnly even before the arrival of the Prophet. The day after his arrival in Medina the Prophet assumed full authority, started forming the state, and began the building of the great mosque.

Muhammad's authority in Medina was of an entirely new and original kind: it was at the same time absolute and consultative, theocratic and socialist. It was religious and absolute in its framework, based on revealed commandments and general rules, but socialistic and consultative in the details and the application of the rules.

The Muslim state which the Prophet created in Medina remains the model of every Muslim state worthy of the name. It is unique in human history, for although this Muslim state was fundamentally religious, it established two principles which are not found elsewhere except in a nonreligious state or in a religion which has no state government associated with it. The first is the principle of freedom of religion, a freedom which the Muslim state not only admits and authorizes but must even defend and guarantee. The second is the principle which defines the idea of fatherland or nation in the most tolerant and human sense, a principle which guarantees equality of rights and national duties for those of all races, colours, languages, and ideologies existing in the country.

The first year and a half after the Hijrah were entirely devoted to purely pacific and constructive activities, to the development of religious and social institutions such as fasting, almsgiving, fraternization of the immigrants with the original inhabitants, agreements between tribes, and the like. Thus far nothing suggested the use of force. It was only because they wanted to be indemnified for the loss of their houses and worldly goods, which had been left behind in the hands of their enemies in Mecca, and because they wanted to put an end to the persecution and violence which the enemies were inflicting upon their brethren in Mecca that the Muslims tried several times, unsuccessfully, to intercept enemy caravans passing near Medina. In Ramadan of the second year after the Hijrah the pagans reacted to these fruitless attempts to intercept the caravans by declaring an offensive against Medina. The Muslims thereupon sought to defend themselves, in a rather improvised manner, and although inferior in numbers and weapons they obtained a decisive victory. In the month of Shawwal in the third year the Meccans took their revenge, and for the next few years actions and counteractions followed until in the sixth year a ten-year truce was concluded. This truce was very favourable for the growth of Islam. Not only did it spread among the Arabs of the Hijaz—the western side of the Arabian peninsula—who were in frequent contact with the Muslims, but during this time the Prophet sent his messages and messengers to the Roman Emperor Heraclios, and to the kings and princes in Persia, Egypt, Bahrein, and Yemen.

In the year A.H. 8 the Meccans broke the truce, and this time the Prophet marched victoriously into the capital. The indulgent and merciful character of the Prophet, which he had always shown, was clear to all the people of Mecca after this conquest when, without repressive action or loss of life, he generously pardoned all his former persecutors. The conversion and submission of the whole Arab peninsula came soon after the conquest of Mecca, but in the northern part of the peninsula the Romans (Byzantines) prepared themselves for a strong attack against the young religion. In A.H. 9 the Prophet himself led an expedition as far as Tabouk (halfway between Medina and Damascus) which made the Romans renounce their enterprise. When the Prophet returned to Medina he had concluded non-aggression treaties with the neighbouring countries to the north.

It was also in the ninth year of the Hijrah that the Prophet ordered Abu Bakr, his closest disciple, to lead the pilgrims to Mecca and to proclaim that the approach to the Kaaba from that time onward was to be forbidden to all pagans and polytheists.

In the tenth year after the Hijrah the pilgrimage to Mecca was led by the Prophet himself. This is known as the "farewell pilgrimage," during which the Prophet received the divine message that his mission was fulfilled and foresaw that the end of his life was near. "This day have I perfected your religion for you and completed My favour unto you, and have approved for you as religion AL-ISLAM" (Surah V, 3).

Those who heard his sermon on Arafa day in the tenth year recognized that they were hearing his last will and testament. With great emphasis he reminded all human beings of their brotherly love, their common origin, their equality without distinction except by means of virtue. With clear authority he commanded respect for the person, the family, and for property. With kindly compassion he recommended gentleness toward women. With great vision he enjoined his listeners to retain and transmit his message to all those who have not heard it, for, he said, "Who knows? Maybe I shall not see you again after this year." Finally, addressing himself to the pilgrims who had come from all the surroundings countries in such numbers that they reached the horizon and spread over all the desert, he said, "God will ask you about me: did I transmit to you His message?" "Yes! Yes!" Thereupon, looking toward heaven and pointing his fingers, Muhammad prayed in a loud voice, "My God, be witness."

Less than three months after this sermon, on the twelfth day of Rabi Awwal, A.H. 11 (June 7, AD 632), Muhammad's soul returned to his eternal resting place. The question of miracles in relation to Muhammad has often been debated. Did he perform miracles other than the Quran?

The Quran, revealed to the world by the voice of Muhammad, is a miracle—yes, rather THE Miracle. Everything proves it: its style, its contents, the extraordinary events by which it was revealed, taught, and written down; its constant conformity with past, present, and future truth; its transcendent character which never shows a trace of a particular man, of any one society or epoch of history or specific region of the globe. The Quran is not a passing event in history which appears one day and disappears the next, to be known only by more or less correct hearsay reports. No, it is a fact, stable and durable, which remains unchanged and eternally present for the admiring contemplation of all men.

The Quran is not a temporary wonder which deceives the mind and is alien to the new knowledge which it has come to influence. It is the truth, the truth which proves itself, and while it appeals to reason it transcends reason and thus shows its divine origin.

The recognition of the Quran as THE Miracle does not diminish the value of other material and tangible miracles, known through our senses. These miracles, too, can very well bring us conviction; they are often the best means to reinforce our faith. That is why our earlier prophets have performed miracles. Was it the same with the Prophet of Islam? Has he performed miracles other than the transmission of the Quran? There are current tendencies toward answering in the negative, pretending to find proof in the Quran itself. The Quran, it is said, tells us that the Prophet Muhammad systematically refused to satisfy those who asked him to produce miracles.

> *And they say: We will not put faith in thee till thou cause a spring to gush forth from the earth for us; Or thou have a garden of date-palms and grapes, and cause flyers to gush forth therein abundantly...*
>
> *Or thou have a house of gold; or thou ascend up into heaven, and even then we will put no faith in thine ascension till thou bring down for us a book that we can read. (Surah XVII, 90-93)*
>
> *And they say: Why are not signs sent down upon him from his Lord? Say: Signs are with Allah only, and I am but a plain warner.*
>
> *Is it not enough for them that We have sent down unto thee the Scripture which is read unto them?*
>
> *Lo! herein verily is mercy, and a reminder for folk who believe. (Surah XXIX, 50-51)*

At the basis of the theory that the Prophet refused to perform miracles we find a grave misinterpretation, not only of the meaning of these quotations, but more so of the Islamic conception of the author of miracles in general. In those quotations the possibility of a miracle is not denied. Rather, they point out that miracles come from the supreme authority which alone is capable of any form of creation, and above all of creating supernatural things. It is a matter of demarking the frontier which separates human and divine power. The man is not yet possessed of the true Islamic faith who confounds those two powers, believing that the prophets themselves created their miracles. For the prophets are only human; they cannot overcome physical laws nor can they overcome the laws of the mind. God alone does so, if and when He wants to, in order to prove the divine origins of the message which the prophets transmit.

Therefore, it was not Moses who transformed the stick into a living snake, for this transmutation took place to his great surprise. It was not Jesus, either, who by his own power revived the dead; he did it only by the authority of the Lord. And when he refused the demands of those who once asked him to produce a sign from heaven, does this mean that he no longer performed miracles? Evidently not!

It is the same with Muhammad(Pbuh) in his refusal to comply with certain pagan requests. The answer with which he avowed his own incapability to perform miracles is the same which he gave concerning the Quran. It is not Muhammad who is the author of the Quran, but it is "the faithful spirit"; it is the Archangel Gabriel who, on God's command, brought the Quran down from heaven and deposited it in Muhammad's heart so that it may guide and rejoice those who believe in it. Not only could Muhammad not modify an iota of it, he did not even expect to be its bearer and was not sure that he would continue to receive it.

Thus no miracles, material or spiritual, are of human origin, for all are exclusively within God's domain and competence. All prophets have avowed that they are subject to the same limitations. Neither they nor the people to whom they were sent could demand a certain miracle or substitute one miracle for another according to their preferences. God gives His mandate to whomsoever He wills, in the form which He deems proper to persuade any epoch of history or any age of humanity. To each epoch its book. To each people, its guide.

> *And verily We sent messengers (to mankind) before thee, and We appointed for them wives and offspring, and it was not (given) to any messenger that he should bring a sign save by Allah's leave. To each epoch, its book. (Surah XIII, 38)*

In Islamic terminology a miracle is most often defined as a fact contrary to general rules, opposed to the normal course of events, with a cause which escapes human comprehension; and this fact is also a challenge to anyone who doubts it. Now the only fact which most obviously fulfills all these conditions is, of course, the Quran, which repeatedly and in many ways cries out its challenge to all beings visible and invisible and predicts their impotence to prove that it is not the miraculous message of God. It invites them first to imitate its text in its entirety, then to create ten Surahs similar to those in the Quran or to create but a single similar Surah, and finally asks but for a Surah only slightly resembling one in the Quran.

The question as to whether or not the Prophet performed any miracle other than the revelation of the Quran thus depends on the definition of a miracle.

If it is required that such a challenge must have been explicitly expressed, then it must be said that in Islam there has been no miracle other than the Quran. But once we eliminate the arbitrary stipulation that the challenge must have been expressed, we find an uncountable number of miracles performed by the Prophet. Some of those miracles are mentioned in the Quran itself:

The Prophet's(Pbuh), journey made by supernatural means from Mecca to Jerusalem in a single moment of the night; a journey during which he saw many divine signs, and distinguished clearly all topographical details of the place, details which he later described, to the surprise of all (Surah XVII, 1).

The prediction of a cleavage on the surface of the moon, a celestial phenomenon which indeed took place immediately in the presence of the crowd of people he was addressing and which was observed and confirmed by travellers (Surah LIV, z). The miraculous victory over the army of his enemies which was accomplished by a small number of faithful, poorly armed followers, but men who were assisted by divine power (Surah VIII, 17).

The fact that the society in Medina, which had been divided and eaten by hatred and civil war for dozens of years, became overnight a united group of intimate friends—a sudden change of mind which could not have been accomplished by earthly forces (Surah III, 103; VIII, 63).

The revelation by the Prophet of secret facts which had been carefully hidden from his knowledge (Surah IV, 113; LXVI, 3). Innumerable predictions fulfilled, such as the announcement of the precise date of a coming victory of the Romans over the Persians (Surah XXX, 2-6).

Also innumerable truthful reports of historic facts which were unknown to him and his people (Surah XI, 49; XII, 102; XXVIII, 44-46).

Among other miracles not mentioned in the Quran only a few can be cited here. The knowledge of these miracles, performed publicly by the Prophet, has been transmitted from generation to generation by reporters who have been identified and are known to be trustworthy historians. These examples are taken from the first chapter of al-Bukhari's *Alamate El Noboua:* The prediction that the Roman and Persian empires would cease to exist immediately after the death of their emperors who were contemporaries of the Prophet.

The announcement of the death of the King of Abyssinia on the date of his death. The assurance he gave that, after the battle against the pagans of Mecca in the fifth year of the Hijrah, the Meccans would never again march against Medina and that Mecca would be conquered by the Muslims.

The prediction that his grandson al-Hasan would re-establish unity and end the conflict between two great parties of Islam, a prediction which was fulfilled in the days of Muawiya, the fifth Caliph.

A miracle which was often repeated during times of drought and general thirst in the army was the production of an abundant yield of water from a little vessel which the Prophet blessed by putting his fingers in it. Fifteen hundred soldiers were able to quench their thirst, perform their ablutions, and water their animals with the water from that little vessel.

During a Friday sermon, when a Bedouin complained about the continuing dry weather and the famine which would ensue, the Prophet prayed for rain, and storm-clouds gathered from all directions, bringing rain which continued until the following Friday.

The next Friday the same Bedouin complained of the destruction being caused by the rain, and after the Prophet prayed the sky above Medina cleared immediately.

Once when the Prophet had been sitting on a tree stump and then abandoned it for a higher seat in order that the increased number of listeners might hear him better, all the audience heard the wailing complaint of the stump, a wailing which continued until the Prophet took the stump in his arms and consoled it as one would console a baby.

These are only a few of the many authenticated examples of miracles, other than the great miracle of receiving the revelation of the Quran, which were performed by the Prophet Muhammad, the Messenger of God.

THE QURAN

The greatest miracle was the revelation of the Quran which was transmitted by the Prophet in passages of unequal length at different times over a period of twenty-three years.

As soon as the Prophet received each inspired message he recited it to his audience and they in turn repeated it to the community, which was made up of people who were fond of literature and eagerly awaited each new message, whether they were partisans or adversaries.

As the Prophet dictated each new passage it was written down by the scribes on anything within reach, on thin white stones, pieces of parchment, wood, leather, or whatever was available. Tradition counts up to twenty-nine different persons in Medina who served as secretaries; a lesser number of scribes recorded the revelations received in Mecca. From the very beginning the faithful never failed to record the revealed messages, even during the persecutions. Among these scribes were included the first five Caliphs: Abu Bakr, Umar, Uthman, Mi, and Muawiya.

Thus the holy book of Islam became known in both an oral and written form. In its oral form it was called *Quran,* that is, Recital. In its written form it was called *Kitab,* or Scripture.

At the beginning the written extracts were not put in order or even gathered together, for other messages were expected.

As time went on several groups of verses began to grow up and tended to become independent unities as new verses were added according to the instructions given by the Prophet, who was following the orders of the Revealer Spirit. Although the text was originally scattered in its written form, it always had a definite order in the Prophet's mind and in the minds of the faithful, with each verse or group of verses fitting into its proper place in the structure of the whole. In the Prophet's lifetime there were hundreds of his Companions, called "Quran bearers," who were specialists in reciting the Book and knew by heart every Surah in its proper place in the structure.

At the death of the Prophet the Quran was preserved in the memories of the faithful as well as in writing. While in its oral form every Surah was complete and in its proper place in the order known today, in its written form it was nothing but scattered documents written on many different materials. During the year following the death of the Prophet no one worried about the written form because there were innumerable oral witnesses among them as living copies of the Quran complete in its final form. But about a year after the Prophet's death seventy of the Quran bearers were killed in the battle with Musailima, the false prophet, and it became clear that it would be necessary to guard against the loss of the oral tradition by gathering the written documents into a book easy to handle and use for reference. The idea of preparing the book was suggested by Umar and carried out by Zaid Ibn Thabit, a Quran bearer who had attended the last recital of the Quran by the Prophet and a man known for his intelligence, integrity, and competence.

Under the guidance of Zaid Ibn Thabit the correct written form of the Quran was determined by including only those passages which were verified by two witnesses as having been written down at the dictation of the Prophet and as being in the oral text of the last recital by the Prophet. This official collection is distinguished from the other personal, oral versions by an absolute rigorism which excluded from the text any explanatory notes and even eliminated the Surah titles. When the written form was completed it was given to the first Caliph, Abu Bakr, who entrusted it to Umar when he designated him the second Caliph. Since the third Caliph had not been chosen at the time of Umar's death, he gave it to his daughter Hafsah who was one of the widows of the Prophet.

The universal authority of the written form of the Quran dates from its publication by the third Caliph, Uthman, who received it from Hafsah and ordered four secretaries to write as many copies of the document as there were big towns in the Islamic Empire. From that time the Uthman edition has been the only one in use in the Islamic world.

Ever since the earliest days the question has been raised as to whether the Quran was of divine or human origin. The explicit and implicit testimony of the Quran is that the author is God Himself. It is never the Prophet who speaks in the Quran. The Scripture either refers to him in the third person or addresses him directly—O Prophet, O Messenger, We reveal to thee, We send thee, do this, recite this; such is the language of the Quran.

The direct proof of the divine origin of the Quran is manifest all through the Scripture itself. It is also shown by the peculiar phenomena which accompanied every revelation of the Quran, according to the testimony of the true tradition. The Prophet's contemporaries were objective witnesses of the visible, tangible, and audible signs of the mysterious accompanying phenomena which made evident the real source of the Quran and opened the eyes of the truth-seekers. In the presence of the Revealer Spirit the Prophet's inspired face was illumined, like a mirror; there was silence; conversation stopped as if in moments of absence of mind; his body relaxed as if in sleep and a mysterious buzz was heard around him—as in a telephone conversation where the one listening is the only one who can hear distinctly enough to understand. There was nothing voluntary about these phenomena, for the Prophet could neither avoid them when they came nor bring them into being when he earnestly desired to receive a message. On many occasions the Prophet sought a revelation but it was not given; then, sometimes after an interval as long as a month, the mysterious phenomena would come, appearing suddenly and vanishing abruptly, after which the people with him would listen to the wonderful text.

The literary style and contents of that text are conclusive evidence of the divine origin of the Quran, but before considering that evidence let us turn to the arguments by which attempts have been made to prove that the origins were human. It is to the honour of Islam that the Quran records all hypotheses, reasonable or absurd, by which the contemporaries of the Prophet attempted to establish human origins for the Scripture. If the origins were human, they must have come from Muhammad's environment, from other religions in that environment, or from the meditations and reasoning of the human author. Let us examine the activities of the Prophet before and during his apostolate and see what he could have learned from his surroundings or from his own meditations.

It is scarcely necessary to point out that at the beginning of Islam neither the ideas nor the practices of the people of Mecca show any resemblance to the teachings of the Quran. There is no relation between the pure unitarian system, the most perfect and refined ethics of the Holy Book of Islam, and the ignorance, paganism, superstitious idolatry, arrogant materialism, infanticide, prostitution, incest, dowry extortion, oppression of orphans, disregard for the poor, and scorn of the weak which were characteristics of Mecca in those times.

An effort has been made to show that the teachings of the Quran are similar to those of the Sabians, a sect well-known in Mecca at that time. But the Sabians were idolatrous and polytheistic, worshiping the stars and angels with a mixture of pagan, Christian, and other rites. Their pilgrimage was not to the Kaaba, but to Harran in Iraq, and their prayers were to the stars at sunrise, at noon, and at sunset—three times when prayer is prohibited in Islam.

It was also suggested that Muhammad might have been influenced by the travellers and immigrants who came to Mecca: the Abyssinians or Romans, the labourers or wine merchants. It is clear that our Personage could not have known the vulgar class of immigrants for he lived either alone, in complete solitude, or as a shepherd, or as a big merchant in a caravan, or in the high society with the leaders of the community. Even if he had any contact with such people, their lack of religious knowledge would have been evident, and as the Quran points out, their foreign language would have made communication impossible (Surah XVI, 103).

It has been argued that in Muhammad's travels he became acquainted with Arab tribes which had been converted to Christianity and got his ideas from them. Many scholars, ancient and modern, have pointed out that such contact with Christianity is unlikely but that, even if it did happen, the Christianity practiced in that part of the world was so debased that it was indistinguishable from paganism. The fourth Caliph, Ali, said that the tribe Taghlib had taken from Christianity nothing but the habit of drinking wine. Wherever Muhammad traveled he found beliefs to be rectified, deviations to be brought back to the right way. Nowhere did he find a moral or religious model which could have been copied for his work of reform.

Again, it has been suggested that the Prophet gleaned his teachings from the reading of books recording previous revelations. But the Quran categorically denies that he knew how to read or write (Surah XXIX, 48). Furthermore, the Bible was not available in Arabic until many centuries after the Prophet's time, and the Bible in other languages was out of reach of the common people. The few biblical ideas which may have circulated among the common people were so vague and often contradictory that they cannot be the basis for the precision, extensiveness, unity, and vigour of the material in the Quran.

Nor can it be argued that Muhammad(Pbuh) was influenced by Jewish teachings after he came to Medina, where he was in contact with Jewish scholars. Even before the Hijrah the Holy History had been revealed in all its true details in the Meccan Surahs, and the Quran had condemned the believers in the Pentateuch as followers of satanic inspiration, unworthy of being accepted as teachers or examples (Surah XVI, 63). In the revelations in Medina the Quran goes even further in its condemnation of the followers of the Pentateuch (Surah II, 79-80; III, 75; IV, 161). The psychological attitudes on both sides made Jewish influence on Islamic thought practically impossible. The majority of the Jewish scholars adopted an antagonistic position which was far from the benevolent attitude of teachers. Those of the Israelite scholars who were impartial enthusiastically welcomed the Prophet in Medina and declared their conversion to Islam, thereafter as disciples recognizing him as their Master. Between the two categories of the hostile or the submissive, there was no place for a third group of friendly tutors.

Thus it is clear that the teachings of the Quran cannot be attributed to the influence of the environment on Muhammad. There remains the question as to whether or not he could have created the Quran by himself through the use of meditation and reason. To a limited extent, reason could have revealed the falseness of idolatry and the senselessness of superstition, but how could it know how to replace them? It is not by mere thinking that facts can be known, that previous events can be described, yet the Quran was always in perfect accord with the essential data of the Bible, even those hidden from Muhammad by scholars. Mere intellect by itself could not have given such details. The Quran confirms that before the revelation Muhammad did not know any book nor even the meaning of faith (Surah XLII, 52). He could not possibly have guided others, for he did not even know how to guide himself in religious matters. He was ignorant of all the legislative, moral, social, and ritual details which are included in the revelation of the Quran. It was not by reason, or by the study of books, but only by revelation that Muhammad could know the creative God and the divine attributes. Only as it was revealed to him could he define the relation between God and the visible and invisible worlds and specify the future reserved to man after death. We have seen that the Quran could not have human origins traceable either to the experience of Muhammad in the environment of his time or to his ability to construct the Holy Book by use of his reason. We have seen that the divine origin of the Quran is attested by the mysterious phenomena which always preceded a revelation. Now let us look further and consider the internal evidence for the divine origin in the literary form and contents of the Quran.

The literary form of the Quran is distinguished clearly from all other forms, whether they be poetry, rhythmic or non-rhythmic prose, the style of the common people, or that of the Prophet himself. The exceptional eloquence of Muhammad was always acknowledged and is known to us in countless instructions which he gave after careful thought, or dictated as non-Quranic insights. In all such passages there is not the slightest resemblance between them and the revealed messages.

We feel such ascendant power in the revealed texts that they penetrate the soul. The infidels in the time of the Prophet considered the form of the text such an extraordinary phenomenon that they used to call it magic. Even in modern times those who can understand the Arabic text recognize its sublime character without being able to explain it.

In our lectures on exegesis at Al Azhar University in Cairo—the oldest university in the world—the following analysis is used to point out the ways in which the literary form of the Quran transcends the powers of man and defies imitation.

The form of the Quran reflects neither the sedentary softness of the townsman nor the nomadic roughness of the Bedouin. It possesses in right measure the sweetness of the former and the vigour of the latter. The rhythm of the syllables is more sustained than in prose and less patterned than in poetry. The pauses come neither in prose form nor in the manner of poetry, but with a harmonious and rhythmic symmetry.

The words chosen neither transgress by their banality nor by their extreme rarity, but are recognized as expressing admirable nobility. The sentences are constructed in a dignified manner which uses the smallest possible number of words to express ideas of utmost richness. The brevity of expression, the conciseness, attains such a striking clearness that the least learned man can understand the Quran without difficulty.

At the same time there is such a profundity, flexibility, suggestivity, and radiance in the Quran that it serves as the basis of the principles and rules for the Islamic sciences and arts, for theology, and for the juridical schools. Thus it is almost impossible in each case to express the ideas of a text by one interpretation only, either in Arabic or in a foreign language, even with the greatest care.

Quranic speech appears to be superhuman in its transcendence of the psychological law that intellect and feeling are always found in inverse proportion to each other. In the Quran we find constant cooperation between the two antagonistic powers of reason and emotion, for we find that in the narrations, arguments, doctrines, laws, and moral principles the words have both a persuasive teaching and an emotive force. Throughout the whole Quran the speech maintains a surprising solemnity and powerful majesty which nothing can disturb. Finally, when we pass from the structure of a sentence, or a group of sentences dealing with the same subject, to the structure of the Surah and of the Quran as a whole, we find an over-all plan which could not have been created by man.

We know that the Quran was revealed in long and short fragments over a period of twenty-three years and that they have been arranged according to neither their chronological order nor their subject matter but in an independent, complicated order which appears to be arbitrary. As each revelation appeared it was placed in its fixed place, given its number among the verses, and its place was never changed. Thus, for every revealed verse there are two different orders, the chronological order based on the date of its revelation and the architectural order which determined its place in the composition of the Book. Throughout the long period of the revelations these two orders were strictly followed for every verse, every Surah, and the whole work.

In the chronological order, every revelation meets the need of the hour and links with the previous and following ones in a gradual progress in teaching and legislation. For instance, consider the main outline of these successive stages: it begins with the simple command, "Read!" (Surah XCVI, 1); then goes on to the apostolic charge, "Preach!" (Surah LXXIV, 2); then the call at first to the near relatives only (Surah XXVI, 214), extended next to the whole town (Surah XXVIII, 59), then to the neighbouring towns (Surah VI, 92), and at last to humanity (Surah XXI, 107). Consider also the general outline of the progress in teaching in its two big divisions: first the fundamental bases of the work in the Surahs of Mecca; then the codified application of those general principles in the Surahs of Medina. This long course of events continued from the day of the grotto, when Muhammad was simply warned that he would receive a divine teaching, until the day of the last pilgrimage, when he was told that his mission was accomplished and he had nothing else to do on earth. After receiving the revelations for twenty-three years, he was called back.

Nothing, therefore, has been improvised in the Quran. Everything was foreseen and formed as a whole and in every detail, from the beginning to the end, including the death of the Prophet. Who could have formed and carried out such a complete plan? Who other than God from whom came this heavenly mission?

In addition to the chronological order there is the architectural order in the Quran. The very texts which follow in the chronological order the most wise educational plan were taken from their historical positions and fixed in the architectural order, every one in a definite frame already built to receive it, taking its place in those units of different length called Surahs. What makes it so wonderful is that once each Surah is completed from those scattered parts it is a unit faultlessly formed, artistically, linguistically, and logically. A special musical rhythm runs equally through all parts of the speech; there is a common, harmonious style, and a logical plan in the development of the ideas expressed.

It is clear that to establish such a scheme in advance the author would have had to foresee not only the problems which would arise from the events of the next twenty-three years, and their solutions, but also the literary form, the musical tone and rhythm in which it would be expressed, the appropriate structure for all the revelations yet to come, and the precise spot in that framework where each revelation would be fixed. It must be confessed that no man or any other creature is capable of knowing the future in such detail or creating such a Book. Only the Divine Omniscience could be the creator of the Quran.

The teachings of the Quran are universal, addressed to all people throughout the world regardless of their origins and revealed to mankind to enlighten man's spirit, to purify his morals, to unify his society, and to replace the domination by the powerful with justice and fraternity. As is confirmed in Surah XVI, 89, all human problems can be solved through the Quran, either directly or indirectly: "And We reveal the Scripture unto thee as an exposition of all things."

This revelation in the Quran deals primarily with the Supreme Truth and with virtue. All the rest of the contents of the text—such as knowledge of the soul, the sciences of the nature of the heavens and the earth, history, prophecy, warnings, and the like—are only means to strengthen the message of the Quran, to give it more weight and conviction. The great theologian al-Ghazali, who died A.H. 505 (AD 1111), pointed out in his *Pearls of the Quran* that 763 verses are concerned with knowledge, and 741 verses with guidance in virtue. For him these 1504 verses represent the most precious substance of the Book, while the remaining 5112 verses are, so to speak, the envelope or shell of the teachings. According to the Quran, the act of faith must include these three elements:

Belief in God

Belief in His messages addressed to humanity

Belief in the Day of Judgment.

The starting point in Islam is belief in God, the Almighty, the Benefactor, the Creator of everything, the only proper object of worship. In the attempts to persuade the polytheists to accept this pure monotheism, the chief point at issue is the question of the proper object of worship. The Quran in many passages points out that the pagans confess that there is but one Creator and Administrator of the universe (Surah XLIII, 9), but their mortal mistake is that in their worship they associate secondary gods with God and claim that those secondary gods are capable of interceding with Him on their behalf and winning His favour. The Quran uses arguments based on reason and on tradition to bring back those who have strayed from monotheism into polytheism.

In the rational arguments directed at the polytheists, the Quran emphasizes their agreement that creation and providence are attributed exclusively to God and seeks to persuade them to the exclusive worship of God. How can one equate the creature to the Creator? Is it conceivable that the being which has created nothing equals the One who has created everything? (Surah XVI, 17).

Is it not illogical to invoke that which never answers us, which never even hears our appeal? (Surah XLVI, 5).

Is it not ungrateful on our part to forget the Benefactor who grants us our happiness, the Benefactor to whom we address all our supplications in times of disaster? Is it not ungrateful to associate with Him in worship others who are incapable of either good or evil actions? (Surah XVI, 53-54). And finally, those polytheists who pretend that any man or saint or other being has the power of mediation or intercession with the great God must prove that it can be done (Surah II, 255; XIII, 33; XXXIX, 3).

In addition to the rational arguments against polytheistic worship, the Quran points to the unanimous testimony of the prophetic traditions. "There has not been one previous prophet to whom We have not revealed this truth that there is no God but Me, therefore worship Me" (Surah XXI, 25). "Ask the divine messengers who preceded you: Have We allowed them to worship other gods than the Merciful?" (Surah XLIII, 45).

While the starting point of faith is belief in God as the Creator, the Benefactor, and the only object of worship, it must be recognized that God is also the Legislator. He commands our actions and our emotions. He requires our trust and obedience. This truth can be known by natural intelligence, by common sense and conscience, and also by the confirmation given in the Quran. God has given man the natural power to discern good and evil, justice and injustice (Surah XCI, 7-8), but the experience of all time shows that passions, work, and material and worldly preoccupations sometimes turn our minds away from the highest ideals and lead us to erroneous judgments and practical mistakes. Therefore the Divine Mercy did not abandon us to our natural intelligence alone. To check any tendency in us toward declining our responsibilities, God has reinforced our natural intelligence with revealed Truths (Surah XXIV, 35).

In order that His commandments might be known to men without dependence on reason alone, God chose among men and Angels those worthy of receiving and transmitting the divine light, sending to every nation or large tribe His warning (Surah XVI, 36).

Those who refuse to believe in any spokesman of God refuse to believe in God himself, for every divine messenger has been given proof of the divine origin of his revelations (Surah LVII, 25).

The first two elements in the faith of Islam—belief in God and in His messages—are not complete without the third: belief in the Day of Judgment. God is Creator, God is Legislator, and God is also the supreme Judge. He is the beginning and the end; to Him all men must turn to give an account of their deeds and to receive from Him equitable retribution according to their merits (Surah XL, 16; LVII, 3; II, 281).

The doctrine of life after death includes belief in the survival of the soul and the resurrection of the body. The belief in the survival of the soul did not give rise to difficulties, but the impious objected with irony to the doctrine of the resurrection of the body: "Give us back our fathers if you speak the truth!" (Surah XLIV, 36).

The Quran opposed such superficial reasoning by pointing out the argument from nature, how the earth is at one time dead and dry and then living and fertile. (Surah XXII, 5-7; XXX, 50).

The Quran establishes that resurrection is not only possible, it is certain. It is certain because God has promised it, and it is certain because it is required by wisdom and justice in order to give to each creature a just retribution for his deeds. Otherwise, the creation of man would have been in vain. "Deemed ye then that We had created you for naught, and that ye would not be returned unto Us?" (Surah XXIII, 115).

Nor should it be thought that good and bad men would be treated in the same way, giving them similar life and death (Surah XLV, 21).

In the Day of Judgment, justice will be given to all men. Belief in God the Creator, God the Legislator, and God the Judge is not enough in itself. The Quran teaches that a genuine believer must have that faith and must also observe the law; it requires sincere belief and laborious obedience. In giving its commandments it awakens in us a sense of good and evil, of beauty and ugliness. "God could not order indecent things" (Surah VII, z8).

"Tell them: My Lord forbids only what is indecent done in public or in private; deeds of the limbs or of the heart, such as any impious action and any unjustified violence" (Surah VII, 33).

"The faithful do not defame the reputation of those who are absent. Would any one of you like to eat his dead brother's flesh?" (Surah XLIX, 12).

The Quran points out that such ideals of universal duty were always taught by wise men and the saints. The names of Abraham, Isaac, Ishmael, Jacob, Moses, and Jesus are often mentioned as having taught such virtues and the necessity for prayer, charity, fasting, and the like.

Thus it is clear that the Quran has preciously preserved these previous teachings concerning virtue which were true, but we must notice that the Quran does not synthesize the sometimes divergent previous teachings; it marks out its own way by a spontaneous impulse. While it preserves the religious and moral patrimony, it adorns it more, crowning the divine building on which all the prophets have collaborated. By means of a variety of proofs convincing to the mind and attractive to the heart, the teaching concerning the divine attributes, the destiny of the soul, and the moral duties of man is much more developed in the Quran than anywhere else.

For instance, instead of only prohibiting drunkenness, the Quran stops the evil at its source by strictly forbidding the use of all intoxicants. Again, after reconciling the two apparently opposed principles of the Old and New Testaments, the principles of Justice and Charity, the Quran adds quite a new dimension which can be called the Code of Politeness, Discretion, and Propriety (Surah IV, 86; XXIV, 27-28, 31, 58-62).

With the Decalogue of Moses, we are still in the fundamental and elementary laws, as if on the ground floor of morality. With the Sermon on the Mount we already find ourselves on a very high level at which charity excels justice and the heavenly kingdom scorns the earthly realm. Finally, through the laws of the Quran we reach the summit where charity and justice are combined and there is a total disinterestedness which aims at the absolute Good which is God. It is God Himself who must be borne in mind while carrying out His will by living a virtuous life.

In the revelations of the Quran, as in every previous revelation, a new and original contribution is added to the earlier ones. It is the purpose of the Quran to "confirm and to safeguard the former books" (Surah V, 48).

"Safeguard," in that verse, means to discard the alterations and false interpretations unjustly attributed to the earlier revelations (Surah XVI, 63-64).

The text of the Quran itself is safeguarded against any additions or changes because God Himself promised to be its protector (Surah XV, 9). As for the other books, they were written by men and left to their protection (Surah V, 44).

In addition to the Quran's primary aim of revealing religious and moral truths, there arc secondary objectives designed to strengthen faith in the Creator or to support the faithful in their hope. It is striking to discover the extent to which the explanations of the natural world, God's creation, correspond precisely with the latest discoveries of cosmology, anatomy, physiology, and the rest of the positive sciences. For instance, consider these remarkable examples of scientific knowledge: the sphericity of the earth (XXXIX, 5), the formation of rain (XXX, 48), fertilization by the wind (XV, 22), the aquatic origin of all living creatures (XXI, 30), the duality in the sex of plants and other creatures, then unknown (XXXVI, 35), the collective life of animals (VI, 38), the mode of life of the bees (XVI, 69), the successive phases of the child in his mother's womb (XXII, 5; XXIII, 14).

A constant support to the faithful in their hope is the fulfillment of prophecies. In a short passage in Surah XLIV the Quran predicted accurately the different stages through which the Islamic preaching would pass and the different attitudes toward it which would be taken by the first adversaries, how they would at first be heedless and careless, then conciliatory and interested, and finally opposed and obviously hostile. At the same time it was predicted that the ungrateful town of Mecca would at first endure an awful misery which would bring some of the people from incredulity to an attraction of their souls toward heaven, then it would have prosperity which would make them forget God, and finally Mecca would suffer a humiliating defeat in the first battle (Surah XLIV, 9-16). Other verses announce the triumph of Islam, the permanence of its doctrine, the growth of the empire of young Islam, and the inability of any earthly power to annihilate Islam (XIII, 18; XIV, 24; XXIV, 55; VIII, 36).

The Quran also predicted the eternal schism in Christendom (V, 14), the dispersion of the Israelites (VII, 168), their world (VII, 167), their everlasting need of a protecting ally (III, 112), and the dominance until the day of resurrection persecution until the end of the world (VII, 167), their everlasting need of a protecting ally(III, 112), and the dominance of the Christians over the Jews until the day of resurrection (III, 55).

It must be noted that not only have the prophecies of the Quran been confirmed, but the Quran has thrown out this challenge: nothing can ever contradict the prophecies of the Quran, neither in the past, the present, nor the future (XLI, 42).

Who could ever give guarantees against space and time other than the Master of Space and Time Himself?

The divine origin of the Quran is evident for all the reasons which have been considered in this discussion. The possibility of human origin has been eliminated. Nowhere in the Quran is the personal character of the Prophet reflected, nowhere is there an echo of his daily joys and sorrows or of his earthly surroundings. There are no indications of geographical, atmospherical, racial, tribal, or individual peculiarities in the subjects treated. Only that which is necessary for the education of humanity is found in the Quran. The revelations were accompanied by visible signs of their divine origin. The linguistic and stylistic form of the Quran give positive signs of its divinity. The religious and moral teachings are clear evidence of its divine origin, free from the possibility of borrowing from other books.

It is for this reason that the Quran holds the highest place in Islam. For Muslims, the Quran is not only the text of prayers, the instrument of prophecy, the food for the spirit, the favourite canticle of the soul; it is at the same time the fundamental law, the treasure of the sciences, the mirror of the ages. It is the consolation for the present and the hope for the future.

In what it affirms or denies, the Quran is the criterion of truth. In what it orders or prohibits, it is the best model for behaviour. In what it judges, its judgment is always correct. In what it discusses, it gives the decisive argument. In what it says, it is the purest and most beautiful expression possible in speech. It calms or incites most effectively.

Since the Quran is the direct expression of the divine will, it holds supreme authority for all men. The obedience due to our parents, our superiors, our community, or the Prophet himself is given only when it is based on a principle found in the Book of God. Their commands are obligations to us only so long as they transmit the divine commandment or do not contradict it.

It is edifying to know how the Prophet himself regarded the text of the Quran. He could not by his own will retouch it in the slightest; he interpreted it exactly as any commentator would a text which was not his own. And when he postponed carrying out any of its commandments even for a short time, in order to treat kindly the souls of the faithful and to forestall the objections of adversaries, we see the Revelation reproaching him most severely. Those reproaches he accepted with resignation and left engraved forever in the text (Surah XXXIII, 37). This constantly humble, submissive, and reverential attitude toward the words of God is sincerely confessed in the Quran itself: "Recite: my prayer, my acts of devotion, my life and my death belong exclusively to God, the Ruler of the Universe, lone Ruler and without partner. Of this I received the order and I am the first of the submissives" (Surah VI, 163-64).

SUNNAH

The prophetic teachings outside the Quran are called the *Sunnah,* the Traditions. The base of Islam, as we have seen, is the Quran, and nothing is believed or commanded which is contrary to any revelation in the Holy Book. The Sunnah is the derived law of Islam which every Muslim is obliged to obey.

The Prophet taught in three ways: by oral instructions; by the example of his personal behaviour; and by his silence, his tacit approval of other people's actions, by letting others do as they pleased without comment or reproach. These three aspects of the Prophet's teaching—speaking, acting, and approving—are the basis for the Muslim tradition called the Sunnah, and are considered to be the second source of Islamic legislation and instruction.

The Prophet draws this triple authority from the Quran itself, for it commands us to obey the Messenger's orders (Surah IV, 59; XXIV, 56), tells us that he who obeys the Prophet obeys the very commandments of God (Surah IV, 80), and recommends that we follow his example (Surah XXXIII, 21). In the Quran the Prophet is commanded to behave in such a way that his behaviour will be a model for believers (Surah XXXIII, 37). It also describes the Prophet as one who gave to mankind all good instructions and forbade all bad actions; therefore, the action he does not forbid is permitted (Surah VII, 157).

The great majority of Muslim learned men hold, with good reason, that the Prophet's teachings follow either the directive of divine, though nontextual, inspiration or, if it was a personal, purely human effort, he applied the very essence or spirit of the law of the Quran. If in his instruction as a human being, without specific revelation, he ever was in error, he was immediately brought back to the truth through a revelation (Surah IV, 106-13; VIII, 67; IX, 43, 113).

In the absence of such correcting revelations, all his orders, permissions, judgments, and behaviour are rightly considered as implicitly approved and having full legislative and educative authority, subject only to the condition that they have been transmitted through authentic and strictly verified sources. Thus the Muslim tradition in Islam is related to the Quran as a nation's laws are related to its constitution.

It is a significant fact that regarding our two most essential practical duties—prayer, which is our obligation to God, and alms, which is a duty to our fellow men—the Quran refers us directly to tradition for detailed instruction. Speaking of prayer, the Quran says explicitly, "Do that which God has taught you" (Surah II, 239).

Again, speaking of alms, it says that it is a "precise and known" right of the needy to receive a share of the possessions of pious men (Surah LXX, 24-25).

And similar references are found concerning the season of pilgrimage and the sacred months. Now, in the absence in the Quran of any further elaboration on these subjects, any clear details as to how these duties are to be performed, it is obvious that through these references the Quran establishes the authority of the Sunnah, and grants to it the right to elaborate and define the general precepts of the Quran. Without the Sunnah, these texts would have been incomprehensible, stating as known things which were not known.

The role of the Sunnah is not limited to clarifying the duties implied in general commandments revealed in the Quran. Often the Sunnah establishes new obligations and prohibitions for which no clear reference can be found in the Quran. This is not, however, an addition to the legislation of the Quran, for a careful study will show that each of these traditions expresses the spirit of a more general teaching in the Book, even though the ties connecting each tradition with its appropriate foundation in the Quran are not easily discovered.

For example, the Quran made compulsory the alms deducted from gold, silver, and the crops, using also the more general terms "possessions," and "things granted by God"; the Prophet added the requirement that alms should be deducted from the herd. The Quran instituted the fast during the month of Ramadan as training in piety and patience and an opportunity to express thankfulness for divine blessings; the Prophet added the requirement that alms be given at the end of the fast of Ramadan as an act which is an additional means of accomplishing those purposes. The Quran forbids usury; the Sunnah forbids those usurious sales in which the increase in price has the same effect. Since such sales, halfway between a legitimate sale and forbidden usury, fell within a doubtful and suspect area of business activity, tradition rightly forbids them under the legislation of the Quran which recommends that we abstain from any action when in doubt. Again, the Quran prescribes scourging as the punishment for lewdness, while the Sunnah specifies scourging for unmarried persons and calls for death by stoning for adultery—justified by the passage in the Quran which says that the punishment for lewdness in women should be confinement to the house up to death, until the time when another punishment should be revealed.

The Sunnah, based on the verified traditions concerning the teachings, actions, and tacit approval of the Prophet, is justifiably binding on all Muslims. Since the Quran gave the Prophet full power to enlighten men concerning the meaning of the revelations, he was the best qualified to legislate in matters requiring clarification. The Prophet knew better than any other possible legislator the essence and spirit of the Law. Therefore, it is not surprising that he took new legislative steps, creating the Sunnah, the Traditions binding on all Muslims, through legislation *by* analogy, by precise definition, and by extension of the revelations given in the Quran.

Conclusion

We now see how Muslims regard the Quran and the Prophet(Pbuh).

The Quran is a purely divine work, a textual revelation which reached the world through a heavenly Messenger, the Faithful Spirit, the Archangel Gabriel, who deposited it in the heart of Muhammad.

Muhammad's(Pbuh) role was limited to receiving the revelation, learning it, writing it down, transmitting, explaining, and applying it. Muhammad could not go beyond or change or modify the Quran in any way, nor can any other believer.

Any human work can be discussed, controverted, or contradicted by events in the past, present, or future. But the Quran, the Word of God, is perfection itself; it is unchallengably true, infallibly just, and inimitably good and beautiful.

The Prophet Muhammad(Pbuh) was but a man, of a purely human nature. He was neither a great god, nor a small god, nor a sub-god, nor even an auxiliary of God.

He could not acquire any good or avoid any evil except through God's will. He knew only so much of the past or the future as God revealed to him. He was infallible in his judgments only when sustained by revelation.

But he was set apart from the rest of mankind by an excellent inborn morality, by the divine knowledge granted to him, and by the dignity of his apostleship: he is the head of all believers. As the faithful interpreter and living example of the Quran, we owe him obedience, respect, and love. The Quran urges us to treat him with particular reverence.

The Prophet led us out of the darkness of ignorance into the light of truth. Lost and vicious as we were, he brought us back to the straight path of Islam.

But however great our respect for him may be, and however deeply we may love him, in our eyes he is not raised above the level of man. Muhammad never aspired to the rank of divinity; he was God's apostle and servant.

In our confession of faith, the Prophet's role as a servant surpasses his role as apostle. For us, he is not an object of worship; we do not pray to him, but pray to God for him, asking God to heap blessings on him.

Islam's monotheistic system is infinitely pure and unmixed.

There is no God but Allah.

Muhammad(Pbuh) is his servant and apostle.

All men are brothers.

Such are the three elements of the Muslim creed, as they are stated in three successive Surahs of the Quran (XLVII, 19; XLVIII, 29; XLIX, 13).

Such is the straight path of Islam, the path of those who submit to the will of God as revealed in the Quran, God's Word as given by the Archangel Gabriel to Muhammad, the Messenger of God.

2

The Islamic Code

In the name of God, the Merciful, the Most Compassionate

In the introduction to this chapter it was stated that the Quran, the all-embracing source of the true concept of Islam, says that Islam is both a faith and a code. Up to this point we have discussed the beliefs that must be held with the head and the heart if one is to be a Muslim. The acceptance or rejection of these beliefs determines the dividing line between loyalty to Islam and infidelity. The Islamic code is the name given to the principles and laws which God revealed and which He requires all Muslims to adhere to strictly in all their actions, whether in their relations with Him or in their dealings with mankind.

The actions through which Muslims draw near to their Lord, recall His greatness, and show their trust in Him by their observance of His divine rules are known in Islam as *worship of God*. The actions through which Muslims uphold their interests and repel evils in themselves, between themselves and their neighbours, and between Muslims and non-Muslims, the actions through which they prevent maltreatment, preserve rights, fulfill the general good, and establish peace and security, are known in Islam as *dealings*.

The great number of laws which make up the Islamic code are classified under these two headings: worship and dealings.

Worship of God

The worship of God is made up of prayers, fasting, payment of religious tax, and pilgrimage. Basic to the worship of God is the acknowledgment of God's oneness and Muhammad's heavenly purpose in life, the cleansing of the heart and soul, the strict observance of obedience to God in all actions. This is the foundation, these are the pillars on which Islam is built. Therefore the Prophet (may God bless him) has said,

> *"Islam is put upon five principles: belief In the single God and in Muhammad as His Messenger, performance of prayers, payment of religious tax, keeping of the month of Ramadan, and pilgrimage to the Holy Mosque by whoever finds the way clear to do it."*

Prayer

Prayer is a form of physical worship assigned to the Muslim five times a day at specified times. In prayer he stands wherever he happens to be at the appointed time and turns his face toward the Divine Mosque in Mecca. He begins his prayer by saying in a fairly loud voice, "God is the Most Great," praying reverently with profound intent to worship God. He then recites the Good Book's first Surah, along with a passage of the Quran which he has learned by heart, trying to understand its inner meaning. He then bows by bending until his back makes a straight horizontal line, holding his knees with his hands, and saying to himself as he bows, "Great God."

Then he lifts his head, saying, "God the Most Great," and kneels down, touching his forehead to the floor, saying as he goes down, "God the Highest." He then lifts his head, saying "God the Most Great," and sits comfortably on his heels. Then he touches the floor with his forehead a second time. This process is called one kneeling. There are five daily prayers: First is the morning prayer which the Muslim performs at the beginning of his day between the small hours of the morning and sunrise.

It is made up of two kneelings, at the end of which the worshiper sits to salute his Lord, admitting His oneness and the mission of His Prophet in a manner which has been universally copied from Muhammad (may God bless him). He then salutes the right side and the left side with the words, "Peace be upon you together with God's blessings." The second prayer is the midday prayer which is performed from noon until halfway between noon and sundown. The afternoon prayer comes between midafternoon and sunset. Each of those prayers is made up of four kneelings. The early evening prayer is three kneelings and is offered between sunset and the vanishing from the horizon of the twilight. The late evening prayer is performed after the twilight disappears; it is the last prayer of the day when the Muslim welcomes the night, and is made up of four kneelings.

With these prayers the Muslim thinks of his Lord five times during each day and night, appearing before his Lord repeatedly and saluting His name within his heart and soul, submitting himself to God, looking forward to His favour. Therefore he perseveres in obeying His commands.

The Muslim can perform these prayers anywhere—at the mosque, at home, in the field, at the factory, in the office—wherever he happens to be when the time falls due for prayer. He can pray alone, or he can pray with others standing in a line or lines arrayed closely in straight formation, like a highly-disciplined military parade, behind a leader who is followed by the congregation in all that he does. Congregational prayer in Islam is the best form of prayer because it encourages acquaintanceship, intimacy, cooperation, joint entreaty, remembrance, and cheerful submission to God, the Lord of all peoples.

Muslims are reminded of the time for prayer by the call to prayer which is given from the minaret of the mosque in the form taught by the Prophet, "God is Most Great. God is Most Great. I avow that there is no God other than Allah. I avow that there is no God other than Allah. I declare openly that Muhammad is the Messenger of God. I declare openly that Muhammad is the Messenger of God. Welcome prayer. Welcome prayer. Welcome good fortune. Welcome good fortune. God is Most Great. God is Most Great. There is no God but Allah."

Islam also has a weekly prayer, known as the Friday prayer because it is performed at noon on Friday. It is a congregational service with preaching before the prayer, which is made up of two kneelings. There are also two other prayers like the Friday prayer which are performed twice a year on the mornings of the two Islamic feasts, the first day following the month of Ramadan and the tenth day of the month of Dual Hijja. These two prayers are known in Islam as the prayers of the two feasts, Ramadan and al-Qurban. In addition to the daily prayers, the Friday prayer, and the prayers of the two feasts, there is in Islam the funeral prayer, a religious ceremony expressing the Muslims' loyalty toward their dead. Muslims are required to prepare their dead for burial by cleaning the body and wrapping it from head to foot in unstitched cloth; the body is then placed on a bed and the mourners stand in line and, led by one of them, join in the prayer for the dead person. They repeat four times the phrase "God is Most Great" and recite together the preface to the Quran; then they ask God's blessing on the deceased. The body is later buried. According to Islam the grave may be in the ground or on the surface level, but should not be elevated either for a member of the masses or for a prophet who has completed a heavenly mission.

In this connection it should be pointed out that Islam has no other funeral ceremonies than those mentioned above. The elaborate rituals, the special places for ceremonies, the special funeral processions which are sometimes seen, the domes built over graves, all these have nothing whatever to do with Islam. Nor is there any basis in Islam for the great respect paid to certain mausoleums with the object of securing blessings. Islam has nothing to say about visiting graveyards for inspiration or blessing. These customs have been copied by Muslims from others.

Islam is also opposed to the practice of withdrawing into monasteries or caves to repeat prayers. It looks upon the daily work to support one's family and to improve the life of the community as an obligation as important as prayer. Indeed, the daily prayers are assigned merely to fulfill the debt owed to God, and as a means of securing His aid in the daily struggle in the world. The Islamic code states clearly the everyday obligations of the Muslim which provide him with food for the soul through worship and further his material standing as an individual and promote the welfare of his community. Islamic law provides the best way for a man to maintain the right relationship with his Lord and a proper participation in the life of the world. This is not possible except for the Muslim. Except for the five daily prayers which distinguish the Muslim from the non-Muslim, the daily routine of the Muslim is like that of other men. He carries on the business for which his talents qualify him, earning his livelihood, guarding his family and his interests, and abstaining from sin in matters of food and drink and evil amusements. Then he retires at night to relax from work and fatigue. Islam does not prevent the Muslim from enjoying the beautiful things of life and the favours of God. "Say: Who has forbidden the adornment of Allah which He has brought forth for His bondmen, and the good things of His providing?" (Surah VII, 32).

Fasting

Prayer is the first form of physical worship. The second is fasting—refraining from eating, drinking, and sexual intercourse all day from dawn to sunset during the whole month of Ramadan each year with the intention of showing submission to God's command. The act of fasting during Ramadan is the means by which the Muslim recognizes the favour God did to His subjects in the month of Ramadan when He began the revelation of the Quran to the Prophet Muhammad (may God bless him).

Fasting is the means by which the Muslim voluntarily abandons certain legitimate frivolous enjoyments as a means of putting his soul to a test and promoting its capacity for perseverance, thus strengthening his will to keep away from sins, both obvious and obscure. The Muslim thereby samples enough of starvation to make him a warm-hearted, hospitable person, sympathetic with the poor who are in constant want. This is precisely the spirit Islam endeavours to create in the Muslim's heart and mind by requiring fasting as a mode of worship. Therefore, Islam attaches no significance to the kind of fasting that does not inspire this great humanitarian spirit, and a person fasting for any other purpose has nothing to gain except hunger and thirst.

Religious Tax

The third form of worship is the religious tax, *zakat*. This is a fiscal worship by which Islam requires the well-to-do to care for the needs of the poor and to pay a subsidy to maintain public benefits like hospitals, educational institutions, and a defense force. It is a sacred duty incumbent upon the rich to pay out of their possessions in excess of their requirements, and those of their dependents, portions which are universally recognized by Muslims as fair, and which in the aggregate meet the needs of the poor and the general interests of the community without adversely afflicting the owners. It is customary to give one-tenth of the product of the land if it is watered by rain and one-twentieth if it is irrigated by human effort; two and one-half per cent of savings is suggested, with equal proportions of the increase in cattle or in trade in goods. The motive for giving the religious tax is internal; there is no external pressure.

Worship through the giving of the religious tax is the best means of promoting the welfare of society, linking the classes of the community with reciprocal sympathy and compassion, and spreading throughout the people a sentiment of love and cooperation. Through the religious tax the nation protects itself from creating financial tyranny through the concentration of the bulk of the national income in the hands of a few individuals, or of the ruler who might claim it in the name of the state. The divine legislation which requires the religious tax preserves for the ordinary man freedom of choice as to his means of livelihood and at the same time provides the community with the aid and cooperation owed it by the individual. The Muslim who fails to pay the religious tax is failing in his religious duty and undermining one of the main pillars of Islam.

Pilgrimage

Pilgrimage is also a form of physical, or external, worship in Islam. The pilgrimage is an annual form of congregational worship in which those Muslims who are able to make the trip assemble from all over the world at Mecca, the home of the revelation to Muhammad (may God bless him). There they visit the Holy Mosque and pray to God in Arafat, a narrow defile some thirteen miles from Mecca. It is a public worship expressing the full equality among Muslims gathered together from all over the world with a common objective—all performing the same actions, all seeking to gain God's favour. At Mecca all pilgrims stand on equal footing whether rich or poor, rulers or ordinary people, scholars or labourers. There all of them, wearing similar white, seamless robes and shorn of class distinctions, assemble around a single centre which inspires them with a strong sense of unity. There their views and aims are unified and their resolution is strengthened to work cooperatively for the fulfillment of the general good. This, then, is worship in Islam—based on the beliefs required of all Muslims, worship is performed through prayer, fasting, payment of the religious tax, and pilgrimages. These forms of worship are required by Islam as owed to God in order that Muslims may please Him, observe His commands, and show their gratitude to Him. As Muslims perform their worship they always think of God and of His gifts related to the body, wealth, and society. At the same time the Muslim realizes that these ceremonies performed in honour of God are of benefit to himself. Prayer and fasting give the Muslim discipline which he needs and further the development of his spiritual life; the religious tax encourages communal cooperation to meet the requirements of the poor and of society; and the pilgrimage widens the circle of acquaintances and increases mutual understanding and cooperation under the shadow of revelation and divine guidance.

The Mosque

Although the prayers may be performed at the appropriate times wherever a Muslim happens to be, the mosque has since the dawn of Islam been the best environment for Islamic learning and the performance of religious ceremonies. It has been the centre for preaching and guidance, it has served as a court of law where disputes are reconciled, and has been like a social club where Muslims assemble to discuss topics of common interest. The mosque was not invented by Islam but is copied from ancient divine establishments. The Quran states that the first building set aside for worship for the people was the Holy Mosque erected by Abraham and his son Ishmael. The Good Book says of mosques in general, "He only shall tend Allah's sanctuaries who believes in Allah and the Last Day and observes proper worship and pays the poor-due and feareth none save Allah. For such (only) is it possible that they can be of the rightly guided" (Surah IX, 18).

The Quran mentions two mosques by name, the Divine Mosque in Mecca and the Aqsa Mosque in Jerusalem.

> *"Glorified be He who carried His servant by night from the inviolable Place of Worship [Mecca] to the Far Distant Place of Worship [Jerusalem], the neighbourhood whereof We have blessed" (Surah XVII, 1).*

Among the first things the Prophet did on his return to Medina was to establish his own mosque as a means of bringing the Muslims closer together and forming the Muslim community, and as a place for performing the magnificent communal prayer.

Following the example of the Prophet, the Caliphs set up mosques where Muslims worshipped their Lord on an equal footing without any distinctions whatsoever. Today mosques are found throughout the Islamic world as the symbol of Islam, the centre for Islamic worship, teachings, and service.

DEALINGS

Within the Islamic code, which provides guidance for all human activities, the distinction between worship and dealings is made for convenience in the exposition of Islam. We have seen the nature of the true worship of Islam; in considering the dealings we shall be concerned with the dealings within the Muslim community—the family, monetary affairs, relations with fellow Muslims, and government—and dealings with non-Muslims both as individuals and nations. Islamic law has clearly stated the obligations of the Muslims in all areas of life and the penalties to be inflicted for offenses and irregularities.

Under the guidance of its code of laws Islam preaches the one God and, by acknowledging the principle of equality, asserts the unity of the human race and denounces discrimination based on colour, racial, or regional differences. It aims at justice through the eradication of oppression and tyranny. It mistreats no stranger merely because he is a stranger in a strange land, nor the infidel because of his infidelity, nor the enemy because of his enmity; nor is a near relative given special treatment in Islamic law because of his relationship, nor is a friend shown partiality for his friendship, nor is a Muslim treated leniently because of his adherence to Islam.

> *"Be steadfast witnesses for Allah in equity, and let not hatred of any people seduce you that ye deal not justly. Deal justly, that is nearer to your duty" (Surah V, 8).*

The family. Marriage in Islam requires the full agreement of both parties without compulsion being brought to bear on either person. A marriage which takes place forcibly is considered null and void. When an agreement is reached between the two, the man pays to the woman the bride money, which is a token of admiration, not a purchase price or a form of remuneration. The actual amount of the bride money is determined by agreement and is the exclusive property of the prospective wife; the husband is not entitled to use it in any way without her consent.

The marriage contract is repeated in the presence of two or more witnesses. The bride says, "I marry you to myself," and the groom replies, "I accept your marriage to me." It is quite in order for the two accredited agents for the bride and groom to repeat the phrases of the marriage contract also. If the contract is not authenticated by two witnesses it is unlawful, and no marriage exists between the two. Properly witnessed, this verbal contract completes the marriage and the man and woman may establish their home.

In Islam, the husband, by virtue of his physical strength and ability to secure means of livelihood, is given the responsibility of guardianship of the wife and of the home, within the framework of their reciprocal legal rights and obligations. Such guardianship is not an autocratic authority which excludes the wife from expressing her views or from the right of consultation; it is merely a rank of honour and control which must respect the wife's point of view.

Thus it is seen that the marriage in Islam is a simple agreement between two parties without any participation by religious or civil authorities. Nor does it curtail the wife's freedom of action or her control of property, so long as she lives up to the responsibilities of married life and cares for the home and children.

Islam authorizes a man to marry a second wife in special circumstances in which the objectives of the initial marriage, such as the begetting of children, cannot be fulfilled. There can be no doubt that marriage to a second wife is the best solution to the problem in cases in which the first wife, if divorced, might not be able to remarry or might have no one to look after her. Islam permits a man to have not more than four wives and stipulates that he may have not more than one wife unless he is able to discharge the rights of each wife and maintain absolute equity between them. Islam authorizes the woman to bring her case before justice if she believes that by marrying another wife her husband sought to injure her.

Islam permits marriage with Christians and Jews. In the Quran He says, "This day are (all) good things made lawful for you. The food of those who have received the Scripture is lawful for you, and your food is lawful for them. And so are the virtuous women of the believers and the virtuous women of those who received the Scripture before you" (Surah V, 5). But Islam forbids Muslims to marry disbelievers or polytheists, for He says, "Wed not idolatresses till they believe; for a believing bondwoman is better than an idolatress though she please you; and give not your daughters in marriage to idolaters till they believe, for lo! a believing slave is better than an idolater though he please you" (Surah II, 221).

Islam seeks to stabilize married life and reconcile differences between the husband and wife. It orders, for instance, that when there is a disagreement between husband and wife they should turn to their family or near relatives for arbitration. But if ill feelings gain such a hold on the married couple that their union is endangered, and no arbitration can succeed, and married life develops from a state of tranquillity, love, and compassion into one of anxiety, hardship, and boycott, and indeed is almost hell, then in such a situation, and only in such a situation, the husband is allowed by Islam, against its better judgment, to seek the remedy of divorce. Strictly speaking, divorce is a right bestowed on the husband in view of his ability to shoulder the marriage obligations and because of his aptitude for better self-restraint than the wife can display.

If the shock of divorce fulfills the purpose for which it is intended and both the husband and wife return to their senses, then they are permitted by Islam to resume their marriage within the terms of the Islamic code. Islam permits the husband to resort to the remedy of divorce twice, and to remarry each time if a satisfactory reconciliation is attained, but a third divorce is decisive and a woman so divorced cannot be made a legitimate wife a fourth time unless she first marries a different man and is then divorced by that man of his own free will, and there have been no consequences of that marriage. If that marriage had been arranged with the intention of divorcing him so that she might go back to her original husband, the contract for the second marriage was unlawful.

It is thus seen that Islam has not allowed divorce in order that a man may use the threat of divorce as a sword which he waves in the woman's face. On the contrary, Islam allows divorce as a bitter medicine to be used by a man to cure a situation or get rid of an association that defies remedy. Islam holds that if a man trespasses on a woman's rights by divorcing her without cause he is abusing his power and is therefore liable to be held responsible for committing a breach of duty. Islamic courts are allowed to censure the man for misusing the right of divorce.

The law of Islam permits the woman to ask the courts of law to look into her case if her husband maintains an unpleasant association with her, or causes real hardship to her unjustifiably, or if she finds that he suffers from a disease of the body or mind which prevents him from preserving her chastity. The court is authorized to order her to be divorced if she is justified in her contentions and her husband refuses to divorce her.

Just as Islam maintains equality between husband and wife in married life it insists on equality in the termination of the marriage. It does not allow the man in any circumstances to take undue advantage of the woman's innate weakness to deny her any of her rights or to abuse the rights which she owes to him. At the same time, it does not require a woman to go beyond her obligations to keep intact her purity and to preserve her husband's property and the home.

The family bears a special responsibility for the education of the children in Islam. The training begins with teaching the child to repeat lessons concerning Islamic beliefs and to perform correctly the worship rites. The family is also responsible for seeing that the child receives further training in the school and the mosque where legitimate and illegitimate actions and beliefs are expounded so that when the child attains maturity he will have been guided along the way to a true understanding of Islam.

Monetary Affairs: Inheritance in Islam is based on the blood relationship of parents, brothers and sisters, and children, and on the marriage relationship of husband and wife, without regard for sex or age in the right of inheritance. The parents, the children, and the consorts do not in any circumstances lose this right, though the amount of their share may be affected by the number of heirs. However, brothers and sisters are not entitled to inheritance in case the parents are living. If men and women are both heirs, the man receives twice as much as a woman except in the case of maternal half-brothers and half-sisters, who each get an equal share.

Islamic law has ruled that, since the man bears the support of the woman and the expenses of her children as well as the cost of her marriage, his share of the inheritance should be double that of the woman. Her share is allowed to stand her in good stead in case she loses the source of her livelihood. Islam has taken into consideration the fact that to allocate the inheritance among blood relatives and consorts strengthens bonds of affection and promotes among relatives a reciprocal interest in their common good. Jealousy would prevail and the family structure would be exposed to disintegration if favouritism were allowed among heirs of equal standing. Thanks to this system, Islamic society has been guarded against the threat of financial tyranny which may result when the entire inheritance goes to a single person. It is also guarded against the danger which would come from paying the inheritance into the state treasury, for that would deprive members of the family of the results of the efforts made by parents, children, relatives, husbands, and wives, and would be damaging to society.

Islamic law also sets the standards for financial dealings through its regulations governing such things as the terms of sale and lease, things liable to sale and lease and those liable to neither, ways to employ capital, conditions regulating deposits, authentication of debts, and like matters which could become sources of controversy. All these financial dealings must be based on truthfulness, fidelity, and a willingness to discharge obligations.

Government: The necessity for some sort of government in the Muslim community is indicated by many texts in the Quran, such as, "Retaliation is prescribed for you in the matter of the murdered" (Surah II, 178). "Lo! Allah commandeth you that ye restore deposits to their owners, and, if ye judge between mankind, that ye judge justly" (Surah IV, *58)*. The obligations imposed upon the community by the Quran can only be discharged by the community deputizing a spokesman from its midst, a man possessing the mental qualifications, will power, and skills which enable him to secure unity of thought and cooperation in carrying out the tasks required for the common welfare. Such a man is known in Islam as the Caliph or Imam.

It is the duty of the Caliph or Imam, the leader in Islam, to consolidate public opinion, execute judgments, administer state machinery, encourage the faithful in the practice of their faith, such as prayers and the religious tax, and look after affairs of public interest with the guidance of a parliamentary democracy, the basis of government in Islam. The Caliph, in Islamic practice, is subject to control by the nation; he has no authority other than that given to him as a representative of the people and that which is required of him as the enforcer of supernatural laws. If he violates the terms of national representation or breaks God's orders, it is up to the nation to depose him and replace him. The Caliphate or Imamate in Islam is not based on a heavenly sanction which gives the Caliph power from God to rule the nation; he has no divine authority which makes it the duty of the people to obey him at any cost. The Caliph or Imam is only a member of the society whose actions are determined by divine laws and orders. The Caliph and the nation form an inseparable whole linked together by the strong tie of religious faith, worship of God, fair dealing, and interest in the public welfare. The Prophet (may God bless him) says, "The Muslims are equal before God." The first Caliph in Islam said, "Obey me so long as I obey God and the Prophet in dealing with you. Once I cease obeying them you are no longer obliged to obey me."

Thus in Islam we find no distinction in community life between that which is called religious and that which is outside religion. In Islam religion is concerned with faith and worship, and also with the upbringing, education, and guidance of the people, and with all economic and social dealings as to those which are legitimate and illegitimate, sound or corrupt; and religion is concerned with the government of the people and the administration of state machinery, with the operation of all the functions of the community or nation. Religion provides the guiding principles for the individual and for the state. There can be no state which has a separate framework for the government and for religion. Those Islamic regions which separate the state from religion are following a mere private school of thought, contrary to the teachings of Islam.

Islam recognizes equally the rights and responsibilities of the individual and the community. It has built its legislation on the recognition that a man has a personality independent of his compatriots and his community, a personality which forms an element in the social structure. He has rights and obligations as an independent individual and rights and responsibilities as a part of the nation to which he belongs. As an independent person, man is required by Islam to believe in God, worship Him, and to live in a manner which assures him a clear conscience; it is incumbent upon him to work for a living, to control himself and his children, and to realize his interests and maintain his existence without encroaching upon the life and welfare of other people. It is his right to own property and to enjoy the legitimate pleasures of life. As a member of the community it is the divine duty of man to contribute to the general good, to guide and aid his fellow men, to do his full share in furthering the social amenities of the community, and to take part in fighting the common enemy.

In return for the individual's fulfillment of his obligations, the community is required by Islam to protect the individual's life and property, and to safeguard the chastity of his womenfolk. Islam has legislated for this purpose, clearly defining the functions of the legitimate ruler who is representative of the community, and outlining the penalties which the ruler must enforce.

Within the Islamic framework the individual and the community have defined for them the rights and obligations which ensure life and happiness through cooperation and equity in assigning privileges and tasks without encroaching upon the rights of the individual or the community. Should the individual deny to the community any of the rights due to it, he deserves God's denunciation, and it is the duty of the ruler to censure him on behalf of the nation. And if the society, as represented in the ruler, fails to ensure the rights of the individual, then the individual is entitled to insist upon his rights, and the ruler deserves God's condemnation and anger. When the ruler does not protect the rights of the individual, the community is empowered to depose him and to replace him with a man who is able to live up to the functions of his high office.

Dealings with non-Muslims: Islam does not hold any enmity or hatred toward non-Muslims. It stands for peaceful coexistence and cooperation in daily life with them. For thus the Quran says, "Say: O disbelievers! I worship not that which ye worship; Nor worship ye that which I worship. And I shall not worship that which ye worship. Nor will ye worship that which I worship. Unto you your religion, and unto me my religion" (Surah CIX). "Unto this, then, summon (O Muhammad). And be thou upright as thou art commanded, and follow not their lusts, but say: I believe in whatever Scripture Allah has sent down, and I am commanded to be just among you. Allah is our Lord and your Lord. Unto us our works and unto you your works; no argument between us and you. Allah will bring us together, and unto Him is the journeying" (Surah XLII, 15). When non-Muslims are resident in the same country with Muslims, the most important thing is to ensure freedom of belief and the opportunity for non-Muslims to worship God in their own sanctuaries and hold their religious ceremonies, and to maintain full equality between them and their Muslim compatriots in public rights and obligations.

As we have seen, Muslims are permitted to marry Christian or Jewish women, and such wives enjoy the same rights and duties as Muslim wives with full liberty to cherish their own religion and perform their religious duties.

Even if parents are polytheists and even if they strive to mislead their Muslim son to follow them, he is commanded by the Quran to be good to them and to treat them gently, for Allah says, "And We have enjoined upon man concerning his parents... But if they strive with thee to make thee ascribe unto Me as partner that of which thou hast no knowledge, then obey them not. Consort with them in the world kindly, and follow the path of him who repenteth unto Me" (Surah XXXI, 14-15). It is said in history that Abu Talib, the Prophet's uncle, who was a polytheist until his death, was a good helper and protector of Muhammad.

Islam is strongly averse to resorting to force to expound its cause or to compel people to embrace its faith. Islam's invitation to non-Muslims to embrace Islam is made by an explanation of its advantages—its easily understandable faith, its simple obligations in religious ceremonies and dealings, its tolerant ethical principles, freedom of research, deep understanding of the universe, and the fact that it makes no distinction between men except by virtue of piety and good achievements. It points out that in Islam no man has authority over another person's beliefs, and that only God has authority to introduce beliefs and to require or receive worship.

Islam bases its policy for relations between Muslims and other people of varying beliefs on acquaintanceship, cooperation, and working for the common good. Non-Muslims who live in the community in cooperation and peace are looked upon by Islam as equal to Muslims, each of them holding to his faith and preaching its aims with wisdom and friendly argument without bringing pressure to bear on anyone or encroaching on each other's rights. Islam requires of non-Muslims only abstention from hostility to Muslims and from sedition or opposition to the Islamic way of life.

In the relations between Muslim and non-Muslim states, Islam stands for "inviting the world to do good." Islam permits treaties and cooperation with non-Muslim powers in time of peace so long as the treaties do not contradict the basic principles of Islam. "Allah forbiddes you not those who warred not against you on account of religion and drove you not out from your homes, that ye should show them kindness and deal justly with them. Lo! Allah loves the just dealers. Allah forbiddes you only those who warred against you on account of religion and have driven you out from your homes and helped to drive you out, that ye make friends of them. Whosoever maketh friends of them—(All) such are wrong-doers" (Surah LX, 8-9).

Islam does not turn from friendly relations with non-Muslim countries unless it is the victim of an aggressive attack, or obstacles are placed in the path of Islam, or attempts are made to seduce the people. When Islam is exposed to such hardships, its believers are permitted, and indeed it is made incumbent upon them, to repel aggression, to restore peace, and to establish a just situation in which people can think and act freely. Islam forbids Muslims to launch aggressive war motivated by a spirit of cruelty, or a desire to drain the resources of a people, or to cause suffering, or to eject people from their homes. After an approved war breaks out, Islam rejects devastation or extermination as methods of war. It does not permit the killing of members of the civilian population who are not actively engaged in hostilities, such as women, children, the old, and the disabled. The Prophet said, "Do not exterminate the young ones." When he was asked, "Aren't they the children of the infidel?" he replied. "Are not the best among you children of infidels?"

Islam does not permit participation in war until after the causes are clearly known and the enemy has received a warning. Islam condemns maltreatment of prisoners of war, their persecution, or their murder. It is made clear in the Quran that the prisoners must be fed in order to win God's satisfaction. "And feed with food the needy wretch, the orphan and the prisoner, for love of Him" (Surah LXXVI, 8). The termination of an approved war does not require that the enemy forces embrace Islam. It is considered sufficient if the enemy stops his evil aggression and signs a treaty which preserves the rights of the people, and protects them from tyranny or sedition.

Such are the principles which govern the relations of Muslim and non-Muslim nations and the code of *jihad*—the Holy Struggle. The basis for the Islamic code of war was laid in the Quran and it was carried out in practice by the Prophet and his foremost successors.

Penalties and Rewards: Up to this point we have been discussing the Islamic code—worship and dealings. The code also states the rewards and penalties which are in store in this world and in the Second World. Islam has specified the death penalty for murder, the cutting off of the hand for theft, and flogging for adultery and slander. The punishment is definitely stated for these three categories of offences only; the penalties for other offences and irregularities are left to the ruler who is representative of the nation and who acts after consultation with the people.

Concerning the rewards and penalties in the next world, Allah has said, "Whoso obeys Allah and His messenger, He will make him enter Gardens underneath which rivers flow, where such will dwell for ever. That will be the great success. And whoso disobeys Allah and His messenger and transgresses His limits, He will make him enter Fire, where such will dwell for ever; his will be a shameful doom" (Surah IV, 13-14). The penalty for the aggressor and the corrupt is stated in God's saying, "The only reward for those who make war upon Allah and His messenger and strive after corruption in the land will be that they will be killed or crucified, or have their hands and feet on alternate sides cut off, or will be expelled out of the land. Such will be their degradation in the world, and in the Hereafter theirs will be an awful doom" (Surah V, 33)

Thus we see that in both worship and dealings man stands before his Lord and receives rewards or punishment in the afterlife according to his merits. In Islam, both worship and dealings are religious ceremonies and the Muslim must answer for all his actions before God in the Second World just as he must answer before a court of law in this world.

If a Muslim commits a breach of divine law through intent and premeditation, it constitutes a dangerous sin for which he alone is responsible. Even an accomplice who seduces him to commit the sin cannot relieve him of responsibility; he must, as an accomplice, bear his own sin. According to the Quran it is a law of God of long standing that it is only the sinner who bears responsibility, "That no laden one shall bear another's load" (Surah LIII, 38). One of the clearly established principles of Islam is that only God forgives sins, and that God has given no authorization to anyone whatsoever to pardon sins, "Who forgives sins save Allah only?" (Surah III, 135). Another principle is that all sins are pardoned by God as he pleases except the sin of infidelity This is expressly stated in the Quran, "Lo! Allah pardones not that partners should be ascribed unto Him. He pardones all save that to whom He will" (Surah IV, 116). Infidelity includes doubt in God's oneness and divinity. Therefore those who denounce the Creator, and those who worship other than God, and those who disagree with God's legislation as to that which is legitimate or illegitimate are all infidels.

It is also a principle of Islam that if a sinner repents and abstains from committing further sins because of fear of God and a determination to uphold His orders, God has pledged to forgive the sin. "And He it is Who accepts repentance from his bondmen, and pardones the evil deeds, and knows what ye do" (Surah XLII, 25). And Islam holds to the principle that man is born free from sins and remains free of sin until he is mature and has heard God's teachings. If, then, he closes his eyes to God's teachings and refuses to observe them, only then is he regarded as a sinner, with exclusive responsibility for his sins.

THE MORAL FRAMEWORK

Thus far in this chapter we have dealt with Islamic beliefs, Islamic worship, and Islamic dealings. The moral framework of Islam is a fourth element of equal significance in the life of a Muslim, entailing reward or punishment in the afterlife according to its observances or neglect. The moral principles of Islam strengthen the Muslim's resolve to adhere strictly to Islamic teachings and rules of conduct for polite society. They consolidate the bonds of understanding and unify sentiment and common feeling among Muslims. Allah urges Muslims to speak the truth, forget and forgive, and display compassion, mercy, valor, and love in all their relations with others.

The moral framework of Islam states the principles of etiquette for polite society for the common people as well as for the most advanced. The Quran says concerning the etiquette of walking and modesty in one's bearing, "Turn not thy cheek in scorn toward folk, nor walk with pertness in the land. Lo! Allah loves not each braggard boaster. Be modest in thy bearing and subdue thy voice" (Surah XXXI, 18-19).

Concerning the etiquette of calling on one's neighbours, "Lo! those who call thee from behind the private apartments, most of them have no sense" (Surah XLIX, 4). And also, "Enter not houses other than your own without first announcing your presence and invoking peace upon the folk thereof" (Surah XXIV, 27).

And in closing the door to sexual irregularities, the Quran says, "Tell the believing men to lower their gaze and be modest. That is purer for them. Lo! Allah is Aware of what they do. And tell the believing women to lower their gaze and be modest" (Surah XXIV, 30-31). And concerning unkind conversations, "Lee not a folk deride a folk who may be better than they (are), nor let women (deride) women who may be better than they are; neither defame one another, nor insult one another by nicknames" (Surah XLIX, 11).

By these and similar rules of social etiquette Islam guided the steps of people in backward stages of development, urging them to rise to an appropriate standard and attain the level of the more advanced social classes. At the same time Islam invites men of all levels to live up to the highest point of ethical and spiritual progress. "Keep to forgiveness (O Muhammad), and enjoin kindness, and turn away from the ignorant" (Surah VII, 199). "The good deed and the evil deed are not alike. Repel the evil deed with one which is better" (Surah XLI, 34). "Those who spend (of that which Allah has given them) in ease and adversity, those who control their wrath and are forgiving toward mankind; Allah loves the good" (Surah III, 134). "If ye publish your alms-giving, it is well, but if ye hide it and give it to the poor, it will be better for you" (Surah II, 271).

In calling upon the people to guide their lives by these ethical principles, Islam insists, in the main, that they should be moderate in all things, sparing themselves misery and not lowering their status in life. Islam requires courage of Muslims and warns them against cowardice and extravagance. It demands forgiveness and renounces both submissive humbleness and revenge. It upholds hospitality and condemns spendthrift and miserly economy. It preaches perseverance and rejects panic and defeatism. It constantly urges, "Give the kinsman his due, and the needy, and the wayfarer, and squander not (thy wealth) in wantonness" (Surah XVII, 26). It praises moderation in all things, "And those who, when they spend, are neither prodigal nor grudging; and there is ever a firm station between the two" (Surah XXV, 67).

These illustrate, briefly, the ethical principles which guide the actions of the Muslim.

SOURCES OF ISLAMIC LEGISLATION

The fundamental source of Islamic legislation is the Quran, which has been proved beyond all doubt as God's own book brought down by His Prophet to guide the people to obey its commands and to refrain from actions which it prohibits. The legislation of the Quran is of two kinds: that which has a crystal clear and decisive meaning not open to debate, and legislation liable to have two or more meanings.

The secondary sources of Islamic legislation are the Sunnah and the schools of thought, dealing with those areas not decisively covered in the Quran, the areas of probable meaning. After the Quran, the chief interpretative authority for Islamic legislation is the Sunnah—Muhammad's own sayings, deeds, and legislative decisions which have been correctly and authoritatively transmitted. If a problem arises which is not dealt with clearly in the Quran or in the Sunnah, the answer is sought in the schools of thought, the theories worked out by "leaders of thought" who have been careful students of the Quran and the Sunnah, have thought profoundly about their inner meanings and understand their general principles, and who have special knowledge of virtue and the general welfare.

The order of merit of the three sources of Islamic legislation has been recognized by Muslims from the days of the Prophet. They will continue to be the basis of Islamic legislation to the end of time.

The Quran: In the previous discussions of the Quran we have seen that it contains many specific passages calling upon the people to follow its teachings and be guided by its legislation. "Lo! We reveal unto thee the Scripture with the truth, that thou may judge between mankind by that which Allah shows thee" (Surah IV, 105). "These are the limits (imposed by) Allah. Transgress them not. For whoso transgresses Allah's limits: such are wrongdoers" (Surah II, 229).

The Quran legislates concerning worship, enjoining fixed hours for prayer; it prescribes fasting, the giving of alms, and pilgrimage. It lays down the regulations for family life—marriage and divorce. It gives clear directions concerning financial dealings, contracts and pledges, relations with the people of the scriptures and with infidels, holy war and fighters and non-fighters, the administration of community life, sources of legislation, and the penalties for disobedience.

Thus the Quran is established as the foundation of the faith and of the code of legislation. Although the legislation in the Quran which may have two or more meanings is the subject of theory and study, the legislation which is explicit and open to only one meaning is binding on all Muslims. Should the Muslim fail to follow such legislation in his practical affairs, he is looked upon as rejecting Islam. Whoever alleges that the Quran is the product of a particular people, or a special age, or a limited aspect of human life is a disbeliever in Islam and in God's Book.

The Sunnah: There are two aspects to the Sunnah: legislation given by the Prophet on matters not specifically detailed in the Quran, and traditions based on the actions and utterances of Muhammad as a human being.

The legislation given by the Prophet is illustrated by the rules stating the form of prayer, the pilgrimage rites, and giving in detail the limits of legitimacy in marriage. For instance, marriage is illegitimate between two people who in their infancy fed from the same breasts, and a man may not be married at the same time to a woman and to her aunt. This type of teaching is based on the tradition of Muhammad's instructions on matters not specified in the Quran.

The second aspect of the Sunnah is not associated with legislation. It deals with the traditions based on the actions and teachings of Muhammad concerning the affairs left to man's discretion, affairs for which God has given no definite command as to their legitimacy or illegitimacy, such as when to stand up and when to sit, the etiquette pertaining to eating and drinking and sleeping, and matters to be dealt with on the basis of experience or expert knowledge like agriculture, industry, medicine, military discipline, and tactics. It is authentically related that the Prophet, in the course of one of his battles, ordered an army contingent to be dispatched to a particular point, but a group of his disciples objected, "Is it a position God commanded you to choose, or have you chosen it as a strategist?" He replied, "No, it is one of my own choosing." His disciples pointed out that it was not an ideal position and gave their reasons for preferring an alternate location. The Prophet was convinced and dropped his plan. At another time he expressed his views as to the proper way to fertilize palm trees, but the trees failed to produce fruit. When he was informed of the result, he said, "You are better acquainted with your own worldly affairs."

Knowledge which depends on human experience and traditions related to the Prophet concerning such matters are not the basis for Islamic legislation. Traditions attributed to the Prophet can only be a source of legislation that must be obeyed if they are based on revelations given to him to guide the people according to God's laws.

The Sunnah as a source of legislation is always subordinate to the principles and fundamental laws of the Quran; its importance lies in the fact that it expounds specific aspects of the general principles of the Quran. Sometimes the expounding may be done by the example of an action; in the case of prayer, the Prophet showed how it is performed, the number of kneelings required for each prayer, and the proper time limits for its performance. The expounding may also be done by adding certain ceremonies not expressly described in the Quran. Expounding is also done by the Prophet in expressing opinions concerning general rules, such as the opinion that the simpler of two possibilities should be chosen in following a general principle stated in the Quran.

Hence we may assert that the legislative Sunnah is an attempt on the part of the Prophet to teach the real meaning of the Quran, its inner implications and aims. Thus, the legislation based on the Sunnah really springs from the Quran.

God's policy in relation to the Prophet's endeavour to interpret the Quran was to endorse his endeavour if it was right and proper, and to direct his attention to the correct interpretation and even to censure him if he was in error. Once when the Prophet out of dutiful regard for his faith was wilfully denying himself certain good things allowable by God, He said, "O Prophet! Why bannest thou that which Allah has made lawful for thee, seeking to please thy wives?" (Surah LXVI, 1). This and similar instances in which the Prophet tried to get at the correct answer but failed provide the best proof that the Prophet used his discretion to determine things about which no revelation was forthcoming, and that whenever he made a mistake God directed him along the correct path.

Thus the Prophet used his discretion and received God's endorsement when he was right, and the result became law, binding on the people. So, also, his disciples copied his example and used their discretion when necessary, and on being informed of the outcome of their efforts the Prophet endorsed them if they were in order and God agreed with his approval. If they were in error, the Prophet directed his disciples' attention to the correct answer to which God guided him. In this way the results of his disciples' endeavours in his time were associated with his own efforts to interpret the Quran and became legislative Sunnah which it is incumbent on the people to respect. Thus we see that during the Prophet's lifetime there was no source of legislation other than the Quran and the Prophet's interpretation of it either through revelation or discretion.

The authenticity of the Sunnah is proved by the Quran, for it orders that the Prophet should be obeyed and it made obedience to him a form of obedience to God and a recognition of His love, "But nay, by thy Lord, they will not believe (in truth) until they make thee judge of what is in dispute between them and find within themselves no dislike of that which thou decides, and submit with full submission" (Surah IV, 65).

If the purpose of the legislation of the Sunnah is to expound the legislation of the Quran, and if God's policy with His Prophet was to endorse Muhammad's interpretation when it was correct and to guide him to what was right when he made a mistake, then the Sunnah legislation is the same as the legislation of the Quran, and equally binding on all Muslims.

Schools of Thought: In the time of the Prophet there were two sources of Islamic legislation: the fundamental source in the Quran, and the interpretative source in the Sunnah. After Muhammed's death his disciples found themselves in an expanding Islamic world, facing new issues for which they needed the guidance of explicit legislation. They would refer to the Quran and if they failed to find a satisfactory answer there they would turn to the Sunnah, which was preserved for them by reliable men who were fully acquainted with the Prophet's interpretations. If they did not find the answer to their question in either the Quran or the Sunnah, they pondered the points at issue—guided by their knowledge of the aims and guiding principles of Islamic legislation—and came to conclusions which are consistent with the Quran and the Sunnah, and have the authority of legislation. In this way the schools of thought, under carefully controlled conditions, became a third source of Islamic legislation.

The schools of thought, in their interpretations of the probable meanings of passages in the Quran and the Sunnah and in their rulings concerning issues not definitely dealt with in those sources, adopted certain general principles found in Quranic legislation as a guide. These are some of the principles on which the schools of thought based their decisions: all things are fundamentally allowable, unless specifically prohibited; toleration and the lifting of restrictions should be the aim of legislation; eradication of mischief is the aim of administration; necessity permits benefiting by things not otherwise allowable; necessity is given due appreciation; preventing mischief has priority over bringing about welfare; commit the lesser of two evils; mischief is not removed by mischief; one should suffer private damage to avert general disaster. Such general principles are the guides for the creation and interpretation of Islamic law.

Under the first two Caliphs: Abu Bakr and Umar, it was the policy when deciding public issues to consult with the leading disciples who were recognized for their accurate thinking, appreciation of the interests of the people, and grasp of the spirit of the legislation of the Quran and the Sunnah. When unity of view was achieved among those responsible leaders of the Muslim community, it was put into practice. In this way, the adoption of a law through consultation and a consensus *(ijma)* of the opinions of the leaders of Islam became a new source of Islamic legislation after the Prophet's death, covering all matters which were not expressly mentioned or clearly implied in either the Quran or the Sunnah.

The authenticity of the legislation of the schools of thought is assured by the Quran, for it says that the affairs of the people are matters of counsel and it orders that the people should obey the authority of those who are responsible for the common good and are known for sound interpretation. Such legislation is also authorized by the Sunnah, for the Prophet dispatched his lieutenants to remote regions with authority to use their discretion when guided by the consensus of opinion on all issues not defined in the Quran and Sunnah.

During the regimes of the first two Caliphs the differences of opinion were quite limited because of the trouble they took to ascertain the authenticity of the Sunnah and the importance they gave to consultations among the students of the law from among the Prophet's disciples, most of whom were resident at the Caliph's headquarters. It is important to note that the regimes of the two Shaikhs Abu Bakr and Umar are the only ones which define the correct use of discretion as a source of legislation. They show that discretion as a source of legislation must reach its conclusions through consultation which arrives at unity of view among Muslims of authority who are qualified to decide issues. Thus unity of view, considered by Islam to be a source of legislation in cases where neither the Quran nor the Sunnah is applicable, is the agreement reached by investigation and study by men of thought who understand the spirit of Islamic legislation and are responsible for guiding the interests of the people in the community.

Unity of view as a source of Islamic legislation is not the same as complete agreement among all members of the nation, whether men of thought or mere laymen, scholars or ordinary people. Such general agreement about Islamic principles definitely known to have been enacted is not the subject of thought and discretion and should be held equally by all Muslims. It is simply the general acceptance of the beliefs and code of legislation required of all members of the Islamic community.

For the unity of thought which is considered to be a source of binding legislation, the agreement or disagreement on the part of those not qualified to state views has no weight. Unity of view which can be the source of legislation must be attained through the use of methods of thinking and investigation which have been approved as valid; it must be reached by a limited number of men from among all classes of the nation, whose qualifications for the use of the approved methods are recognized; the views of all the qualified men must be ascertained; and unanimous agreement on a specific ruling must be sought. The unanimous agreement is difficult to attain because of the varying abilities of the men participating and the diversity of interests and regional circumstances influencing each investigator. Therefore it is recognized that unanimity can be achieved only on the basis of the principles that "there is no knowledge of any dissidents," or of "agreement by the preponderant majority." This is all that can be done to attain unity of view which can be a basis for legislation. "Allah tasks not a soul beyond its scope" (Surah II, 286). However, in seeking unity of thought as a basis for legislation, freedom of thought must be ensured for all those participating and no authority should bring to bear any pressure which would restrict the liberty of thought.

Islamic legislation based upon the consensus of opinion of the leaders qualified to decide is subject to review and alteration. The interests on which the leaders were called to rule vary in different areas, places, and conditions, making it allowable for the successors of the original leaders to review the position in the light of new circumstances and to make a new decision if the changed situation requires it. The new unanimity replaces the former legislation and becomes the new law which ought to be followed.

Individual Private Discretion: In addition to the discretion employed in communal consultations concerning issues not specifically covered in the Quran or the Sunnah, there is the private discretion of the individual man in which decisions are reached by independent thinking. Private discretion *(ijtihad)* is not binding on anyone except the individual who uses it. Islam recognizes that the right of private discretion belongs to any individual who possesses the capacity for clear thinking and study, whether man or woman, ruler or subject, leading government civil servant or private citizen. Just as they have an equal right to engage in individual discretion, so do they have equal responsibility for making mistakes. Islam knows of no one who is immune from committing errors except the Prophet insofar as revelation was concerned. If the Prophet was liable to make mistakes in trying to find the correct answer—and indeed he did try and did make mistakes—then other Muslims, even those of great accomplishment or near relationship to Muhammad, are more liable to commit error.

The exercise of individual discretion was widespread after the time of the first two Caliphs, particularly after the great sedition arising out of the assassination of the third Caliph, Uthman. In its extreme form it transmuted Muslims into contending sects following their own private tendencies in determining schools of thinking and in conveying prophetic sayings.

It should be clearly understood that Islam does not set aside a specific person with the right to interpret the Quran or the Sunnah, nor does it make it a duty of the people to adhere to any person's individual views on questions which are open to private opinion. Every Muslim qualified to investigate questions has the right to do so. Muslims who are not qualified ought to enquire concerning the qualifications of those who speak concerning the obligations of Islamic law. Islam does not bind any Muslim to follow a particular person, for no duty is owed other than those duties which were assigned by God and the Prophet. Nor did God or the Prophet order anyone to follow a given religious school of thought—with the result that since the dawn of Islam Muslims have been asking for right answers from any well-known students of religion they meet, without binding themselves to any specific teacher. Therefore Islam does not recognize as legitimate any tendency to imitate a given school of thought. All those who have legitimately used their discretion have warned others against copying their example unless they have been convinced by proof of the validity of their findings. They have said, "If this talk proves untrue, then it is just my own theory, and it is up to you to disregard all that I have said."

Thus it is understood that the men who hold religious positions in Islam, such as the Caliph or Imam, have no monopoly on thinking and understanding, nor are they immune from making errors, nor do they receive revelation or special inspiration. Such leaders can only advise, and guide, and administer justice within the limits of Islamic laws. The Caliph or Imam is elected to his office by the nation, and he represents the nation while in office. So long as he discharges his functions within the framework of God's orders, the nation aids and obeys him—and it deposes him if he deviates from the right course.

The position of the Judge (*Qadi*), or the *Mufti*, the *Shaikh of Islam*, and the *Mullak* is similar to that of the Caliph in matters of understanding and legislation. The Judge's responsibility is limited to passing judgment on disputes between parties in accordance with the laws of Islam. The Mufti's function is to explain questions put to him. If he happens to be a man of discretion, the Mufti expresses his own views; otherwise he copies someone else's opinions. However, his answers to questions are not binding on those who resort to him; they have the right to insist on proof that the answers are correct and his tradition is authentic, and they are entitled to ask the same or other questions of someone else in whose knowledge they have confidence.

Shaikh of Islam and *Mullah* are titles which gained popularity among Muslims in certain regions and eras, conferred on men who distinguished themselves in religious and legislative knowledge. Neither of them is depended upon for decisions in legislative matters, and they are not immune from committing mistakes. Islam does not recognize one Shaikh or one Mullah who has authority in Islamic knowledge, and certain religious sects which claim such leadership are deviations from Islamic teachings far from being in order.

Within the area in which private discretion is appropriate, whoever believed himself competent to think clearly did his best to understand the correct implications of Islamic teachings, each thinker following his own style of study and inference. Some thinkers confined themselves to a limited number of prophetic sayings, because of the spread of invented sayings which cast doubt on many widely accepted sayings. They preferred to rely upon general rules and the spirit of Islamic legislation. Such thinkers are known in the history of Islamic jurisprudence as rationalists, or men of thought. Others, known as students of the prophetic sayings, convinced themselves of the authenticity of the transmission of many more of the prophetic sayings and preferred to rely upon them for their decisions. Other thinkers based their judgments on the traditions prevailing in Medina because it was the environment where legislation was made at the time of the Prophet and during the first two Caliphates before the outbreak of the sedition.

Out of such varying uses of the right of private discretion there grew up schools of religious thought which in time gained popularity in Islam and were allowed to spread. In modern times there are four of these schools of interpretation, or schools of Islamic law, which are found living amicably together in the Islamic world. The Hanafi 'school was founded by Imam al-

Numan Ibn Thabit, who died in Baghdad in the year 150 (AD. 767*)*, based on the teachings of Abu Hanifah; the Maliki school was founded by Malik Ibn Anas, who died in Medina in 179 (AD. 795 the Shafii school was founded by Muhammad Ibn Idris al-Shafii, a native of Gaza who died m Cairo in 205 (AD. 820); and the Hanbali school was founded by Imam Ahmad Ibn Hanbal, a Persian who died in Baghdad in 241 (AD. 855).

These four schools of thought are still taught in most institutions of learning in Islamic countries. The Hanafi school is found chiefly in India, the countries which were under the Ottoman Turks, and China; the Maliki school is found today in North Africa and Upper Egypt; the Shafiis are found in Indonesia, southern Arabia, lower Egypt, and parts of Syria; the Hanbali school is influential in Saudi Arabia.

The fact that Islam has permitted individual as well as communal discretion—limited only by the original definite legislation of the Quran and the Sunnah, which define the roads to justice—enabled students of the Islamic code to choose freely the laws regulating the affairs of Islamic society. Such toleration has been the basis for the everlasting usefulness of the Islamic code and for its fitness to regulate the affairs of life everywhere and at all times.

3

Islamic Beliefs and Code of Laws

In the Name of Allah, the Beneficent, the Merciful

Islam is the religion of Allah revealed to the Prophet Muhammad (Allah bless him and give him peace) in order that he might proclaim it to all mankind and men might be able to believe in it and put its teachings and regulations into practice.

The Apostle transmitted the Scripture precisely as it was revealed to him, explained its fundamental teachings, and in his own life followed the principles and regulations of the Holy Revelation.

Since the time of the Prophet, Muslims have for generation after generation received the Quran as it was given to the Apostle himself from Allah, passing it on precisely as it was taught at the beginning—whereof there is no doubt whatsoever. It has been definitely proved that the Quran could not possibly be the work of Muhammad or of any other human being, as is clearly seen when one considers its style, the treasures of teachings contained in it, and the environment in which Muhammad lived.

In the Scripture itself Allah defiantly stressed the impossibility of imitating the Quran when He said to the unbelievers, "And if ye are in doubt concerning that which We reveal unto Our slave (Muhammad), then produce a surah of the like thereof, and call your witnesses beside Allah if ye are truthful.

And if ye do it not—and ye can never do it—then guard yourselves against the fire prepared for disbelievers, whose fuel is of men and stones" (Surah II, 23-24).

Such a final demonstration that the Scripture was revealed by Allah to Muhammad is the Muslim's authority for recognizing the Quran as the principle source of Islamic beliefs and the Islamic code governing practices. After the Apostle had been called by Allah, the *ulama*—those leaders who were well-versed in Islam—recognized that there were two types of texts in the Quran: those which are clear and definite and those which could have more than one meaning.

The Quranic texts which are clear and definite are concerned with the basic beliefs like belief in Allah and the Last Day. These texts also cover the origin of law, whether religious laws governing prayer, religious tax, and fasting, or prohibitions against such acts as manslaughter or attacks on the chastity of a woman, and laws governing the use of property. For them no freedom of interpretation is allowed. The texts which could have more than one meaning are concerned with subsidiary aspects of Islam, but not its fundamentals, and have given rise to a plurality of Muslim theories and attitudes which are more or less personal points of view and are far from being obligatory. Islam, except in matters concerning its basic beliefs and the principles of its code of practices, is not limited to one type of thinking or one specific legislative method.

It is a tolerant religion which authorizes and permits wise liberality. As it has demonstrated throughout the Muslim world, Islam fits into all major cultures and constructive civilizations—and will continue to do so forever. The Quran, the principal basis of Islam, shows us that Islam cannot find its way into any heart or mind without the acceptance of its two basic branches: the beliefs and the code of laws.

Islam requires, first of all, a deep belief in it without any doubt or suspicion, as is made clear in many texts of the Quran and in the general agreement of the ulama of Islam. This emphasis on the primacy of belief was the first message of Muhammad to the Arabs, just as it was the message of all apostles and prophets; as the Quran says, "Say (O Muslims): We believe in Allah and that which is revealed unto us and that which was revealed unto Abraham, and Ishmael, and Isaac, and Jacob, and the tribes, and that which Moses and Jesus received, and that which the Prophets received from their Lord.

We make no distinction between any of them, and unto Him we have surrendered" (Surah II, 136).

The code of laws provides the regulations which create the proper relations between man and God, such as saying prayers, fasting, and other religious duties; they guide man in his relations with his brother in Islam or the non-Muslim community, in organizing the structure of the family and encouraging reciprocal affection; they lead man to an understanding of his place in the universe, encouraging research into the nature of man and animals and guiding man in the use of the benefits of the natural world.

The Quran makes clear that the result of belief is faith, and the result of the code of laws is good behaviour, as is shown in many texts: "Lo! Those who believe and do good works, theirs are the Gardens of the Paradise for welcome, Wherein they will abide, with no desire to be removed from thence" (Surah XVIII, 108-9). "Lo! Those who say: Our Lord is Allah, and thereafter walk aright, there shall no fear come upon them neither shall they grieve" (Surah XLVI,13).

Islam is both belief and legislation which organizes all the relationships of man. Belief is the basis of the code of laws and the code of laws is the result of belief, for legislation without belief is a building without a foundation—and belief without a code of laws to put it into effect would be merely theoretical and ineffective. Thus, in Islam there is an intimate interrelation between belief and the code of laws governing all conduct, and those who deny this can by no means be considered to be Muslims.

Islam calls upon all people to accept its beliefs and code of laws regardless of race, sex, colour, rank, or any other difference. All people are equal before Allah and must bear their own responsibility to accept the revelations of the Quran: "O mankind! Lo! We have created you male and female, and have made you nations and tribes that ye may know one another. Lo! the noblest of you in the sight of Allah, is the best in conduct" (Surah XLIX, 13). "It will not be in accordance with your desires, nor the desires of the People of the Scripture [*i.e.*, Jews and Christians]. He who does wrong will have the recompense thereof, and will not find against Allah any protecting friend or helper. And whoso doeth good works, whether of male or female, and he (or she) is a believer, such will enter paradise and they will not be wronged the dint in a date-stone" (Surah IV, 123-24).

Those two verses make clear that the descendants or relatives of any of the apostles have no more rights in His sight than any common believer. They also emphasize that men and women bear equal religious responsibility, regardless of their sexual differences. The woman's responsibility is quite independent of that of her mate; his good behaviour will not benefit her and his bad actions will not harm her. Each will receive in the eternal abode the reward or punishment which his—or her—actions merit. "Allah citeth an example for those who disbelieve: the wife of Noah and the wife of Lot, who were under two of our righteous slaves yet betrayed them so that they (the husbands) availed them naught against Allah and it was said (unto them): Enter the Fire along with those who enter" (Surah LXVI, 10).

The son is also responsible for himself once he attains majority. The belief and behaviour of his parents neither benefit nor harm him, nor does his belief and behaviour benefit or harm his parents. Thus says the Quran, "O mankind! Keep your duty to your Lord and fear a Day when the parent will not be able to avail the child aught, nor the child to avail the parent" (Surah XXXI, 33).

Thus it is clear that it is the individual responsibility of each person to accept the revelation of Allah—the Islamic beliefs and code of laws governing conduct—regardless of sex, rank, race, or any other difference.

The Fundamental Beliefs of Islam

A man announces his acceptance of the beliefs of Islam and his commitment to its code of regulations, he manifests the existence of Muslim beliefs in his heart, when he repeats the Word of Witness: *I witness that there is no God but Allah and that Muhammad is His Prophet.* To witness that Allah is One includes a perfect belief in Him as the source of creation and knowledge and the object of worship. To witness that Muhammad is His messenger includes a perfect belief in the

Angels, the Scriptures, the messengers, the Day of Resurrection, and the principles on which the code of laws is based. This witness is the key to Islam, subjecting one to its beliefs and regulations. "The messenger believes in that which has been revealed unto him from his Lord and (so do) the believers. Each one believes in Allah and His angels and His scriptures and His messengers—We make no distinction between any of His messengers—and they say: We hear, and we obey" (Surah II, 285). "It is not righteousness that ye turn your faces to the East and the West; but righteous is he who believes in Allah and the Last Day and the angels and the Scripture and the Prophets" (Surah II, 177).

We must believe in the existence and oneness of Allah, that He is the only creator and disposer of the universe, that He has no partner, that there is no comparable being, and that none but Allah is worthy of worship. "Say: He is Allah, the One! Allah, the eternally Besought of all! He begottes not nor was begotten. And there is none comparable unto Him" (Surah CXII). "Say: Shall I seek another than Allah for Lord, when He is Lord of all things?" (Surah VI, 165). "Say: Shall I choose for a protecting friend other than Allah, the Originator of the heavens and the earth, who feedes and is never fed?" (Surah VI, 14).

We must believe in all the messengers of Allah of whom we are informed by the Quran from Noah to Muhammad (Allah bless them and give them peace). Allah selects some of his slaves and prepares them through ideal education to be His messengers to mankind. Some of these apostles are mentioned in the Quran and other are not mentioned; we must believe in all of them.

We must believe in Angels, the ambassadors of the revelation from Allah to His apostles, and, of necessity, in the Scriptures, His messages to humanity. The principles of legislation of Allah are His laws that we must follow; we must not sanction that which Allah has forbidden, nor forbid that which He allows us to do. We must believe in the contents of all the messages concerning the code of laws which aims at the organization of human life in a way which meets the needs of mankind and promotes human welfare in accordance with His justice and mercy.

We must believe in the Day of Judgment and the Other World, which is the only eternal life and is the life of reward and punishment.

We have to believe in all of these facts.

Anyone who denies one of these Muslim facts cannot be treated as a Muslim nor subjected to the Muslim rules. Yet it does not follow that he who does not believe in any of these facts would be considered a nonbeliever by Allah and would therefore suffer eternal damnation. It simply means that he would not be treated as a Muslim; he would not be under any obligation to worship Allah according to Muslim rules. He would not be prevented from doing things prohibited by Islam—such as drinking wine or eating pork—and on death he would not be washed and prayed for by Muslims.

Man will, however, be considered to be an unbeliever if, after having been freely convinced of the truth of these beliefs, he rejects them, or any part of them, through obstinacy, pride, love of mammon or the pomp of power, or the fear of being criticized. But if these beliefs had not been presented to him at all, or were presented in a hateful way, or were presented in a true and right way but he was incapable of fully understanding them, or even if he were capable but died before being fully convinced—in such cases a man is not an unbeliever according to Almighty Judgment and will not suffer everlasting punishment. The only disbelief mentioned in the Quran for which man will suffer judgment is a disbelief arising from obstinacy and pride. Hence the distant peoples to whom Islam has not been introduced, or those to whom it has been introduced in a hateful way, or those who have not understood the evidence even though they tried, will not suffer judgment. But they will by no means be treated as Muslims for they have not adopted the Word of Witness; they have not said with conviction, "I witness that there is no God but Allah and that Muhammad is His Prophet."

Islam, when it invites one to adopt its beliefs, does not use any compulsion, for it detests compulsion. Faith cannot be attained by force; there can never be true faith through obligation. The Scripture says, "There is no compulsion in religion" (Surah II, 256). "And if thy Lord willed, all who are in the earth would have believed together. Would thou (Muhammad) compel men until they are believers?" (Surah X, 100). Not only is there no compulsion to adopt Islam, but Islam does not lead people to faith through spellbinding miracles which seek to convince without thought or the exercise of free choice. "If We will, We can send down on them from the sky a portent so that their necks would remain bowed before it" (Surah XXVI, 4).

Islam, in its invitation to accept its beliefs and to submit to its rules, rejects any methods which are not based on liberality and freedom of choice. Everyone has full liberty to embrace Islam voluntarily and through conviction. Thus Islam supports its beliefs through sound evidence and completely logical proofs. The Quranic evidence for the revelation of Allah-concerning belief in the One God, in Angels, the Scripture, the prophets, and the Last Day—is the Quran itself, the Word of Allah, whereof there is no doubt, as we have already seen. The logic of this belief is that all that is mentioned in the Quran is a matter of fact because it is supported by a standing miracle which will never cease, the Quran itself. "And thou (O Muhammad) was not a reader of any scripture before it, nor dids thou write it with thy right hand, for then might those have doubted, who follow falsehood. But it is clear revelations in the hearts of those who have been given knowledge, and none deny our revelations save wrong-doers. And they say: Why are not portents sent down upon him from his Lord? Say: Portents are with Allah only, and I am but a plain warner. Is it not enough for them that We have sent down unto thee the Scripture which is read unto them? Lo! herein verily is mercy and a reminder for folk who believe" (Surah XXIX, 48-51).

BELIEF IN ALLAH

The basic belief in Islam is belief in Allah—His existence, His unity, and His perfection. The evidence by which the Quran draws people's attention to the belief in Allah is based on reason and inner consciousness or intuition.

The rational evidence for belief in Allah is based on Islam's call to ponder on the nature of the universe—the earth, the heavens, the mysteries, the natural laws, the harmony and unity of the universe. Thus one comes to see that it is impossible that the universe could be self-created, or created by opposed or contradictory forces, or purposeless. This universe was created by an ultimate creative force; it was created by a supernatural force which guides and manages it through ultimate knowledge and wisdom. This universe is attaining its purposes through the will of the Almighty Creator. One of those purposes is its ultimate dissolution, after which comes the eternal abode, as we are told in many places in the Quran.

> *When the heaven is split asunder, And attentive to her Lord in fear, And when the earth is spread out. And has cast out all that was in her, and is empty. And attentive to her Lord in fear! (Surah LXXXIV, 1-5)*
>
> *When the heaven is cleft asunder, When the planets are dispersed, When the seas are poured forth, And the sepulchres are overturned, A soul will know what it has sent before (it) and what left behind. (Surah LXXXII, 1-5)*
>
> *When the sun is overthrown, And when the stars fall, And when the hills are moved, And when the camels big with young, And when the wild beasts are herded, And when the seas rise, And when souls are reunited, And when the girl-child that was buried alive is asked, For what sin she was slain, And when the pages are laid open. And when the sky is torn away, And when hell is lighted, And when the garden is brought nigh, (Then) every soul will know what it has made ready. (Surah LXXXI, 1-14)*

By such rational evidence we are instructed in the Quran as to the ultimate end toward which the universe is moving, the final destruction which awaits all created things. In almost every Surah we find rational evidence proving that the universe was created and is sustained by Allah. "Lo! in the creation of the heavens and the earth, and the difference of night and day, and the ships which run upon the sea with that which is of use to men, and the water which Allah sendes down from the sky, thereby reviving the earth after its death, and dispersing all kinds of beasts therein, and (in) the ordinance of the winds, and the clouds obedient between heaven and earth: are signs (of Allah's sovereignty) for people who have sense' (Surah II, 164).

"And in the Earth are neighbouring tracts, vineyards and ploughed lands, and date-palms, like and unlike, which are watered with one water. And We have made some of them to excel others in fruit. Lo! herein verily are portents for people who have sense" (Surah XIII, 4). "We have built the heavens with might, and We it is who made the vast extent (thereof) And the earth have We laid out, how gracious was the Spreader (thereof)! And all things We have created by pairs, that happily ye may reflect" (Surah LI, 47-49). These are only a few examples illustrating the many texts which give rational evidence of the creative power of Allah.

The intuitional evidence for belief in Allah, the belief based upon the recognition of Allah by our inner consciousness, is brought to our attention in the Quran by pointing out the important psychological fact that there is an instinctive feeling of faith in Almighty Allah, the Creator of the universe, which comes to men when they are free from inclinations, or the distractions of dull routines, or when surprised by the question of the origin of the universe, or when faced with hardships or misfortunes which they cannot overcome by themselves. These facts are illustrated by many texts of the Quran. "And if thou (Muhammad) ask them: Who created the heavens and the earth, they will surely answer: The Mighty, the Knower created them" (Surah XLIII, 9). "When We show favour unto man, he withdraws and turnes aside, but when ill touches him then he abounds in prayer" (Surah XLI, 51). "And if a wave enshrouds them like awnings, they cry unto Allah, making their faith pure for Him only. But when He brings them safe to land, some of them compromise. None denies Our signs save every traitor ingrate." (Surah XXXI, 32).

The Quran illustrates this sudden, instinctive faith in Allah by describing in detail Pharaoh's feeling when he was faced with death by drowning and realized the impossibility of escape, "And We brought the Children of Israel across the sea, Pharaoh with his hosts pursued them in rebellion and transgression, till, when the (fate of) drowning overtook him, he exclaimed: I believe that there is no God save Him in whom the Children of Israel believe, and I am of those who surrender (unto Him). What! Now! When hitherto thou has rebelled and been of the wrong-doers? But this day We save thee in thy body that thou may be a portent for those after thee. Lo! most of mankind are heedless of Our portents" (Surah X, 91-93). Thus we see that the belief in Allah is based on both rational evidence and intuitive insight, evidence which is available to all men who are not heedless of the Divine portents.

The Scripture also guides us to the Names and Qualities of Allah, all of which refer to His power, His wisdom, and all His perfections. Many of the Names are difficult to translate from the Arabic, for example, Allah is the One, the Eternally Besought of All, the First, the Last, the Beneficent, the Powerful, the Almighty, the Wise, the Knower, the Creator, the Shaper out of Naught, the Fashioner, the Guardian, the Majestic, the Superb, the Glorified. The Creator names Himself in this manner, "He is Allah, than whom there is no other God, the Knower of the invisible and the visible, He is the Beneficent, the Merciful. He is Allah, than whom there is no other God, the Sovereign Lord, the Holy One, Peace, the Keeper of Faith, the Guardian, the Majestic, the Compeller, the Superb. Glorified be Allah from all that they ascribe as partner (unto Him). He is Allah, the Creator, the Shaper out of naught, the Fashioner. His are the most beautiful names. All that is in the heavens and the earth glorifies Him, and He is the Mighty, the Wise" (Surah LIX, 22-24).

These names which show His superiority, mercy, and perfection are recognized by wise men to be true and justly applicable, because a true understanding of the nature of the universe indicates that these are the qualities of Allah. The wise man recognizes also that no other being in the universe is worthy of such names, for all these beings are creations—changeable, needy, and deficient. In the Quran the proper and comprehensive name which emphasizes His individuality is the *Ultimate Being,* known to Muslims as Allah, or the name of the Almighty and the Sublime.

Muslims call Him and worship Him by such names. For thus He says: "Allah's are the fairest names. Invoke Him by them. And leave the company of those who blaspheme His names. They will be requited what they do" (Surah VII, 80). It is forbidden for a Muslim to invoke Him by a name or an adjective that is not mentioned in His Scripture or by His Apostle.

The Ultimate Being can be described, but not conceived by man. When the Quran guides men to belief in Allah, it aims at turning man's thought from the fruitless attempt to know the essence and reality of His Ultimate Being and instead to guide men to know His creative ability and the activities which reveal His qualities, His might and perfection. The Quran shows that He is above all qualities possessed by His creation, that His qualities are divine and superior and that attempts to know His essence, to describe Him by such concepts as monism or pantheism, will fail. For He says, "Such is Allah, your Lord. There is no God save Him, the Creator of all things, so worship Him. And He takes care of all things. Vision comprehends Him not, but he comprehends (all) vision. He is the Subtile, the Aware" (Surah, VI, 103-4).

The story of Moses (the Blessing of Allah be upon him) when he asked his Creator to show him Himself, is a good illustration of the impossibility of knowing the essence of the Ultimate Being. "And when We did appoint for Moses thirty nights (of solitude), and added to them ten, and he completed the whole time appointed by his Lord of forty nights; and Moses said unto his brother: Take my place among the people. Do right, and follow not the way of mischief-makers. And when Moses came to Our appointed tryst and his Lord had spoken unto him, he said: My Lord! Show me (Thy self), that I may gaze upon Thee. He said: Thou wilt not see Me, but gaze upon the mountain! If it stand still in its place, then thou wilt see Me. And when his Lord revealed (His) glory to the mountain He sent it crashing down. And Moses fell down senseless. And when he woke he said: Glory unto Thee! I turn unto Thee repentant, and I am the first of (true) believers" (Surah VII, 142-43). It is by such texts that the Quran makes clear that Allah can be described, His qualities can be partially known, but His essence cannot be conceived of by man.

One final point should be stressed in relation to the Islamic belief in Allah. Islam rejects all forms of polytheism. Allah is One. The Quran often reprimands those who believe in the existence of two gods, or in Trinitarianism, and those who worship any part of His creation such as the sun, the moon, or idols. The Quran calls upon such polytheists to consider the numerous evidences of His ultimate Unity. "If there were therein

Gods beside Allah, then verily both (the heavens and the earth) had been disordered" (Surah XXI, 22). "Allah has not chosen any son, nor is there any God along with Him; else would each God have assuredly championed that which he created, and some of them would assuredly have overcome others. Glorified be Allah above all that they allege" (Surah XXIII, 91). "Say: O People of the Scripture: Come to an agreement between us and you: that we shall worship none but Allah, and that we shall ascribe no partner unto Him, and that none of us shall take others for lords beside Allah" (Surah III, 64). "Lo! I have turned my face toward Him Who created the heavens and the earth, as one by nature upright, and I am not of the idolaters" (Surab VI, 80). Thus it is seen that Islam clearly rejects all polytheism, Trinitarianism, and idolatry and worships only the One.

Belief in Angels, Jinn and the Soul

The first of the basic beliefs of Islam is the belief in Allah, as we have said. The second basic belief is the belief in Angels. The Scripture describes Angels as supernatural and says that such is their real nature that they do not appear in the material world generally, but only by divine command. The Quran says, "And they say: The Beneficent has taken unto Himself a son. Be He glorified! Nay, but (those whom they call sons) are honoured slaves; They speak not until He has spoken, and they act by His command" (Surah XXI, 26-27).

The Angels' functions are concerned with spirits and souls. Some of these functions, through which they carry out His orders and His will, are recorded in the Quranic texts. Some of the Angels carry His revelations, His orders, His messages to His prophets and apostles: "And lo! it is a revelation of the Lord of the Worlds, Which the True Spirit has brought down Upon thy heart, that thou may be (one) of the warners" (Surah XXVI, 192-94).

Other Angels support the prophets and make the believers stand firm. "And we gave Jesus, son of Mary, clear proofs (of Allah's sovereignty) and We supported him with the holy Spirit [*i.e.*, the angel Gabriel]" (Surah II, 253). "When thy Lord inspired the angels, (saying:) I am with you. So make those who believe stand firm. I will throw fear into the hearts of those who disbelieve" (Surab VIII, 12).

Other Angels are preachers who preach the true and the good and encourage believers by His good tidings of His eternal Paradise. "Lo! those who say: Our Lord is Allah, and afterward are uptight, the angels descend upon them, saying: Fear not nor grieve, but hear good tidings of the paradise which ye are promised. We are your protecting friends in the life of the world and in the Hereafter. There ye will have (all) that your souls desire, and there ye will have (all) for which ye pray" (Surah XLI, 30-31). Others are Angels of Death, such as Azrad. "Say: the Angel of death, who has charge concerning you, will gather you, and afterward unto your Lord ye will be returned" (Surah XXXII, 11). "Those whom the angels cause to die (when they are) good. They say: Peace be unto you! Enter the Garden because of what ye used to do" (Surah XVI, 32).

"Lo! as for those whom the angels take (in death) while they wrong themselves, (the angels) will ask: In what were ye engaged? They will say: We were oppressed in the land. (The angels) will say: Was not Allah's earth spacious that ye could have migrated therein? As for such, their habitation will be hell, an evil journey's end" (Surah IV, 97). Other Angels are registers of the deeds of human beings, preserving the records until the Day of Judgment when they are shown to man. "Lo! there are above you guardians, Generous and recording, Who know (all) that ye do" (Surah LXXXII, 10-12).

Such exemplary functions, like all other functions of the Angels, are supernatural. The Quran describes Angels as "Messengers with wings and force." "Allah chooses from the angels messengers, and (also) from mankind" (Surah XXII, 75). "Praise be to Allah, the Creator of the heavens and the earth, who appointeth the angels messengers having wings two, three, and four. He multiplies in creation what He will. Lo! Allah is Able to do all things" (Surah XXXV, 1). As has been demonstrated previously, the Quran is the basic resource of Islam and therefore the Muslim's belief in Angels must be fully limited by definite Quranic texts, which are the only source of such supernatural facts. Another kind of supernatural creature is the Jinn. The Quran differentiates between Jinn and Angels in several ways. Concerning the substance of the Jinn, the Quran states several times that He created them from fire. "And the Jinn did We create aforetime of essential fire" (Surab XV, 27).

Some of the Jinn are virtuous, others are wicked. According to the Quran, speaking of the Jinn, "And there are among us some who have surrendered (to Allah) and there are among us some who are unjust. And whoso has surrendered to Allah, such have taken the right path purposefully. And as for those who are unjust, they are firewood for hell" (Surah LXXII, 14-15). In contrast, we have seen above that the Angels are "honoured slaves."

Angels, as we mentioned previously, are the messengers of Allah to His prophets and apostles, but Jinn, like mankind, receive the revelations through His apostles. This is shown in the Quranic text, addressed to Muhammad, "And when We inclined toward thee (Muhammad) certain of the Jinn, who wished to hear the Quran, when they were in its presence, said: Give ear! and, when it was finished, turned back to their people, warning. They said: O our people! Lo! we have heard a Scripture which has been revealed after Moses, confirming that which was before it, guiding unto the truth and a right road. O our people! respond to Allah's summoner and believe Him. He will forgive you some of your sins and guard you from a painful doom" (Surah XLVI, 29-31).

Jinn share with mankind the responsibility of hearing and believing Muslim teachings. On the Judgment Day, both mankind and Jinn will be called by Allah in the same way and will be responsible in the same degree. "In the day when He will gather them together (He will say): O ye assembly of the Jinn! Many of humankind did ye seduce. And their adherents among humankind will say: Our Lord! We enjoyed one another, but now we have arrived at the appointed term which Thou appointed for us. He will say: Fire is your home. Abide therein for ever, save him whom Allah wills (to deliver). Lo! thy Lord is Wise, Aware" (Surah VI, 129). But the Angels do not share with mankind the same responsibilities. The Quran makes it clear in many passages that Angels possess all the spiritual virtues and none of the shortcomings of human beings, while the Jinn are described as sometimes being whisperers and provocators—evils which are sometimes found in men.

Concerning the soul, or spirit, the Quran says very little. "And (remember) when thy Lord said unto the angels: Lo! I am creating a mortal out of potter's clay of black mud altered, so, when I have made him and have breathed into him of My spirit, do ye fall down, prostrating yourselves unto him" (Surah XV, 28-29). There is another text in which He says, "Why, then, when (the soul) comes up to the throat (of the dying) And ye are at that moment looking" (Surah LVI, 83-84). All that we can deduce from such texts is that the soul is the source of life, and that it is the vital force of existence without which beings become lifeless. As to the precise nature of the soul, the Quran says nothing. However, there is no Quranic text which prohibits searching for such a supernatural spirit, whether or not such researches might be fruitful. His saying, "They will ask thee concerning the Spirit.

Say: The Spirit is by command of my Lord, and of knowledge ye have been vouchsafed but little" (Surah XVII, 85), indicates that the identification of the soul is His own concern and that the human mind is too limited to understand such a supernatural reality. This has been a subject of scientific research, but up to now those who have studied the problem have not reached a clear understanding about the soul. Concerning the soul after death, the texts of the Scripture and the sayings of the Prophet say nothing except that the soul remains after death, either living in ease and comfort or in torment. Thus He says, "Think not of those, who are slain in the way of Allah, as dead. Nay, they are living. With their Lord they have provision. Jubilant (are they) because of that which Allah has bestowed upon them of His bounty" (Surah III, 169-70).

Belief in the Apostles

Belief in Angels is the highest stage of belief which leads to the right way, the belief in Allah. Belief in apostles is not a belief in the supernatural, for they are men with the same human nature that other men have. They differ from other men in that they have been selected by Allah and authorized to receive His revelations through His Angels in order that they may proclaim them to mankind and lead men in practising their teachings. Such a divine selection preserves them from error in all that they proclaim of His divine messages. At the same time, their very human nature and qualities make it easy for believers to accept what they say and imitate what they do. He says, "And We sent not (as Our messengers) before thee other than men whom We inspired. Ask the followers of the Reminder [*i.e.*, the Jewish Scripture] if ye know not? We gave them not bodies that would not eat food, nor were they immortals" (Surah XXI, 7-8).

It is a divine fact that in all ages Allah has sent His messages to men through His apostles to direct and strengthen human beings toward good. Since the dawn of creation it has been the aim of the divine will to further the spiritual progress of man by providing the guidance which enables man to arrange his daily affairs so that he lives wisely and correctly, "and there is not a nation but a warner has passed among them" (Surah XXXV, 24). Thus messages have been revealed again and again with the one purpose of guiding man to perfection. Each age had its message and each generation had the chance to hear His words. In all these messages, the principles taught were the same. "He has ordained for you that religion which He commanded unto Noah, and that which We inspire in thee (Muhammad), and that which We commanded unto Abraham and Moses and Jesus, saying: Establish the religion, and be not divided therein" (Surah XLII, 13).

The Messenger Muhammad(Pbuh) illustrated the unity of divine messages by saying that all the apostles are builders of one house, the earlier apostles laying the foundation for the later ones who build upon their foundation. The Quran calls upon mankind to believe in all His messengers as well as in the scriptures revealed to them. To believe in some apostles and reject others is a fallacy from the Islamic point of view. The Quran says, "Say (O Muslims): We believe in Allah and that which is revealed unto us and that which was revealed unto Abraham, and Ishmael, and Isaac, and Jacob, and the tribes, and that which Moses and Jesus received, and that which the Prophets received from their Lord. We make no distinction between any of them, and unto Him we have surrendered" (Surah II, 136). "And who believe in that which is revealed unto thee (Muhammad) and that which was revealed before thee, and are certain of the Hereafter" (Surah II, 4).

Those who believe in some apostles and reject others will be punished, for the Quran says, "Lo! those who disbelieve in Allah and His messengers, and seek to make distinction between Allah and His messengers, and say: We believe in some and disbelieve in others, and seek to choose a way in between; Such are disbelievers in truth; and for disbelievers We prepare a shameful doom" (Surah IV, 150-51). On the other hand, those who believe in all of His apostles will receive their reward. "But those who believe in Allah and His messengers and make no distinction between any of them, unto them Allah will give their wages; and Allah was ever Forgiving, Merciful" (Surah IV, 152).

The message of the Apostle Muhammad(Pbuh) includes the foundations of all the previous messages which guide humanity to perfection and open the way to human progress, both materially and spiritually. Islam calls mankind to believe that Muhammad is the last of all prophets and apostles, as is made clear in the Quran, "Muhammad is not the father of any man among you, but he is the messenger of Allah and the Seal of the Prophets; and Allah is Aware of all things" (Surah XXXIII, 40). "This day have I perfected your religion for you and completed My favour unto you, and have chosen for you as religion AL-ISLAM" (Surah V, 3).

Muhammad's(Pbuh) message, or Islam, is addressed to every human being in all ages and all over the world, regardless of colour, race, nationality, or any other difference. "Say (O Muhammad): O mankind! Lo! I am the messenger of Allah to you all" (Surah VII, 158). The messages of the apostles before Muhammad differed from his in that they were limited to the apostle's people or tribe, as the Quran shows. "We sent Noah (of old) unto his people, and he said: 0 my people: Serve Allah. Ye have no other God save him" (Surah VII, 59).

"And unto (the tribe of) A'ad (We sent) their brother, Hud" (Surah VII, 65). "And to (the tribe of) Thamud (We sent) their brother Salih" (Surah VII, 73). And the Quran reveals concerning Jesus (the Blessings of Allah be upon him): "Allah createth what He will. If He decreeth a thing, He says unto it only: Be! and it is. And He will teach him [Jesus] the Scripture and wisdom, and the Torah and the Gospel. And will make him a messenger unto the children of Israel" (Surab III, 47-49). Thus we see that Muhammad(Pbuh), the last of the prophets, brought a message which was unique in that it was addressed to all men everywhere.

It should be clearly understood that, according to the Quranic texts, the function of the apostles is limited to guiding and educating people through revelation. They are worthy of the highest degree of honour and respect, for they are fully authorized to assume spiritual and educational leadership for all men, but they have no authority over people's beliefs, minds, or hearts. They are in no way responsible for the unbeliever. They have no power to confer any benefit or to inflict any punishment on themselves or other human beings. He says, "We have not sent thee (O Muhammad) as a warden over them" (Surah XVII, 54). "Thy people (O Muhammad) have denied it, though it is the Truth. Say: I am not put in charge of you" (Surah VI, 66). "Say: For myself I have no power to benefit, nor power to hurt, save that which Allah wills" (Surah VII, 188).

THE APOSTLES ARE HUMAN BEINGS

The Quran asserts that the fact that their messages were divine revelations did not change their human nature or make them into supernatural beings. They were highly honoured to be selected as messengers, but they remain human; their only infallibility is that given them by Allah concerning the religious facts revealed through them. The Quran says, "Say: I am only a mortal like you. My Lord inspireth in me that your God is only One God. And whoever hopes for the meeting with his Lord, let him do righteous work, and make none share of the worship due unto his Lord" (Surah XVIII, 111). As human beings, in all matters other than the messages of Allah, apostles can be right or wrong like any other human beings. It is recorded in the Quran that Allah admonished His Apostle Muhammad for some of his actions, as for instance when the Apostle was distracted from his responsibilities to the Muslims by his honourable aim to preach to the idolators (Surah LXXX, 1-10).

We have seen that worship may be offered only to Allah. Islam states that no Angel or human being is entitled to any kind of worship. No human being can be of any assistance in the Day of Judgment, nor can a human being remit any sins, for himself or for others. Only Allah has the power to pardon or punish, only Allah is entitled to worship. And just as no Angel or prophet is entitled to worship, so also no worship may be offered to any of the educated believers, the leaders in Islam, no matter how distinguished. Islam has no saints in the sense of beings with intercessory powers who may be worshipped. Rather than saints in that sense, Islam has Allah's *Aoulia,* that is, His constant obeyers, His favourites. According to the Quran they have no special distinction which gives them any sort of saintliness or supernatural ability such as the authority to intercede or remit sins. The constant obeyers, or favourites of Allah, are true believers who follow the apostles in all that is revealed to them by Allah, obeying the divine commands and avoiding that which He prohibits.

Some people, influenced by non-Muslim sources, say that Allah has, in addition to the apostles, His distinctive slaves who are authorized by Him to rule the universe and to respond and fulfill the people's demands. It is even said that when such "saints" die they should have distinctive tombs, high domed, and lighted at night; that one should seek their blessings, offer them pledges, and bow before them. Such errors have become popular among some Muslims and in other religious congregations, but all such errors are entirely rejected by His religion in all His messages.

Belief in the Scriptures

To accept and believe in the messages of Allah is a mere logical consequence of belief in Angels and apostles. The messages are the contents of all His scriptures, which include instruction concerning true beliefs and the fundamental principles for codes of law which guide men in distinguishing the approved from the forbidden in human actions. Islam calls mankind to believe in all His scriptures which have been revealed through the apostles—such as Abraham's Books, Moses' Bible, Jesus' Gospel, and Muhammad's Quran. From the Muslim point of view, no one who denies any of these scriptures is considered to be a believer.

It also follows that if Muhammad is the final Apostle, the Quran is the final Scripture. The Quran, as is known to anyone who is thoroughly acquainted with its contents, States the basic beliefs, the basic principles of worship and of human dealings, and the ideals of morality. The Quranic texts do not give in detail the code of laws regulating dealings—human actions—but they give the general principles which guide people to perfection, to a life of harmony—to an inner harmony between man's appetites and his spiritual desires, to harmony between man and the natural world, and to a harmony between individuals as well as a harmony with the society in which men live. The means of establishing harmony which are revealed in the Quran are based on faith and justice, and a wise understanding of human nature.

It is not the function of the Quran to explain in detail the facts of the universe, its secrets and the useful ways in which it can serve mankind. It does, however, urge men to use their minds and skills to gain understanding of the universe, its secrets and its wonderful phenomena. It opens the way for man to use his mind and powers in whatever vocation falls to his lot, to increase his knowledge, and to strengthen his faith in the Almighty. It guides mankind to individual and social welfare and establishes justice among men. The Quran limits the human mind only in basic beliefs and principles of legislation, a wise limitation which is necessary to guide the people's faith and bring them to submission to Allah.

Belief in the Last Day

The fifth principle of faith in Islam—after faith in Allah, Angels, apostles, and the scriptures—is belief in the Day of Resurrection, the Judgment Day. It is the end of man and His goal in the creation of man. "And that man has only that for which he makes effort, And that his effort will be seen, And afterward he will be repaid for it with fullest payments (Surah LIII, 39-41). What happens to a man on the Last Day—his reward or punishment, his pleasure or pain,—is determined by what he has chosen to do in this world. The Other World is the world of judgment for what man has done. "On the day when We shall summon all men with their record, whoso is given his book in his right hand—such will read their book and they will not be wronged a shred. Whoso is blind here will be blind in the Hereafter, and yet further from the road" (Surah XVII, 71-72). Thus the belief in the judgment of the Last Day is the strongest motive for man to seek perfection and progress in this world in order that he may be accepted and favoured by Allah in the Other World.

The Quran mentions in various places the rewards and sufferings which will come to men in the Other World. Although it uses phrases that are commonly used by man in his daily life, Islamic sources emphasize that life in the Other World is a new life that differs from life in this world in everything except the names.

But for him who feareth the standing before his Lord there are two gardens. Which is it, of the favours of your Lord, that ye deny? Of spreading branches. Which is it, of the favours of your Lord, that ye deny? Wherein are two fountains flowing. Which is it, of the favours of your Lord, that ye deny? Wherein is every kind of fruit in pairs. Which is it, of the favours of your Lord, that ye deny? Reclining upon couches lined with silk brocade, the fruit of both gardens near to hand. (Surah LV, 46-54)

Concerning the sufferings in the Other World, He says, "The guilty will be known by their marks, and will be taken by the forelocks and the feet" (Surah LV, 41). "While the reward of disbelievers is the Fire" (Surah XIII, 35). "And lo! for all such, hell will be the promised place" (Surah XV, 43). Thus in many passages does the Quran describe the blessings and sufferings of the Other World in a way which urges men to believe according to the teachings of Allah's messages and to act in accordance with the principles of dealings laid down in the Quranic texts.

A Muslim never doubts, nor hesitates to hold a firm belief in, the eternity of the blessings of the Other World. He knows that those who obstinately continue to be disbelievers will be punished for that disbelief which contradicts the natural disposition of man. That punishment, according to the Quran, will continue eternally. It is not definitely stated in the Quran whether Hell is everlasting or not, but it is clearly stated that Paradise and its blessings are eternal. In all matters of belief concerning the Last Day and the Other World, the human mind is subject to the definite Quranic texts and the sayings of the Apostle.

These, then, are the beliefs of Islam: belief in Allah the One God, in Angels, in the apostles, in the scriptures, and in the Day of Judgment. These beliefs are, according to Islam, the basis of every divine religion; therefore, the religions which are not founded on them are false religions. Allah rejects the disbelievers, those who are polytheists, who do not believe in Angels, or in the apostles, or in the scriptures, or in the Last Day—and He invites them all to believe in Islam through logical thought and acceptance of the evidence revealed to men.

Man was called by Allah to adopt these beliefs. As an expression of His mercy and His goodness to His slaves, He has made man master of the earth, God's deputy on earth to make use of its blessings by using and developing its natural resources. Allah has called upon man to study the universe in order that he may see and understand the wonders of His creation which confirm man's faith and lead him to spiritual and material progress. The Quran says, "He it is Who created for you all that is in the earth" (Surah II, 29). "See ye not how Allah has made serviceable unto you whatsoever is in the skies and whatsoever is in the earth and has loaded you with His favours both without and within?" (Surah XXXI, 20). "Allah it is Who has made the sea of service unto you that the ships may run thereon by His command, and that ye may seek His bounty, and that happily ye may be thankful; And has made of service unto you whatsoever is in the heavens and whatsoever is in the earth; it is all from Him. Lo! herein verily are portents for people who reflect" (Surah XIV, 12-13).

Islam states that Allah created man with a disposition which leads him sometimes to choose the good and sometimes to choose the evil way of life. His good deeds lead him to his own happiness, to social welfare, and to his being acceptable to Allah, while his evil deeds lead him to unhappiness and to destruction in this life and damnation in the next. For thus says Allah,

> *Did We not assign unto him two eyes, And a tongue and two lips, And guide him to the parting of the mountain ways? But he has not attempted the Ascent—Ah, what will convey unto thee what the Ascent is!—(It is) to free a slave, And to feed in the day of hunger, An orphan near of kin, Or some poor wretch in misery, And to be of those who believe and exhort one another to perseverance and exhort one another to pity. (Surah XC, 8-17)*

The purpose of Allah's messages and revelations is to strengthen the good tendencies of men and guide them to perfection in this life, thus laying the foundations for the next life. Islam points out that each man must choose for himself the way to happiness through good deeds or the way to unhappiness and punishment through wickedness.

Islam, in placing the responsibility on each individual, makes no distinction between human beings; each is given the same rights and responsibilities regardless of his sex, race, colour, or other differences.

Blessed are faithful and true believers. The Quran says, "Whosoever doeth right, whether male or female, and is a believer, him verily We shall quicken with good life, and We shall pay them a recompense in proportion to the best of what they used to do" (Surah XVI, 97).

In the eyes of Islam a man chooses either good or evil by his own free will and is rewarded or punished according to his deeds. He is only guided and advised by the messages of Allah and by the apostles but is still completely free to choose as he wishes.

It is quite clear that if Allah wanted to He would have created man wholly good and completely ignorant of all evil. Since man has been created free to choose between good and evil, he will be rewarded or punished on Doomsday according to what he has chosen.

There is no supernatural force which limits a man or compels him to adopt any mode of behaviour. What is called fate, or testing, is nothing but the operation of natural laws, such as the principles of cause and effect and of the freedom of man.

In former times, disbelievers excused themselves by saying that they had been predestined to certain actions by His will. But the Almighty rejected such an excuse and made it clear that full responsibility is thrown on each man because of his free mind and the guidance given by the apostles.

"They who are idolaters will say: Had Allah willed, we had not ascribed (unto Him) partners neither had our fathers, nor had we forbidden aught. Thus did those who were before them give the lie (to Allah's messengers) till they tasted of the fear of Us. Say: Have ye any knowledge that ye can adduce for us? Lo! ye follow naught but an opinion. Lo! ye do not guess. Say—For Allah's is the final judgment—Had He willed He could indeed have guided all of you" (Surah VI, 149-50). It is true enough that the Almighty foresees how man will act; but this foresight is nothing other than divine knowledge of the freedom of choice, which is a natural law.

Therefore, Islam does not allow a man to wander from the rightful faith and then offer the workings of fate as his excuse. For if that were so, His commandments, the missions of the apostles, the scriptures, and the promise of reward and punishment would all be null and void, impossible to reconcile with the Almighty's Wisdom and Justice.

4

The Rational and Mystical Interpretations of Islam

No account of Islam is complete if it does not take into consideration the extraordinary efforts which the various Muslim sects have made to understand Islam, and the results which they have achieved.

Islam is not merely a body of doctrines expressed in the Quran and the prophetic Traditions; neither is it best represented by the orthodox school at any particular time. It is a living religion which has received and is still receiving its vitality from the people who confess it; it is a great movement which has passed through various stages of development over its long and complicated history, influencing and being influenced by the religious and cultural forces in its environment. Through the interaction between Islam in its original form and those external forces some of the fundamental concepts of Muslim dogmas and practices were reinterpreted and reshaped.

Some of these interpretations are not orthodox, it is true, but they are nevertheless Islamic, at least insofar as they are based on Islamic texts, even though the texts are examined under a different light. It is the purpose of this chapter to discuss the interpretations gleaned from the writings of the old schools of Muslims—mystics and rationalists, including both the theologians and the philosophers—who are not usually regarded by the orthodox school as strict Muslims, but whose influence on Muslim thought and practical religious life is felt even today.

The earliest rationalists were known as Mutazilites, and the mystics of Islam are the Sufis. The discussion in this chapter will be limited to the theological, philosophical, and mystical attitudes toward certain of the fundamental problems of dogmatic beliefs and religious practices in Islam.

THE THEOLOGICAL ATTITUDE

Islam, like all other great religions, has a theology of its own which aims at the establishment of its fundamental articles of faith and the refutation of heresy and innovation. The Prophet Muhammad was no theologian—nor was any prophet before him. In fact, the revelations that prophets have brought into the world defy any serious attempt at a systematic theology. The systematization of religious dogmas in Islam was a task undertaken by the followers of Muhammad when the need for the establishment of a Muslim theology was felt. The criterion for the early theology was taken by writers such as Ibn Khaldun and Adud al-Din al-Iji to be the teachings of the early Muslims and the orthodox party. In the opinion of these writers the Mutazilites (rationalists) and the Shias and many other theological schools are heretical. This is too narrow a view to be adopted, and in dealing with Muslim theology here the term "theology" is used in a wider sense to include the speculative thinking of orthodox and non-orthodox theological schools.

The fundamental principle which Muslim theology has always endeavoured to establish is the principle of the unity of God. On this principle Muslim theologians know no compromise. It is the keynote of Muslim faith and the root from which all other dogmas of Islam are derived. Hence Muslim theology is also called the science of unification (of God), because its object is to determine the nature of God and His attributes, and to explain the relation between Him and His creation, all of which follow as corollaries from a definite concept of Allah as the Absolute One. The Quran, though not itself a book on theology, contains the rudiments of almost all theological problems.

It speaks of God as the only one to be served, the Supreme Master and Ruler of the world. It asserts His absolute transcendence in these words, "Say: He is God alone. God the eternal: He begettes not, nor is begotten; and there is nothing like unto Him" (Surah CXLI). The Quran contains a long list of the attributes of God over which there has been much discussion and disputation among the Muslim theologians. It condemns polytheism, atheism, and deism; and it emphatically denies the eternity of the world. Although on the whole it is sympathetic to Christianity, it rejects the Christian Trinity and all its implications.

In discussing these theological problems the style of the Quran varies considerably. Sometimes it takes the form of a logical argument—a syllogistic proof or an argument based on analogy—but more often it adopts the rhetorical style, calling on man to reflect upon himself and the wonderful world around him so that by means of such reflection he might know his Lord. When dealing with moral precepts the Quran appeals to man's own conscience and bids him reflect upon his actions and the actions of his fellow men.

Such were the seeds from which, under favorable conditions, an elaborate theology developed in the Muslim world. There was no science of theology during the lifetime of the Prophet and the first four Caliphs. The early Muslims accepted the word of the Quran literally. They raised no metaphysical or theological questions. When they were in doubt about a Quranic verse dealing with God or any of His attributes they were told to accept it as it was stated in the Quran with no further explanation or interpretation. The idea was to have faith in Islam, to propagate it, and to defend it, rather than to inquire into its nature. The orthodox party represented by Ahmad Ibn Hanbal (died 241; AD. 855) adhered strictly to tradition and opposed any form of independent thinking.

Later on they even rejected the theological investigations made on strict Quranic lines, and looked with suspicion upon the teaching of the ascetics of their time. They would only allow discussion of questions related to the law (sharia) and the practical affairs of everyday life. But soon after the death of Muhammad political questions relating to his rightful successor were raised, and with them arose certain theological questions concerning the nature of the true Imam (Muslim head of state), the meaning of faith, sin, infidelity, punishment in the Future World, and so on. The interest was primarily political, but the contending parties gave their views a religious colouring, and there was much persecution and bloodshed in the name of religion. Political, or rather political-theological, parties appeared on the scene—the Kharijites, the Qadarites, the Shiites, the Murjites, and the Umayyads, who were the state party and the bitterest opponents of Ali and his followers. This was a period of strife and dissension within the Muslim community during which the whole future of Islam was at stake.

What interests us here is their discussion of faith, sin, and retribution. The Murjites—literally those who postpone; here, those who postpone judgment until it is pronounced by God on the Day of Judgment—were more tolerant than the others in their political views and more liberal-minded on theological questions. They believed that faith alone is sufficient for man salvation. The sinful believer who professes the unity of God and acknowledges His Prophet thus will not suffer everlasting punishment in Hell, a view which was diametrically opposite to that of the Kharijites. They even went so far as to say that a believer need not be a professed Muslim, for faith is a confession of the heart while Islam is an outward or public confession of the tongue.

The question was taken up more seriously later when it lost its political significance and became a theological problem of academic interest. What is the real nature of faith, and what is its relation to religious practice? Does faith admit any degrees? That is, can one man be more faithful than another, or can one and the same person ascend higher and higher in the scale of faith? The Murjites denied the quantitative evaluation of faith, while the rest of the theologians held the view that faith admits increase and decrease. Faith is more nearly perfect when it is accompanied by actions, or better still, when it is so deeply rooted in the heart that it becomes the principle from which righteous actions necessarily follow. Faith which is not accompanied by good works is like a tree which bears no fruit, but true faith becomes a "faculty of the heart"—as Ibn Khaldun calls it—which urges the faithful to perform their religious obligations and to abstain from sin. "A true believer," the Prophet says, "commits no adultery and no theft." In other words, to have real faith and to sin is a contradiction in terms. The theory that faith increases and decreases has its roots in the Quran in such passages as this, "The believers are they whose hearts thrill with fear when God's name is mentioned, and whose faith increases at each recital of His words, and who put trust in their Lord" (Surah VIII, 2).

Such were the beginnings of the era in which Muslim theology was being formed. But these rudimentary and altogether primitive speculations on certain religious problems soon assumed larger proportions when Muslim scholars who were skilled in the art of dialectic and tolerably conversant with Greek philosophy appeared on the scene. There were now two Important factors which helped the development of the new theology, one internal and the other external.

The internal factor is the nature of the Quran itself. As has been pointed out in previous chapters, the Quran contains two different types of verses, those which form the main substance of the Book and are clear and definite in their meaning, and the comparatively few verses which are dubious or less definite. This is admitted in one of the Medina revelations which runs as follows, "He (God) it is who has sent down to thee the Book. Some of its verses are of themselves perspicuous; they are the basis of the Book; and others are dubious. Those whose hearts are inclined to error follow the dubious verses, thereby seeking discord and seeking interpretation. But none knows its interpretation save God. Those who are firm in knowledge say: We believe therein-it is all from our Lord. But none will bear this in mind save men endued with understanding" (Surah III, 7).

The reason for the presence of these dubious verses in the Quran has been discussed by theologians. The majority incline to believe that they are purposely given as a trial in order to test the strength and validity of man's faith. Those whose faith is firm accept them unquestionably, while others whose hearts are inclined to error—as the Quran says—reject them or interpret them in such a way as to cause discord in the Muslim community. Whatever the real reason may be, the fact remains that these dubious verses played an important role in stirring up dispute among Muhammad's followers of the second generation. Out of these disputes emerged different parties, each supporting a different point of view. It is worth while quoting Ibn Khaldun on the subject. He says, in his *Prolegomena:*

In the Quran there are passages which describe God as an absolutely transcendent Being. Their meaning is clear and admits of no interpretation. They are all negative statements; and, on account of their clarity, are accepted by all believers.... The other passages which are comparatively few are suggestive of anthropomorphism [these are the dubious passages]. They were accepted [by the early Muslims] without any enquiry into their meaning. But the innovators of their time resorted to a different method, by subjecting the dubious passages to critical examination. Some exaggerated their anthropomorphic side and attributed to God hands, face, feet, and so on, thus falling into gross corporealism and violating the absolute transcendence of God which is explicitly mentioned in numerous other passages and with such undoubted clarity.... Others admitted anthropomorphism with regard to the attributes of God such as occupying a place, sitting on the Throne, coming and going and speaking in words, and so on. They, like the others, also drifted into corporealism.

The disputes centring around such passages had a far-reaching effect on the course of the development of many theological doctrines which occupied the minds of Muslims for generations. We can even find some traces of these theological disputes in modern times.

The second, or external, factor in the development of Muslim theology is the cultural influences which were brought to bear upon Islam from without. Up to the second half of the second century we meet only the individual men who expressed their opinions on some religious problems. There was no general or recognized system of religious thought; there were no real theological schools, although there were what we might call semi-theological parties.

The course of development changed when foreign influence came into play. Some ethical problems were raised, particularly the problem of determinism and free will. Such metaphysical problems as were inspired by the Quran also came to the fore—the problem of the attributes of God, the divine attribute of speech and the Quran as the eternal word of God, the problem of beholding the vision of God in the next world, and so on. It is significant that most of the major issues in religion were discussed in Syria, which was an important centre of Christian theology. We know that John of Damascus the great doctor of the Greek Church, was a Vizier (Minister) under the Umayyads, and that he and his pupil Theodorus Abucara wrote polemic treatises on Islam summarizing discussions between Christians and Muslims. Some of these treatises were written in a catechetical form: If a Muslim asks you such and such a question, answer so and so. This is taken as an evidence that direct contact between Muslim and Christian scholars must have taken place at an early stage. But while the possibility of such contact is admitted, there is no justification for the exaggerated view put forward by such scholars as De Boer, Von Kremer, and D. B. Macdonald that the development of Muslim theology was largely influenced by Christian thought.

The other foreign factor which influenced Muslim theology, particularly in its mature form, is Greek philosophy. We can see traces of it in almost all the leading theological theories—either in the bearing of some Greek concepts on such theories, or in the way they were presented and discussed. Yet, here again, Greek ideas never remained unaltered; they were given such a turn as to harmonize with the fundamental concepts of Islam.

A consideration of the two major issues in Muslim theology—God and the problem of divine attributes, and man and the problem of free will—will illustrate the significant trends in the development of Islamic theological thought.

The Theological Conception of God

A variety of concepts of God, ranging from crude anthropomorphism to absolute transcendentalism, have their roots in the Quran. V/hen the Muslim theologians began to reflect on the nature of God, they found themselves faced with two types of Quranic verses: those which describe God in relation to His creation, and those which describe Him in Himself. According to the former, God sees, hears, speaks to His people, creates with His hands, sits on His Throne, comes with His Angels, and will be seen on the Day of Judgment. They also ascribe to God typically human qualities such as pleasure and displeasure, love and hatred, and the like. These attributes are some of the ingredients, so to speak, of the personality of the one God who speaks to His servants and hears their call, loves the righteous, and hates the wicked. The Prophet says, "Pray to God as if thou sees Him, for if thou sees Him not, He sees thee." That is, picture God as a person, for you cannot address yourself in prayer to the Absolute.

The second set of Quranic verses, those which describe God in Himself, refer to the divine attributes of transcendence by which God is distinguished from created beings. The question is: Can we predicate attributes of God at all? The Quran certainly does. God is described as omnipotent, as omniscient, as knowing and willing, as eternal, infinite, everlasting, and unlike all created beings. Some of these attributes are positive, others are negative. Can they all be predicated of God in the same way? The orthodox party maintain that they can, but they do not go into what such predication logically implies. The Mu'tazilites examine the implications of such predication. The negative attributes present no difficulty and are therefore admitted by them. The positive ones are either reduced to negations or denied as separate entities distinct from or added to the divine Essence. They do not deny that God knows, wills, and does things, but deny that His knowledge or will or action is different from and coeternal with His Essence. They are all identical with the Essence. To assert the separate existence of the divine attributes which are eternal because they belong to God is to assert a plurality of eternal beings, which is contrary to the oneness of God. Some Mu'tazilites went so far as to deny all positive attributes. To say that God knows such and such a thing, they say, means that He is not ignorant thereof, and the same with the rest of the attributes.

It is interesting to notice that the first Muslim thinker to deny the divine attributes in the above sense was Wasil Ibn Ata (died 131; AD. 748) in his refutation of the Christian doctrine of the Trinity, which he considered a plurality of eternal attributes in one Essence. His view received more elaboration in the later circles of the Mu'tazilites who gave it a more philosophical turn. God was reduced by them to a simple monad stripped of all attributes and qualities. Hence they were called by their opponents *Muattila,* that is, those who render the divine attributes useless or functionless.

The opposite view was held by the orthodox party and later by the Asharite school. Their argument on the whole is not very convincing, and most of it is quibbling with words. God, they say, has attributes, but they are neither identical with His Essence nor different from it. They are "states" which though distinguishable from the Essence are yet inherent in it. The whole trouble, it seems, rested on one fundamental misconception: they personified the attributes but went on thinking they were dealing with the ordinary simple attributes of God. To talk about an eternal attribute which is different from the divine Essence but coexistent with it is to personify it and give it the status of a substance—a position very similar to that of the Christian Trinity. Had these theologians said that the attributes were mere intelligible relations qualifying the Essence, or mere names with which God has described Himself, the question as to their identity or nonidentity with the divine Essence and the other question as to their eternity or temporality would not have arisen.

The failure to realize the significance of describing the attributes of God from two different aspects is responsible for most of the disputes and futile arguments with which Muslim books on theology abound. The two contending parties—the traditionalists and rationalists—concentrated on one set of attributes to the comparative neglect of the other. The result was two extreme views, with corporealism or moderate anthropomorphism on the one side and absolute transcendentalism on the other.

The Mu'tazilites, who were the champions of transcendentalism, resorted to a method of interpretation which explained away all the anthropomorphic passages in the Quran, and they discarded the anthropomorphic Prophetic Traditions as invalid or not authentic. This was necessary to preserve their conception of the absolute unity and transcendence of God. The traditionalists wavered between immanence and transcendence but were more inclined toward immanence.

The rational interpretation of the Mu'tazilites had its advantages as well as its disadvantages. In one respect it helped to liberate Islam from the materialistic and mythological concepts of God by insisting on the more spiritual and abstract attributes. But it was carried to an extreme by some of the rationalists who reduced the Godhead to an abstraction void of all content.

The enquiry into the nature of the divine attributes naturally led to a discussion on the nature of the Quran as the revealed word of God or the external manifestation of the attribute of divine speech. The orthodox, who held the doctrine of the eternity of the attributes, said the Quran was eternal. The rationalists said it was created, or there would be something eternal other than God, and this would be a violation of His oneness. The Prophet to whom the Quran was revealed did not hear the words of God, but heard a voice which God created in a material medium and which conveyed to him the content of the divine mind. The Quran as we know it is therefore created. This was the doctrine of the Mu'tazilites which was championed by the Abbasid Caliph al-Mamun.

When the triumphant days of the Mu'tazilites were ended, the orthodox party saw their opportunity once again and declared that all was uncreated, even the very Word written in the Book and recited in man's prayer. The Asharite school took up the problem later and discussed it on a higher level. They were influenced by older speculations on a similar subject, particularly the Christian and Jewish theories of the Logos, which in their turn were influenced by ancient Greek theories.

The Asharites held that God's speech was eternal. The Quran, the divine command, and the creative Word *Be,* were all forms of the eternal attribute of speech. "The command of God," says the Quran, "is such that when God wills a thing, He says to it: Be; and it is" (Surah XXXVI, 81). The creative command and the creative Word *Be* are therefore prior to all phenomenal existence. The Quran also says, "One of His signs is that the heavens and the earth are sustained by His command" (Surah XXX, 25). Thus the divine command is not only the instrument of creation, it is also the sustaining principle of the created world. Such verses were originally meant to emphasize the absolute sovereignty of God as the supreme Creator and Maintainer of the universe, but a new meaning was read into them by the Asharites in support of a Logos theory comparable in many respects to the Christian and Stoic theories. The divine command and creative Word were personified and given power to create and sustain that which they create. Moreover, the Word, or Logos, is in one respect identical with God, in another different from Him and coeternal with Him. Thus the Word of

God gradually took a place similar to that of the Memra in Jewish theology, and the Second Person in the Christian doctrine of the Trinity.

The Asharites went a step further. They distinguished between two kinds of speech, the external and the internal. The external, which consists of words and sounds and can be put down in writing, is created. The internal, which is expressed by such words and sounds, is identical with the divine consciousness and is therefore eternal. This distinction is certainly borrowed from the philosophy of the Stoics who spoke of potential and actual, or internal and external Logoi. It is also in line with the Christian theory of the Logos which distinguishes the Word which was from eternity with God and was God from the Word which appeared in a temporal manifestation in the form of Christ. Perhaps the earlier Asharites did not express themselves in such plain words. They did not work out the metaphysical implications of their theory. They were more concerned with the problems of the eternity of the Quran which they thought they had proved. What they actually proved is the eternity of the divine mind or the divine knowledge, and the temporal manifestation of this knowledge when revealed to the Prophet. This position was taken up by al-Ghazali and later Asharites.

DETERMINISM AND FREE WILL

The ethical problem of determinism and free will has its roots in the much wider metaphysical problem of the conception of God in His relation to the world in general and mankind in particular. The pessimistic attitude of the Semitic mind toward the world as a fleeting shadow, the notion that it has value only as a place in which man prepares himself for a more permanent life, led to the conception that God is the absolute sovereign power which rules all things, including man and his actions. We have a definite trace of this conception in the Quran. God is the supreme King of Heaven and earth whose authority is not to be challenged. The following examples are typical of a large number of similar texts in the Quran. "He should not be asked concerning what He does" (Surah XXI, 23). "He createth what He will" (Surah XXX, 54) "He it is Who created you from dust" (Surah XL, 67). "He alone misguides whomever He pleases and guides whomever He pleases" (Surah XXXV, 8). And in talking to his people, Noah says, "Nor shall my counsel profit you if God wills to misguide you, though I fain would counsel you aright. God is your Lord, and unto Him shall ye return" (Surah XI, 34). This is one side of the picture; in its theological aspect it emphasizes the absolute-authority of God over His creation, and in its ethical aspect suggests a deterministic theory of man's actions.

The other side of the picture shows the same two aspects closely related to one another. God, who is described as supreme power and will, is also described as just. The following typical passage from the Quran illustrates the justice of God. "We will not burden a soul beyond its power; with Us is a Book which speaks the truth, and they shall not be unjustly treated" (Surah XXIII, 62). "These are the signs of God: we recite them to thee in truth and God wills not injustice to mankind" (Surah III, 108). "God does them no injustice; it is they who are unjust to themselves" (Surah III, 117). "In truth has God created the heavens and the earth that each soul shall be rewarded for what he has earned, and that they shall not be wronged" (Surah XLV, 22). Thus, according to the Quran, justice is an essential attribute of God, and it is inconceivable that God can be the absolute despot who wills and acts as He pleases even if His actions are contrary to justice.

It is obvious that the two opposite theories, determinism and free will, can be traced back to a conflict between two conceptions of the nature of God—God as absolute power and God as just.

The early Muslims who were the true sons of the desert preferred to think of God after the pattern of a tribal God with unlimited authority, a conception from which they derived their ethical theory of determinism. Their God can do everything, even that which is unjust or unreasonable. On the ethical side they taught that man was nothing but an instrument in the hands of his Lord, subjected to the strictest laws of determinism. This theory, known as oriental fatalism, has caused Islam to be stigmatized as a fatalistic religion, but nothing could be farther from the truth, for Islam attaches the greatest importance to the role which man plays in the sphere of his actions.

The Mu'tazilites, on the other hand, emphasized man's responsibility for his own actions. They argued against the despotism of God as well as against determinism and fatalism and put their whole trust in human reason, which to them was sacred. They taught that appeal should be made to reason first, rather than to the religious law. Reason tells us that we are the authors of our own actions and that some of them are right and others are wrong. Perception of right and wrong is an innate power of the human mind not due to knowledge taught by religion. Man therefore is a free agent and the maker of his own destiny. He is also the maker of his own moral law which must coincide with the religious law because the religious law is rational. There can be no religious injunction which is contrary to reason.

Man, however, is not purely rational, according to the Mu'tazilites. There is an irrational element in man to which he sometimes yields. This is why he sometimes goes astray and falls into error and sin, and this is why religion is needed as a reminder to the forgetful and to those whose rational will is thwarted by carnal desires. The Muslim rationalists were certainly on the road to Kant. The good will is the only thing that has intrinsic value in moral life, and it is man's own. Without freedom of the will and personal responsibility, retribution, punishment and reward, and the Future Life with its. Heaven and Hell are all empty words void of meaning.

Rationality is not only the guiding principle in man's actions and beliefs, according to the Muslim rationalists; it is also the ruling principle in the cosmos. This world is the best of all possible worlds because it is the work of a supreme Mini The so-called evil in the world is an integral part of the goodness of the whole.

The root of the doctrine of free will is to be found in the Quran itself and there is no justification for seeking an external source for it. In fact, the Quranic passages in favour of free will by far outnumber those which are suggestive of determinism. "And say: The truth is from your Lord: let him then who will, believe, and let him who will be an infidel" (Surah XVIII, 30). "This truly is a reminder: and whosowills, takes the road to his Lord" (Surah LXXVI, 29). "Say: Everyone acts after his manner; but your Lord knows who is best guided in his path" (Surah

XVII, 84). "He who does evil or acts unjustly against himself, then asks pardon of God, will find God forgiving, merciful. And he who commits a crime, commits it to his own hurt" (Surah IV, 111-12).

According to the Quran man is free to choose his actions and beliefs, and he merits punishment or reward according to whether his choice is right or wrong. It is for God to show the right path, and for man to follow it or not follow it. Everything is predestined in the sense that it is predetermined by man's nature and known as such to God from eternity. The eternal knowledge of God does not interfere one iota with man's choice. Only in this sense can any meaning be attached to moral and religious obligations. Man alone works out his salvation, and this by faith and good deeds. Faith is rarely mentioned alone in the Quran; it is usually coupled with good deeds as the necessary prerequisites for entering paradise. "Bring good tidings to those who believe and do the good things that are right, that for them are gardens 'near which rivers flow" (Surah II, 25). "Those who have believed and done the good things that are right, they shall be the inmates of Paradise" (Surah II, 82).

THE PHILOSOPHICAL ATTITUDE

The attitude of the Muslim philosophers toward Islam is somewhat different from that of the theologians. The main object of the theologians was to defend, in their own way, Islamic dogmas. The philosophers sought to reconcile Islamic dogmas with philosophic ideas, to arrive at a conception of God which would satisfy the requirements of free thought as well as those of religious beliefs. The conception of God as the ultimate ground of all phenomenal existence had, somehow or other, to be brought into harmony with the conception of the personal God of Islam. To what extent the attempt was successful we shall see later.

The first Muslims to philosophize about the simple ideas of Islam were the Mu'tazilites. They were followed by the philosophers al-Kindi, al-Farabi, and Ibn Sina (Avicenna). The philosophers were on the whole contemptuous of their predecessors. Even al-Ghazali could not conceal his disappointment with the method of the theologians. "Their method," he says, "is right only insofar as it accomplishes their own objective; but it is of no avail to anyone who admits nothing but self-evident truths."

Generally speaking one can say that the theological method had no philosophic basis, though this applies more to the school of the Asharites than the Mutaziites. The Asharites were skeptical in their attitude toward sense data. They denied causality and causal necessity and even refused to call God the First Cause. They taught that natural phenomena appear to be uniform not because they are subject to necessary

laws but because the human mind reads sequence into them. At any moment God may interrupt such uniformities and cause miraculous things to happen. Nothing takes place as a result of interrelations between natural phenomena. Everything is fresh creation. Their whole conception of God and the natural world was different from, and directed against, the Aristotelian philosophy which forms the basis of the thinking of the Muslim philosophers.

It is impossible to give an account of the individual systems of all the philosophers of Islam here. In this general treatment of the subject the aim will be to set forth the attitude of the school of al-Farabi and Ibn Sina, who represent Muslim philosophy in its strict and more limited sense. Ibn Sina in particular represents this philosophy in its mature and final form in a clear and well-reasoned manner. His object, like that of all Muslim philosophers before and after him, was to find a formula by which religious dogmas and philosophic principles can be reconciled. In this he was the faithful follower of al-Farabi. For both of them Greek philosophy was almost infallible, yet they acknowledged, in their own way, the basic theological principles of Islam. Their philosophy therefore is a mixture of ideas often irreconcilable except with the help of the drastic method of explaining away the opposite concepts. It is also highly eclectic in character, but eclecticism was not entirely the work of the Muslim mind as some scholars maintain. Two of the most important sources from which the Muslim thinkers drew considerable material reached them in an already eclectic form—Neoplatonism and Hermetic philosophy. Plato and Aristotle had already been brought into some harmony and their ideas interpreted in the light of the ancient wisdom of the Orient with its characteristic religious sentiment. This made them all the more appealing to the Muslim philosophers whose aim was to philosophize Islam.

When Greek thought found its way into the Muslim world, the philosophers found themselves faced with a problem which they attempted to solve. On the one hand Islam called them to a simple faith in God who is the sole creator and sustainer of the world. It offered them no philosophy or even a basis for one. On the other hand, Greek philosophy in the form in which it came to them represented the final achievements reached by the Greek mind in its search for a solution of the problem of existence. It was impossible for Muslims to accept without alteration any religious teaching which, outwardly at least, contradicted their philosophic ideas. But it was equally impossible to go the full length with Greek philosophical theories and accept their necessary consequences. Therefore, the only way left open to them was to reconcile the two. The question was—which of the Greek philosophical theories should they accept? Aristotle's theory of a Prime Mover who set the whole world in motion, then left it to its own fate? Or Plato's theory of God as the supreme Idea of Good—whose relation to the existing world he left unexplained? Or the Stoic's theory of pantheism? Or the Neoplatonic theory of emanation?

Those were the chief Greek theories of the nature of God known to the Muslims, and none of them could possibly be accepted by them without serious modification. The pantheistic view of reality never appeared in the Muslim philosophy of the type we are discussing here, but a full-fledged theory of pantheism was put forward later by the greatest of all Muslim mystics, Muhy al-Din Ibn Arabi. We shall say more about him later. The Muslim philosophers made use of Platonic, Aristotelian, and Neoplatonic ideas in constructing their own metaphysics, in which Islamic ideas also play an important part. But even the Islamic concepts were interpreted in such a way as to make them more philosophical, thus narrowing the gulf between Islamic and pagan thought.

The problem with which Muslim philosophers were faced was that of the relation between the external world, with its multiplicity of spatio-temporal and changeable phenomena, and an ultimate, immutable, and unchangeable First Principle. In philosophical language, the problem was that of the relation between the one and the many, or the noumenon and the phenomena; in theological language it was the problem of God and the universe. The Greek thinkers were far from the idea of the Godhead as explained in revealed religions. Aristotle's philosophy is one of strict determinism in which both the material world and God are subject to a supreme law of self-necessity. The metaphysical-poetical conception of Plato reduces God to a mere abstraction. It was the Neoplatonists who, though in the main adhering to their pagan tradition, put forward some sort of a philosophy of religion. It is no wonder therefore that they paved the way for establishing Christian and Muslim philosophy of religion, and that their influence in Muslim religious thought in particular was predominant.

The attempt to reconcile Islam with Greek philosophy in general and Neoplatonism in particular was an honest but a very daring one. Whether the Muslim philosophers succeeded or failed is another matter, but the fact remains that through making the effort they made their genuine contribution to the history of human thought. They also exposed themselves to the severest criticism of their adversaries. Ghazali's vehement attacks on their views will be referred to later.

Ibn Sina is generally regarded as a true representative of the philosophy which sought to reconcile Islamic and Neoplatonic thought. His metaphysical views are regarded by no less an authority than Ghazali as being the most typical of his school, and when Ghazali launches his attacks against the philosophers he has Ibn Sina in mind all the time. Al-Farabi is also an excellent type, but he lacks the clarity and comprehensiveness of his successor. Al-Kindi is more of a logician, natural philosopher, and theologian. Ibn Rushd's (Averroes) greatness is to be found more in his commentaries on Aristotle than in independent philosophical thought. The rest of the Muslim philosophers of the West are mere satellites moving around al-Farabi and Ibn Sina.

GOD AND THE WORLD

Ibn Sina prefers to call God the Necessary Being, or the Self-Subsistent Being, rather than Allah. His intention is to bridge the gulf between the religious and philosophical concepts of the Deity, and thus to be able to follow up his analysis of being and necessity, or self-subsistence, to their logical conclusions. The name Allah has some Muslim associations which make it unphilosophical.

Ibn Sina starts his analysis of the relation between God and the world with a consideration of the notion of being—a purely ontological procedure—which he divides into necessary and contingent being. The necessary being is that being whose existence is self-necessitated; it exists *per se*; its essence and existence are identical; the supposition of its nonexistence involves contradiction. The contingent being is that which has no essential or necessary reason for its existence; its being or nonbeing are equally possible; its essence is different from its existence. This is the phenomenal world; it is all that is "other than God." Ibn Sina says that the mere fact that we have a notion of the Necessary Being proves that He exists. Existence is a positive quality of perfection, and if we have an idea of the Perfect Being, that Perfect Being must exist, or our idea would be self-contradictory. This is the ontological argument used in modern philosophy by Descartes and Leibnitz, though the consequences which Ibn Sina draws are different.

Ibn Sina also makes use of the Aristotelian distinction between necessity and contingency, but goes far beyond what Aristotle has said in the subject, both in his proof of the existence of God and in his explanation of the relation between God and the universe. He criticizes the cosmological argument of the theologians by which they infer the existence of an eternal Creator from the existence of the phenomenal world. Contingency, he says, not origination in time, is the cause of the dependence of the world upon God. To say that it is origination in time—that is, creation—leads to these absurdities: that God's will and creative power were idle for an infinite time before the creation of the world; that to choose the creation of the world at a certain time, and not before or after that time, must have been due to circumstances outside God's nature, which means that some sort of change must have taken place in Him; and that the world after it has been created could very well be independent of its Creator, since its need of Him is only for creation and not for preservation after creation.

A contingent universe, on the other hand, has no temporal beginning and is dependent for its existence and the continuity of its existence on God. It is an eternal being which derives its existence every moment from God. There is only logical—not temporal—priority between them, the priority of cause to effect. The cause has never existed in time before its effect in this case. We can also call it priority of rank since the cause is usually regarded as superior to the effect. Here Ibn Sina is in complete agreement with Aristotle and in complete disagreement with the theologians who insist on the idea of creation, which is one of the principle dogmas of Islam.

The world, they hold, was created out of nothing by the will of God and at the time He appointed. No question should be asked as to why it was not created before or after, because such relations as before and after have no application within the domain of the eternal Will. This is the argument adduced by Ghazali in his refutation of the philosophers' doctrine of the eternity of the world.

In spite of his theory of the eternity of the world, Ibn Sina describes God as the Maker, the Fashioner, and sometimes the Creator of the world. These epithets occur in the Quran and have one definite sense in common—bringing the world into existence from nothing. Ibn Sina, who believed in the impossibility of creation out of nothing, explains these terms in such a way as to deprive them of their temporal significance. That which comes into being need not always have a temporal beginning, nor need it be the result of an act of will. It can be the result of a spontaneous and necessary overflowing of being from an original source, like the overflowing of the rays from the sun. This is the case with regard to the world in its relation to God. If eternity and necessity are essential attributes of God as the Primary Cause, so must they be attributes of His actions, which are His effects.

Thus we see how far Ibn Sina went in his deterministic philosophy. Necessity is the fundamental law to which both the phenomenal world and God Himself are subjected.

THE ATTRIBUTES OF GOD

The conception of God in Muslim philosophy, in spite of all that has been said, is not quite the same as the Aristotelian conception. God, according to al-Farabi and Ibn Sina, is not a mere principle of action within the material world but is an independent and transcendent Being over and above the material world, forever producing it and preserving it.

Their conception of the Godhead is both theological and philosophical. God has two different kinds of attributes: metaphysical attributes, which can be inferred directly or indirectly from the definition of God as the Necessary Being; and theological attributes with which God describes Himself in the Quran. Even the metaphysical attributes are often tinged with a religious colour and explained in a way which makes them partly ethical and partly theological. This is because these philosophers are forever oscillating between philosophy and religion, although their loyalty on the whole is to philosophy.

According to Ibn Sina the divine attributes are simplicity, oneness, absolute perfection, pure goodness; God is the contemplator and the contemplated; God has no equal nor opposite.

Simplicity logically follows from the definition of God as the Necessary Being; for complexity, whether material, quantitative, or even intelligible, is contrary to necessity and self—subsistence. The complex, whatever it is, is dependent on its constituent parts and on something else to make it a whole. It follows, therefore, that God is not a material substance, is not divisible, is not a compound of two or more substances, and is not definable.

Oneness is an attribute of God, for God is one m every He has no partner who participates either in His or in His attributes. This is the first article of the faith. Plurality of gods contradicts the notion of self-necessity.

Absolute perfection is an attribute of God. God is perfect and complete. In Aristotle's language, God is pure actuality; there is nothing that is possible in Him which is not actually realized—His will, His knowledge, and His action, the whole of His nature. Everything else is in the process of becoming. The perfection of everything other than God is a potentiality which God brings into an actuality.

Pure goodness is an attribute inferred from God's being free from matter and potentiality. Goodness here is equivalent to positive being, the opposite of evil or not-being. All other things possess the two aspects of being and not-being, because in one respect they are actual and in another they are potential. God is not only the pure good, He is also the fountainhead from which good—positive being—is forever flowing into everything in the world. The whole realm of existence turns toward Him in love-like fashion for the good it receives from Him, for the qualities of being through which the world advances along the road to perfection. The world in fact does love God, because it loves the good, and good is the only thing that is loved for its own sake. Through love, therefore, God sets the whole world in motion, and whatever takes place in existence is the fruit of this love.

Ibn Sina, who is not so successful in his theory about God as the Active Cause, admirably succeeds in portraying Him as the Final Cause. His argument here is potent, clear, and free from verbal quibbling. In fact, it is the most beautiful part of his metaphysics; it is here that his philosophy and mysticism meet. The relation between God and the external world is here expressed in terms of love and revelation—love on the part of the world, and revelation on the part of the Beloved. The divine act of bestowing being on things is the very act of self-revelation. God reveals Himself to His creatures in a manner suitable to the requirements of their inner nature, which is fixed and immutable, or in proportion to the degree of perfection which they aspire to achieve. The divine Providence is the work of a mind which comprehends an orderly system gradually unfolding itself. The self-unfolding of the phenomenal world is paralleled in the eternal self-revelation of God, and the two processes are inseparable. Ibn Sina's theodicy, aesthetics, and optimistic theory of the nature of the world branch off from this mystical philosophy. It is here that he seems to be more under the influence of Plato and Plotinus than Aristotle.

For Ibn Sina, God is essentially an intellect whose sole activity is to contemplate Himself. He is the contemplator and the contemplated, the subject and the object in one. There is no duality in Him as there is in other minds. Duality of any kind is contrary to His absolute unity and simplicity.

There is a great deal of discussion about the knowledge of the Divine Mind. The theologians, following the Quran, hold that God knows everything past, present, and future, seen and unseen. They say that He is omniscient, that nothing takes place in the world which is not in accordance with His prior knowledge. The philosophers, on the other hand, maintain that God's knowledge is primarily of Himself and that, knowing Himself, He knows the world in a general way. He is the Ultimate Cause of things, as we have explained, and knowledge of the cause entails knowledge of the effect. They argue that knowledge of individual happenings in the world depends on a temporal relation between the knower and the known and therefore involves change in the knower, but God's knowledge is above time and change.

Ibn Sina also maintains that God has neither an equal nor an opposite. He has no equal because it is impossible for two necessary beings (gods) to be. He has no opposite because two opposites must be similar in one respect and dissimilar in another respect, in which they are said to be opposites—and God has no similar in any respect whatsoever. Therefore He has no opposite.

The Muslim philosophers do not omit the Quranic attributes of God such as omnipotence, omniscience, justice, generosity, and the like, but they interpret them philosophically or explain them away. We have already given the attributes of knowledge and will as examples. So it is quite evident that their concept of God is neither the pagan conception of the Greek philosophers nor the strictly orthodox Islamic conception. The denial of creation in its ordinary sense and the doctrine of the eternity of the world are definitely non-Islamic. In their view, however, they have shifted the problem to a higher plane by maintaining that the world is the outcome of God's inner necessity and the eternal urge within Him to give an outward manifestation of His bounty and generosity.

Although on the theoretical side the Muslim philosophers certainly seemed to be anti-Islamic, at least in some of their views, on the practical side they were true Muslims, insofar as we can gather from their biographies. Al-Farabi is said to have led a saintly life of religious devotion and contemplation. Ibn Sina, though allowing himself some bodily indulgences, is not reported to have neglected his religious duties. It is true that his conceptions of Heaven and Hell and the Resurrection are somewhat unorthodox, but he does not completely deny the orthodox concepts. We will conclude this section with his own words, taken from his *Nine Epistles:* The ultimate object of man wherein lies his greatest happiness in future life is to gain knowledge of the realities of things so far as his nature allows, and do what is incumbent upon him. Only in this way does man's soul become more honourable and perfect, an intelligible microcosm comparable to the existing Macrocosm, and become ready to enjoy the greatest happiness in the world to come.

THE MYSTICAL ATTITUDE

The mysticism of Islam is known as Sufism, a name said to be derived from the Arabic word *suf* which means wool, referring to the woollen mantles worn by the Sufis. With Muslim mysticism we see the climax of the development of religious life and teaching in Islam. Neither the philosophers nor the theologians nor the canon lawyers have contributed so much as the mystics toward deepening the meaning of their religion and enriching its teachings. It is due to them that Islam, in the way they understand it, can be compared with other great religions of the world, for mysticism is the only ground on which the great religions meet.

Muslim mysticism has, from the time of its inception, been a spiritual revolution against a variety of forms and systems, both social and religious. After a long period of hard struggle, Sufism established itself in two quite different ways: as a religious philosophy and as the popular religion of Islam. During some of its flourishing periods, the Sufis were counted by the millions all over the Muslim Empire and in some countries their influence was so great that the heads of their orders were the practical rulers, with supreme authority in every major problem concerning the religious or secular institutions. Such influence can be found even now in some Muslim communities.

As an ideal mode of spiritual life, Sufism has passed through various stages. At some times it was thoroughly orthodox, at others so far removed from orthodoxy as to become a mere system of religious philosophy. It has also undergone some periods of stagnation and corruption during which its followers completely lost sight of the noble and lofty ideals of the original founders, preserving an outward appearance of ritual with nothing to correspond to it in the heart. But these remarks belong more to the history of Sufism. Our immediate object here is to try to set forth the mystical attitude toward Islam so far as it can be gleaned from the lives and teachings of the great Sufi masters, leaving everything else out of our account.

The special attitude of the Muslim mystics toward Islam was quite clear from the time their movement started. Until the end of the second century (eighth century AD) religious laws were based on the literal texts of the Quran and Prophetic Traditions, and scrupulously carried out. They were thoroughly studied and strictly adhered to in practice. Knowledge of the canon law—jurisprudence—was the most venerated of all knowledge, and adherence to its rules was the ultimate aim as well as the true mark of every pious Muslim. When the Sufis appeared on the scene, they came with another religious ideal. To them the examination of the esoteric meaning of the law was a more worthy objective than the study of the law in its esoteric sense. Hence arose the distinction between the outward expression of the law and its inward significance, and with it the distinction between the study of jurisprudence on the one hand and Sufism on the other. The jurists became known as the externalists and the Sufis as the internalists. Gradually the opposition between the two camps grew more and more intense as they realized that they stood for two different conceptions of Islam and its teachings.

The differences between the legalists and the Sufis were apparent in their interpretations of the meaning of religious law and the ways in which it should be derived and justified. They differed as to the nature of worship and the way it should be performed. They did not agree as to which actions are lawful or unlawful or what parts of the law are basic to Islam. Nor did they agree as to the object and value of obligatory and supererogatory religious devotions. Is God the object of formal worship or of love? They differed on many points of Islamic dogma, especially concerning the conception of God in His relation to man, and the meaning of the unity of God.

It is obvious that such disputes touch the very core of Islam, and it is no wonder that the Muslim theologians and jurists became the bitterest enemies of the Sufis and fought them on all fronts for centuries. The first opposition to their movement came from the traditionalist Ahmad Ibn Hanbal (died 241; AD. 855). He could not conceal his admiration for a Sufi like al-

Harith al-Muhasibi (died 243; AD. 857), but admitted that al-Muhasibi spoke in his sermons a language unknown to him, the language of the Sufis. He did not doubt his sincerity but was full of suspicion and apprehension. Relentless persecution of the Sufis was carried on by Ibn Hanbal's party and other theological sects in order to put an end to their growing influence.

Gradually the new mysticism of Sufism—or rather, the new religious spirit—gained ground. It was realized that Islam as understood by the jurists was ultimately reduced to formal ritual which consisted in the performance of certain bodily movements. Prayer, fasting, and pilgrimage were well-defined and measured physical movements, almost void of genuine feeling. Such an attitude toward Islam was sure to satisfy the externalists whose main concern was to give precise definitions to religious terms, lay down general laws, and see that they were strictly observed. It did not satisfy the religious sentiment of the Sufis, who looked for a deeper meaning behind the outward forms. Qushayri tells us that Ruwaym of Baghdad (died 303; AD. 915) said, "All people hold fast to external appearances [of religion], but this community [the Sufis] holds fast to realities. All people consider it their duty to observe the external aspect of the religious law; the Sufis consider it their duty to strive after piety and unremitting sincerity." In these few words Ruwaym sums up the whole situation by pointing out the real difference between the Sufis and the rest of the Muslims in their respective attitudes toward Islam. For the Sufis, Islam is *haqiqa,* a reality hidden behind words and forms, while for the rest of the Muslims it is principally words and forms.

Such a distinction was practically unknown to the early Muslims. The idea started with the Shia who taught that the Quran, like everything else, had two aspects, one external and the other internal. The latter is what the Sufis call the esoteric meaning of the Quran, which is only revealed to the chosen people of God. They extended the idea to everything in Islam. A real contrast was made between the sharia (religious law) aspect of a religious principle or usage and its haqiqa aspect, that is, between the religious law as such and its real meaning.

It is true that the great teachers of Sufism agree that sharia should be strictly observed, and that the abandonment of sharia on the pretext that haqiqa, the reality or spirit of the law, has been obtained is not only impiety but infidelity. Haqiqa without sharia, they say, is baseless, and sharia without haqiqa is meaningless. A reasonable balance between the two is essential for a truly religious life. Such a balance is described by Ghazali in these words,

> He who says that haqiqa is contrary to sharia, and the internal [side of religion] is contrary to the external is nearer to infidelity. Every haqiqa that has no root in sharia should be rejected. Sharia is the law enjoined upon people; haqiqa is seeing the work of Divine Providence. Sharia is worship of God; haqiqa is to behold him. Sharia is to obey the Divine Command; haqiqa is to know by mystic vision what God has predestined, what He has revealed and what He has concealed.

So, according to Ghazali, haqiqa is the spiritual justification and proof of religion. The true meaning of religious teachings is seen by the mystic in his heart. Its real nature is revealed to him. When, for instance, the mystic is called upon to worship God, the meaning of the Godhead and of worship is freshly perceived by the inner light. This is the general attitude adopted by the majority of orthodox Sufis and ardently defended by such men as Tustari (died 273; AD. 886), Kharraz (died 277; AD. 890), Junayd (died 297; AD. 909), and Ghazali (died 505; AD. 1111). But some Sufis went too far in emphasizing haqiqa and minimizing the importance of sharia and were eventually led into various degrees of the erroneous belief that the awareness of inner reality frees one from the moral obligations of the law. They represent the other extreme of Sufism which is condemned by the genuinely pious Muslims. Others among the Sufis held fast to sharia, but understood it in ways which were much wider and more liberal than the interpretation of the orthodox, looking upon the law as either a system of self-discipline or as a set of symbols representing hidden religious meanings.

Those Sufis who regarded the law as essentially a system of self-discipline rejected the claim that the sharia is a collection of norms and codes divided and subdivided into more norms and codes. For them it must not be understood within the narrow limits and strict definitions of the lawyers and theologians. The value of any religious work should not be judged on the basis of its compliance with the law; its value should be determined by the degree to which it fulfills the ideal of the lawgiver.

Voluntary acts of devotion are considered superior to obligatory acts because they fulfill a higher ideal—the love of God—while obligatory acts of devotion only show submissive obedience to God's commands.

The Sufis quote the following Tradition in which God says, "In no way does My servant so draw nigh unto Me as when he performs those duties which I have imposed on him; and My servant continues to draw near to Me through works of supererogation, until I love him. And when I love him, I am his eye, so that he sees by Me, and his ear, so that he hears by Me, and his tongue, so that he speaks by Me, and his hand, so that he takes by Me."

This means that in the act of devotion he becomes completely absorbed in God and loses every vestige of his individual being and feels himself to be one with his Beloved. Such a state is not attained by the ordinary performance of religious duties. The Sufi seeks the attainment of the spiritual benefits which he gains through his acts of devotion, not the mere performance of outward acts as such. Thus the real essence of religion is that which resides in the heart, not that which is performed by the body. The religious command should be addressed to the heart, not to the bodily organs.

This attitude, noble as it is, seems to have paved the way to antinomianism in some Sufi circles. Religious duties, they argued, are a means to an end, and if the end is reached we can very well dispense with the means.

Haqiqa, religious truth, is for them the end and sharia, religious law, is the means. That there were such men even in the golden age of Sufism who allowed themselves all sorts of license and indulgences under the pretext that they had reached their goal is evident from the scathing remarks which we read in the opening chapters of the treatise on Sufism by Qushayri (died 465; AD. 1072).

He attacks most mercilessly the men of his time who believed that haqiqa frees one from the moral obligations of the law, and appeals for a revision of Sufism in the light of the teachings of the old masters, calling upon the Sufis to lead a true religious life in accordance with the Quran and the example of the founders of the Sufi path.

Qushayri's warning was not in vain, for fifty years later it found a remarkable response in the writings of Ghazali who took upon himself the task of reconciling Sufism with Islam. He interpreted the principles of Sufism in the light of Islam and showed their interdependence.

It is true that Ghazali was primarily concerned with the solution of his own spiritual problem when he was in search of the truth, but in solving his own problem he solved the problem for thousands of others who were and still are searching for the same truth. This truth he found in the Sufi way of life lived according to strict Muslim law. Religious truth is the inner meaning of the law revealed in the heart of the Sufi by the Divine Light.

In addition to the Sufis who looked upon the law as a means of self-discipline there were those who looked upon the sharia as a set of symbols standing for hidden religious meanings. Those symbols are of value only as a reminder or an occasion in which the hidden meanings are realized. The pious Muslim should perform the acts of worship prescribed by the sharia with his heart set on their spiritual meanings, otherwise his worship is merely an empty mechanical action.

This attitude takes into account the external, physical acts of worship as well as the internal acts of the heart. The danger is that it might lead to discarding the external acts altogether on the ground that they are superfluous.

The Sufis who insisted on the observation of both the external and internal acts of worship read into the external teachings of Islam meanings undreamed of by canon lawyers. Prayer, for instance, is not regarded as a set of words to be uttered and movements to be performed but is looked upon as essentially a spiritual discourse between man and his Creator. All movements and words are symbols whose meanings form a part of that inner discourse.

Similarly, pilgrimage is not a mere trip to the Holy Shrine of Mecca; it is the spiritual journey of the human soul to God.

Each step of the journey, each of the rites of the pilgrimage—such as circumambulation of the Kaaba, the kissing of the Black Stone, the standing on Mount Arafat—is a symbol of great spiritual significance. Each bodily movement of the pilgrimage has a corresponding movement of the heart.

The mention of God, known as *dhikr,* is another example of the symbolic interpretation of Islamic worship. It is not a mere repetition of the name Allah, but is the silent recollection and contemplation of God, done in such a way that the heart of the contemplator becomes occupied with nothing but Him and the lover becomes completely absorbed in his Beloved.

The Sufis go through the rest of the forms of worship in the same way. The man who performs religious rites without observing their hidden meanings is, according to them, like a child who reads the words of a book without understanding them. His religious life is void because his heart is void. In the case of prayer and dhikr, such a man's heart is occupied merely with the name of God, not with God Himself.

THE SUFI CONCEPTION OF GOD

Just as the attitude of the Sufis toward the religious teachings of Islam was a revolt against the jurists who stifled the true spirit of religion in order to preserve its form, their attitude toward God was also a revolt directed against the theologians and the philosophers.

The barren speculations of the Muslim rationalists deprived the Godhead of its positive content, and God was reduced to a logical abstraction. The orthodox theologians made of Him a despot whose absolute power could do everything, even the impossible and the irrational.

The philosophers, in their attempt to reconcile Islamic dogmas with Greek philosophy, were obliged to abandon many of the theological attributes of God, or explain them away, and put an active or final cause in place of a creator of the world. To the majority of the Sufis, God is essentially a personal being endowed with attributes which determine His relations with the world in general and man in particular. The outline of their picture of God is taken from the Quran, but the details which bring out the main features of the pictures are supplied by them, each in his own way.

God, they say, is the Creator of the world, the Maintainer, the sole Doer of everything, the Light of heaven and earth, the Merciful, the Compassionate, but above all He is the God who abides in the hearts of men. "Neither My heaven nor My earth contains Me," He says in a Tradition often quoted by the Sufis, "but I am contained in the heart of My servant who is a believer." So the Sufi does not look afar for his God, for the kingdom of God is in his heart if he can only see it.

The ultimate goal of the Muslim mystics is to bring this state into full realization, to feel the presence of God in the heart in such a way that nothing else is allowed to occupy it. Their aim is the complete absorption of the individual self in the contemplation of God.

If we pass in review over the long and complicated history of Sufism, we find that three different conceptions of God—ethical, aesthetic, and pantheistic—appear in successive stages of its development. They all had their roots directly or Indirectly in the Quran and Prophetic Traditions, or were brought into relation with such texts by means of interpretation.

The ethical conception of God was predominant in the earliest period of Muslim asceticism. The essence of God was regarded as absolute power and will. God was the supreme author of all things, including men's actions.

The present life was essentially evil and therefore should be abandoned if the everlasting happiness of the Future World was to be attained. The early Sufis had an exaggerated sense of guilt and of the terrible torments that awaited the sinners in Hell. Consequently an overwhelming fear of God and His wrath seized their hearts, and their pious devotions were regarded as a means of escape from the judgment to come.

They had almost forgotten the words of God in which He says, "My mercy embraces all things," and, "God pardons everything except associating other gods with Him." This fear coloured the moral and religious life of the early ascetics, and determined their attitude toward God, the world, and their fellowmen.

The aesthetic conception of God in Sufi metaphysics was based on the idea of reciprocal love between God and man. The root of this doctrine is to be found in the Quran, but further elaborations of it were due to foreign influences coming from Manichaeanism and Neoplatonism.

The first note in this direction was struck by the woman saint of Basra, Rabia (died 185; AD. 801). From the third century onward, the doctrine of divine love became the dominant feature of Sufism. God was the Beloved of the Sufis, and loving Him for His own sake was the end of all their endeavour. It was no longer the fear of Hell or the hope of Paradise, but the hope of obtaining a glimpse of the everlasting beauty of God which motivated the Sufis. Rabi'a says in one of her prayers, "0 God! if I worship Thee in fear of Hell, burn me in Hell, and if I worship Thee in hope of Paradise, exclude me from Paradise. But if I worship Thee for Thine own sake, withhold not Thine everlasting beauty." Also attributed to her is the following verse:

Two ways I love Thee: selfishly, And next, as worthy is of Thee. 'Tis selfish love that I do naught Save think on Thee with every thought. 'Tis purest love when Thou dost raise. The veil to my adoring gaze. Not mine the praise in that or this. Thine is the praise in both I wis. (Translated by R. A. Nicholson in Legacy of Islam, *pp. 213-14)*

As time went on, the idea of divine love went deeper and deeper into the life and thought of the Muslim mystics. On the practical side it became the sole motive of their actions. Moral ideas centred around it, just as they centred around the fear of God in the earlier period. Altruism or selflessness became the highest virtue. This meant the abandonment of worldly pleasures and the absolute denial of selfishness for the sake of God.

"The essence of love is self-denial," says Ghazali. "It is the ultimate end of all mystic stations. Every state that comes after it is a fruit thereof; and every station that precedes it is a step toward it." Jalal al-Din Rumi, the great Sufi mystic, says, "Love is the remedy of our pride and self-conceit, the physician of all our infirmities."

The Sufis devoted their lives to the worship of God because they loved Him and were anxious to win His love. On the theoretical side, divine love was regarded as the sole reason for the creation of the world. Creation is an expression of God's love, it is His eternal Beauty reflected in an external form. The Sufis quote the following Tradition in which God says, "I was a hidden treasure and I loved to be known, so I created the creation that they might know Me."

Moreover they maintain that love is the key to all Heavenly mysteries, and the essence of all true religion. It brings with it, not reasoned convictions, but convictions based on the infallible proof of immediate intuition. It is the celestial light that guides the traveller on his way to God.

Pantheism did not appear in Muslim mysticism—or at least not in a systematic form—before Muhy al-Din Ibn Arabi (died 638; AD. 1240), the greatest of all Arabic-speaking mystics of Islam. Pantheistic tendencies were seen as early as the third century, for instance in some of the utterances of Bayazid of Bistam (died 261; AD. 875), but they were not worked out into a consistent pantheistic doctrine.

Ibn Arabi, on the other hand, was the first to produce a full-fledged pantheistic philosophy which left its indelible marks on the whole of Sufism ever since his time.

The fundamental principle of this philosophy is the principle of the unity of all Being. His understanding of this principle is best summed up in his own words: "Glory to God who created all things, being Himself their very essence." In his *Fusus* he says,

> *O Thou who created all things in Thyself, Thou unitest that which Thou createst. Thou createst what existeth infinitely. In Thee, for Thou art the narrow and the All-embracing.*

In Islamic pantheism the phenomenal world is reduced to a mere shadow of reality, and God is regarded as the only real Being who is the ultimate ground of all that was, is, and will be. There is no actual duality of God and the phenomenal world, but there is an apparent duality asserted by the unaided intellect, which is incapable of comprehending the essential unity of the whole.

It is at most a duality of aspects of One Being—not of two independent beings. Looking at the two aspects within one whole, reality is both God and the universe, the One and the many, the transcendent and the immanent, the internal and the external. If we think—as we usually do—in terms of duality, we predicate of Reality all pairs of opposite attributes. But mystic intuition asserts that God is the only Real Being who is above all description and qualifying attributes, and the world is a mere illusion.

There is therefore a definite place for God in this philosophy, although in some respects He is far removed from the God of Islam. Ibn Arabi makes a distinction which is the dividing line between his metaphysical theory and his theology; it is a distinction between God as the unknowable and incommunicable Reality, and God as the object of belief, worship, and love. His conception of God as the object of belief comes very close to that of the ordinary monotheist, but the gap between pantheism and strict Muslim monotheism was too great for him to bridge.

God is the object of worship not in the sense that He is exclusively the God of the Muslims, the Christians, or the adherents of any other religion, but in the sense that He is the Essence of everything that is worshipped.

He is not to be confined to any particular form of belief or creed. Everything that is worshipped is one of the infinite number of forms in which He reveals Himself. To confine Him to one particular form to the exclusion of all other forms is infidelity, and to acknowledge Him in all forms of worship is the true spirit of religion.

This is the universal religion which the pantheistic Ibn Arabi preaches, a religion which comprises all religions and unites all beliefs. In his *Tarjumanu al-Ashwaq* he expresses this conviction,

> *My heart has become a receptacle of every form; It is a pasture for gazelles and a convent for Christian monks, And a temple for idols, and pilgrims' Kaaba, And the Tablets of the Torah and the Book of the Quran. I follow the religion of love whichever way its camels take; For this is my religion and my faith.*

The religion of love, according to Ibn Arabi, is religion in its widest and most universal sense. All worshippers do in fact worship God, although they appear to worship their particular gods. And since love is the essence of worship—for to worship is to love to the extreme—and since the objects of worship are nothing but the external manifestations of God, it follows that God is both the supremely beloved and the supremely worshipped One.

This brief discussion shows some of the ways in which the interpretations of Muslim theologians, philosophers, and mystics have contributed to the vitality of Islam throughout its long history, making their varied contributions to the development of Muslim thought and influencing Islamic practices.

Although they have often been considered as unorthodox by the leaders of Islam, their attempts to provide a rational basis for Islamic beliefs and a mystical basis for Islamic worship have for centuries enriched and stimulated the Muslim community.

Unity and Diversity in Islam

No one can claim to speak with final authority concerning the diversity found among the more than five hundred million Muslims who seek to follow the straight path of Islam. One can only record some observations concerning the variations in practices among the Muslims from Morocco and the Balkans to China and Indonesia.

It is possible, however, to be much more explicit about the basic unity of Islam, for throughout the Muslim world there is general agreement concerning the sources of Islam, the fundamentals of the faith, and the particular requirements which are the obligations of all believers.

THE SOURCES OF ISLAM

There is general agreement that the sources of Islam are the Quran, the Sunnah, and reasoning about them. Of these, the primary source is the Quran.

Concerning matters not explicitly clear in the Quran, the Sunnah is the secondary, supplementary source; and when the answer to questions needs further clarification the third source for Muslims is reasoning about the intent of the Quran and Sunnah by those men who are recognized as having the training and experience which qualifies them to reason properly. The miraculous revelation of the Quran has been fully discussed in earlier chapters of this book.

It is the final revelation, the Word of God given through His Prophet as a guide to all men everywhere, regardless of race, or colour, or nationality. Within two years of the death of the Prophet it was compiled in book form and has been the primary source of Islam for almost fourteen centuries, without question and without variant versions. Since it was revealed in Arabic it has necessitated knowledge of Arabic, and this has been a unifying cultural factor throughout the Muslim world. It was recognized, however, that the people in the various countries often read the Quran in Arabic without understanding its meaning.

The uneducated people even thought that it was sufficient to pronounce the words correctly, and that such repetition—even without understanding the meaning—would bring them blessings from God and save their souls. Some even used verses of the Quran as amulets against dangers and diseases! Half a century ago the orthodox Muslims believed that it was forbidden to translate the Quran, fearing that translations would supplant the original Arabic version and that versions in different languages would cause disagreements and misinterpretations of the revelation of God. While it is true that because of its very high literary style it is difficult, if not impossible, to translate the Quran into any other language without losing the beauty and vigour of the original, translations in the languages of the people are necessary in order that they may understand the meaning of this book which is the source of Islam. Today the Quran is available in translation in most of the languages of the world.

Sometimes people ask why the Quran was revealed in Arabic if it is intended to be the Holy Book for all human beings. This question cannot be answered definitely, for if the Quran had been revealed in any other language—for example, in English—the question would still remain as to why that one language was chosen. Thus we have to content ourselves with the fact that, regardless of any possible reasons, the Quran was revealed in Arabic.

The second source for Islam is the Sunnah. During Muhammad's lifetime, Muslims could ask him to guide them in solving any problem when they did not find a clear answer in the Quran. For instance, once a man asked him if it would be proper to perform a pilgrimage on behalf of his deceased mother. The Prophet replied that it would be proper since such an act could be compared to a debt which she owed and the son was obligated to pay. When the Prophet was dying, and knew that he would not be present to give such advice, he told the people that they would not go astray so long as they held to the two guides he was leaving for them—the Quran, the Book of God, and the example of his own way of life, the Sunnah. The Quran, in Surah XXXIII, verse 21, establishes the Sunnah as the second source of Islam:

> *"There is a good example in the Apostle of Allah for those who wish to meet God and the Day of Judgment, and to remember God much."*

The Sunnah is made up of the deeds, speech, and approbation of the Prophet. His deeds include the way he prayed, or washed his hands, or took a bath, and the like. His words have been preserved for us, as for example when he said, "I am sent to perfect high morality." By approbation is meant that when Muhammad saw something done, or heard words uttered in his presence and did not object, such actions or words are approved. Approbation was applied chiefly to customs of the Arab society which were not in contradiction to the spirit of Islam. For example, when Muhammad saw a man dancing with a sword he smiled and showed his pleasure, so later jurists concluded that dancing with the sword is permitted. Such approval has been applied to customary practices and laws in all Islamic countries where such customs do not contradict the spirit of Islamic laws—for example, in the marriage ceremonies.

The codification of the Sunnah, the Traditions, began a century and a half after the Prophet when Malik Ibn Anas wrote a compilation of the Traditions concerning Islamic laws. The compilation of the Traditions took final form at the hands of Bukhari and Muslim in the third century (ninth century AD), and today most Muslims recognize their work as the two correct books on Traditions. Those two compilers established conditions for determining which Traditions would be accepted as authentic, conditions which related only to the persons who narrated the Traditions. Such persons must be of good moral character, pious, honest, of sound discretion, and blessed with a good memory; and the series of such transmitters must be continuous from generation to generation. The first generation was called the Companions, the second was known as the followers, and the third as the followers of the followers. Thus a tradition narrated by the followers only would not be accepted by Bukhari because there would be a gap of a generation from the time of the Prophet.

It must be explained, however, that those conditions for the correctness of a Tradition did not touch the subject matter, for internal criticism was unknown at the time. Consequently we find in the two compilations some Traditions, such as those about the signs of the approaching of the Day of Judgment, which we do not understand even yet. The lapse of two and a half centuries between the death of the Prophet and the compilation of the Sunnah has resulted in many differences between Muslims which continue in our time. In the civil war and struggle for power in the time of Uthman, the third Caliph, irreligious elements among the Muslim people did not refrain from fabricating traditions concerning the merits of some political figures. Accurate judgments concerning the narrators of Traditions became difficult because the political feuds sometimes made the judgments far from objective. A knowledge of the way in which the Traditions were compiled and transmitted facilitates an understanding of the various attitudes toward the Traditions which are found in Muslim countries today.

The Quran, which was revealed almost fourteen centuries ago, and the Traditions concerning the Prophet who lived that long ago exclusively in a desert society cannot serve as explicit guides for every situation which might arise centuries later, and especially in the complex societies of the present day. This was recognized by the Prophet himself. Once when he was sending one of his Companions to Yemen to serve as governor, he tested the man by asking him what principles he would follow in his new position. He answered that he would hold to the teachings of the Quran. The Prophet asked, "And if you do not find a particular guide in the Quran?" He replied, "I shall look for it in the Sunnah." Then the Prophet asked, "Well, what *if* you do not find it in the Sunnah either?" He replied, "In such a case, I shall make use of my own opinion." The Prophet was very pleased with that answer and said, "Thanks to God who has guided the messenger of the Messenger of Allah."

Thus a third basis for Islam became established, the basis of reasoning. We find in the Quran many verses which mention reasoning, or thinking, or knowing—verses which exhort us to make use of our brains instead of following blindly the traditions which our ancestors followed. Concerning the Unbelievers of old, the Quran says, "Nay, for they say only: Lo we found our fathers following a religion, and we are guided by their footprints" (Surah XLIII, 22). While exhorting us to contemplate nature, the Quran says, "In the creation of skies and the earth, the difference between night and day, the ships which run at sea carrying that which is useful for mankind, the rain water which Allah sends down from the sky to revive the earth after its death, and to spread animals on it, and the arrangement of winds and clouds between sky and earth, in all those things there are evidences (for the existence of God) for those who make use of their brains" (Surah II, 164). There is even a verse which says that once upon a time the people of Hell said to one another, "If we had made use of our ears or our brains we would not have been the inhabitants of this Hell" (Surah LXVII, 10).

Originally the word used for reasoning, *qiyas,* meant measure, used in the sense of thinking by comparing one thing with another—reasoning by analogy. As the third source of Islamic law it means determining the proper course of action by reasoning from the Quran and the Sunnah. Some men, however, speak of a fourth source of the law of Islam—consensus of opinion, or the agreement of capable men in their judgment on a specific question. This concept was introduced by al Shafii, the founder of one of the schools of law. Some people have misunderstood consensus to mean simply public opinion, and have asserted that if public opinion approves an action it is therefore acceptable to Islam. For Muslim legislators, consensus is the agreement reached among qualified religious leaders in one place at one time. There has never been a means by which such agreement might be found for all Muslims everywhere. True consensus, ijma, was possible only during the time of the first two Caliphs and part of the rule of the third Caliph. Ijma now only means that some agreement has been found in some places concerning the interpretation of certain verses of the Quran. As a basic source for Islam, it is reasoning, not consensus which is the third source. The Quran, the Sunnah, and reasoning are the generally accepted sources of Islam.

There are, as has been seen, some exceptions to the position that these are the three sources of Islam, for some people hold that only the Quran and Sunnah can give us a solid foundation for Islam. Their attitude, however, is easily refuted for it must be admitted that the problems of the world today are very different from those of the time of Muhammad, and their attitude would make Islam a dead religion. Actually, Islam is a dynamic religion, based on the Quran, the Sunnah, and reasoning. Some people confuse ijtihad with reasoning, but if used in the sense of a personal preference it is obviously not the same thing. In the sense of careful reasoning as to the implications of the Quran and the Sunnah, it is the same as reasoning. Unchecked, ijtihad might even lead to disagreement concerning such basic ideas as right and wrong, good and bad! To understand the unity and diversity in Islam it is necessary to understand these three sources of Islamic law: the Quran, the Sunnah, and the proper use of reason.

THE CREED OF ISLAM

The unity in Islam is shown in the acceptance of the six articles of belief, the fundamentals of Islam—belief in God, Angels, revealed scriptures, prophets, the Day of Judgment, and the destiny of man for good or evil. These beliefs are held by all Muslims.

The proof for the existence of God is found in the Quran through meditation on the beauty and order of nature. The harmony of the natural world shows that there is one benevolent Allah who created the universe and all human beings. The oneness of God is His most distinctive characteristic, as is shown in Surah CXII of the Quran, "He is One. He it is to whom we address our demands. He never gives birth and He was never born, nothing is similar to Him." In addition, all good qualities can be ascribed to God, He is the Merciful, the Generous, the Lover, the Great, the High. Some traditions mention ninety-nine names of God, but it is probable that the number is to be understood, not literally, but only as a very great number. Thus a Muslim may choose among those names of God the one which is psychologically relevant in the circumstances, a practice which is common throughout the Muslim world.

Theological treatises mention that there are twenty attributes of God, usually listed in four divisions. The first division includes only the essential attribute of existence. The second division is made up of the five negative attributes—no beginning, no end (eternity), difference from contingent things, independence of existence, unity (uniqueness). The third division includes the seven abstract attributes of power, will, knowledge, life, and the ability to hear, see, and speak. The fourth division, which is called the correlative of the abstract attributes, is made up of present participles of the abstract attributes of the third division—powerful (overpowering), willing, knowing, living, hearing, seeing, speaking. The theologians stressed that the attributes of God are not separate from the essence of God. This division of attributes is arbitrary and not clear, but most of the people consider it to be an essential element of belief. The series of attributes is clearly an artificial reflection of a reaction to Greek philosophy; it is not found in this form in the Quran or the Hadith, and has made people think in an unhealthy way. It is more appropriate to understand the existence of God through contemplating nature, as is revealed in the Quran. The differences of opinion among Muslims as to whether or not God resembles human beings, and the opinion of some common people that God resembles a medieval absolute king, arise only from different patterns of education; they are not fundamental to Islam.

Angels are creatures who serve as liaison between God the Almighty and His apostles, bringing the Godly messages and revelations to them. Some Traditions speak of Angels who guard Hell, some who guard Paradise, some who ask dead people about their beliefs, and some who record all of a man's actions; there is also an Angel who will blow the trumpet to awaken all human beings on the Day of Judgment. Common people tend to understand such Traditions literally, while educated people prefer to understand them figuratively with an interpretation more or less acceptable to reason.

The Quran, the holy revealed Book of Islam, mentions three former revealed books—the Book of David, the Book of Moses, and the Book of Jesus. This does not necessarily mean that there were no other revealed books, but only that we do not know whether or not any other books were revealed. Most people believe that there were no other revealed books than those three and the Quran.

The names of twenty-five apostles are found in the Quran, beginning with Adam. Muslims depend entirely on the text of the Quran for information concerning those prophets since the Quran is the only source about which there is not the slightest doubt. It is fortunate that the career of Muhammad is well-known, that there is nothing vague in the records of his life. The Traditions picture him in a very human way — dealing in commerce, getting married, having children, losing his wife and his sons, sharing all common experiences—in no sense a supernatural being. The only difference between Muhammad and the rest of mankind is that he received the revelations of God. All Muslims recognize Muhammad as a Prophet, and the last of the prophets. They see that the proof of his revelation lies not in external miracles but in the nature of the revelation itself. When the question is asked as to whether or not the teachers of other religions, such as the Buddha or Confucius, were prophets, no clear answer can be given. The Quran is not explicit on that point, for it says, "I have sent many apostles before you (Muhammad). I have told you about some of them, and I have not told you about some others" (Surah XL, 78). Some people conclude that the teachers of other religions are included in the "some others" that God has not told about, but other people say that only by studying the spirit and fundamentals of those religions can one determine whether or not they are of the same spirit as Islam, and their founders might be considered to have been prophets.

The Day of Judgment is mentioned in many verses in the Quran. When the sky is split, when the stars collide, when the mountains are like cotton, when the earth quakes—that is the Day of Judgment. On that day all people are awakened and their deeds are weighed; those having a heavy weight of good records will live happily in Paradise and those who have light weights will go to a Hell full of fire. The descriptions of Paradise are in such beautiful language that they make a deep impression on anyone who listens to the recital of the parts of the Quran which refer to it. On the other hand, Hell is described in a horrible way in many passages in the Quran. Although the common people are inclined to understand the descriptive passages in a literal sense, educated people recognize them as figurative. When the passages which describe Paradise and

Hell are meditated upon it is easy to understand what great power they have to motivate people toward good actions.

The sixth fundamental belief of Islam is the belief in destiny for good or for evil. There has been much misunderstanding of the meaning of the word destiny. Many people have thought that a belief in destiny implies that everything will happen by itself, whether we wish it or not, and that such a belief will make people apathetic and indifferent toward all progress. The real meaning of belief in destiny, however, is that one believes that God created an orderly world and one should act according to the nature of that world. Thus a man with a sense of destiny will be active in doing anything which he judges to be good, knowing that if anything bad happens in spite of all precautionary measures, then there will be no reason for regret or for blaming oneself. Then he would say that it was the destiny of Allah. This meaning was illustrated by the Caliph Umar Ibn al-Khattab when he decided not to visit Palestine while there was an epidemic there. A companion asked him, "Are you evading the destiny of God?" He answered, "Yes. I run from the destiny of God to another destiny of God."

There is no difference among Muslims concerning these six fundamental beliefs of Islam. Every Muslim believes in God, in Angels, in revealed scriptures, in apostles, in the Day of Judgment, and in destiny. The differences are only in the interpretations, as mentioned above, and these differences result primarily from the differences in standards of education.

THE PILLARS OF ISLAM

The fundamental beliefs of Islam have their practical consequences in everyday life. The writers of the other chapters in this book have referred to the practical side of Islam as the consequences of religion, the particular requirements of Islam, or as worship and dealings. Tradition says that the worship obligations, or requirements, of Islam are known as the Pillars of Islam; and the guide for dealings, for the responsibilities of human beings in society, are covered by fiqh, Islamic law.

According to Tradition, Islam is based on five foundations: the confession that there is no God but Allah and that Muhammad is the Apostle of Allah; prayer; almsgiving; fasting during Ramadan; and pilgrimage to Mecca by those who are able to go. Of these five pillars, concerning the first one there is no variation anywhere in the Islamic world. All Muslims know the Word of Witness, the confession of faith in Allah and the recognition of Muhammad as His Messenger, and all Muslims repeat it as their confession of faith.

The prayers are of two kinds, obligatory and optional. The five daily prayers are obligatory, including the obligation to attend the congregational prayer on Friday in the mosque. It is impossible to estimate what proportion of the people perform the five daily prayers regularly, since women usually say their prayers in the home and men may perform the salat at the mosque, at work, or at home. There is no religious superior who checks on the performance of the prayers. It is possible, however, to observe the attendance at the Friday noon prayers in the mosque. Large number of people will be seen at the mosque on Friday in Indonesia, in Turkey, Egypt, and parts of the Maghrib, and in the Shia mosques of Iran, to mention only the most obvious places. The smallest attendance at the Friday service would be found in China, and in the Soviet Union.

The optional, or facultative, prayers are of many kinds, such as the additional prayers before and after the obligatory prayers, prayers on the holiday after the month of fasting, prayers at the festival which marks the end of the pilgrimage, and prayers in times of need—which are offered by anyone at any time or place when the help of God is sought. Prayer for a person who died is necessary, since the spirit of such a person continues to live. Optional prayers can be performed at any time because a Muslim is in constant relation with God.

There are minor differences from country to country in the manner of praying, differences of no importance which have grown up through varying interpretations in the schools of jurisprudence. Some people emphasize the performance of optional prayers after the Friday prayers, while others do not. There are slight differences in posture; for example, in some countries, while standing, the people put their hands one upon the other in front of the lower part of the chest, while others who follow the school of Malik or of the Shias bend their hands down. Such differences are of no importance, and the unity is shown by the complete harmony among Muslims as to the times of prayer, the ablutions which must be performed before prayer, and the facing toward the Kaaba in Mecca.

The mosques are the centres for prayer, teaching, and service in the Muslim world and are recognized as the distinctive symbol of Islam even though they differ considerably from country to country. Originally the mosque was very simple, for any ground can be made a place for prayer. The first mosque built by Muhammad in Medina was a simple plot of ground with clay walls on all sides and a roof of palm branches. As Islam spread to other countries the mosques adopted the architecture of those countries. In China, for example, we find mosques which resemble pagodas in many ways; in Indonesia most mosques are built near streams which the people can use for ablutions; in Arab countries the big mosques have one section roofed for winter use and an open area for use in summer. In recent years the greatest activity in building new mosques has been in Turkey and Indonesia.

There is great variety in the minarets which are used for the call to prayer. They may be simple square or round towers, as in the Levant; or elaborate architectural designs as in Egypt; or the slender, pencil-shaped minarets of Turkey; in Iraq and Iran the minarets in Shia mosques are often beautifully decorated with colourful ceramic tiles; in Indonesia they stand as separate towers, or in the villages may even be a chair in a high tree; and in China the government did not permit the building of minarets. Indonesia is unique in using drums for the call to prayer.

It is generally agreed that a Muslim should give alms which amount to a tenth of the agricultural yield immediately after harvest, and a fortieth part of his wealth of goods, or of gold after a lapse of one year if it reaches the quantity of thirty.-eight grams—and about the same proportion of wealth in animals. The Quran specifies that such alms are to be given to the poor, the needy, the collectors of zakat, those whose hearts are to be appeased, slaves, travellers, debtors, and those who are on the path of God. While the source and the recipients of zakat are generally agreed upon, there are variations in the practice of distribution, largely because most Islamic countries do not have official collectors or an official organization for administering almsgiving. Turkey has a ministry of waqfs, as a part of the government; some of the Arab countries have governmental departments which are concerned with the administration of religious endowments; but in most countries almsgiving in goods or money is a voluntary gift either to individuals or to pious foundations. In Arabia they still give animals as alms since they have official collectors, but there is no almsgiving of goods or gold. In Indonesia people pay zakat on agricultural products to the religious men in the Islamic country reaches the proportion imposed by religion.

Pilgrimage remains a very important force making for unity in the Muslim world. Each year Muslims from all over the world, Muslims of every colour and race, gather in the Holy Land to fulfill their obligation to make the pilgrimage. After almost fourteen centuries the pilgrimage retains its importance for Islam in spite of the development of new means of communication, for there Muslims from all over the world, religious leaders and common folk, meet and exchange views. Such personal contact is necessary to keep the spirit of universal brotherhood alive. The minor details in practices associated with the pilgrimage are only variations which developed in the different schools of law and are not significant. In modern times the improvement in travel facilities has made it possible for large numbers of people to make the pilgrimage even from distant lands, an important factor in bringing the Muslims of the Far East into closer relations with their brothers of the Turkish and Arab areas of Islam. In recent years the major obstacles to the pilgrimage, other than the ever-present difficulty of being able to afford the expense, have been currency restrictions and the limitations imposed by the governments of the Soviet Union and China. Pilgrimage remains one of the vital pillars of Islam, wisely instituted by the Quran and Sunnah as a form of worship which brings Muslims closer to God and to each other.

ISLAMIC LAW

As we have seen, the practical consequences of the six fundamentals of Islam include both worship, as outlined under the five Pillars of Islam, and dealings, or the responsibilities of Muslims in their everyday life. These practical consequences, the particular requirements of religion, have been codified in the four schools of law which exist amicably side by side in the Muslim world. The Maliki school which was founded during the second century after Muhammad shows preference for the Traditions and practices of Medina where the Prophet lived for thirteen years; it is found today chiefly in North Africa, some parts of Egypt, and in the Sudan. Also in the second century there lived in Baghdad a silk merchant named Abu Hanifah, a rationalist who based his teachings concerning the consequences of religion on the Quran and the Traditions. He wrote no book himself, but his disciples spread his liberal teachings and founded the Hanaifi school of jurisprudence which is found in Turkey, Afghanistan, Central Asia, Pakistan, India, and Egypt. Another of Abu Hanifah's disciples, Muhammad Ibn Idris al-Shafii, founded the Shafii school in the third century; he was a great systematic jurist who took an Intermediate position between extreme legalism and traditionalism. The school of Shafii interpretation is predominant in South Arabia, South India, Thailand, Malaya, Indonesia, and the Philippines. The fourth school of law was also founded in the third century after the Prophet by Ahmad Hanbal, a resident in Baghdad; he stressed the Traditions and distrusted the use of reason. The Hanbalis arc found in Central Arabia, Syria, and some parts of Africa.

These four schools of law—covering the four divisions of rites, contracts, matrimonial law, the penal codes—were worked out so completely by their founders over a thousand years ago that those who came after them found fully adequate systems of law which met all the requirements of their times. A Muslim was free to choose any one of the four systems for his personal guidance, but the prevailing practice was to choose the school of law which was followed in the place of a man's birth. Thus a man born in Indonesia is usually a follower of Shafii law, while a man born in Turkey will be a Hanafite.

The influence of birth was so great that many Muslims later became convinced that one did not need to look back to the original sources of the Quran and the Sunnah, for they believed wrongly that no one in these Later days has a capacity for reasoning equal to that of the founders of the schools of law. They became imitators of their predecessors on the basis of a belief that every period since the time of the Prophet has been inferior to the earlier days. While it might be true that those who lived in the time of the Prophet could understand religion better than the people of today who must study Islam by means of documents only, we cannot ignore the considerable change in the social situation and world conditions during the past fourteen centuries. The insistence on imitating the predecessors reflects a loss of self-confidence which was at one time widespread in Islamic communities. The texts of the Quran are still and will always be valid, but we should understand them in the light of present knowledge. One of the great tasks facing religious scholars in our time is the re-examination of the jurisprudence of Islam in the light of reason and modern knowledge. Since Islam does not make a distinction between the secular and the religious, and since a large part of the Muslim world has but recently attained political independence and is now playing a significant role in world affairs, this re-examination of Islamic law is all the more urgently needed.

The relation between Islamic law and the law of the government is a pressing issue in modern times. In Turkey the national law is avowedly secular and even the waqf funds are administered by secular authorities. In Egypt, Pakistan, and India the problem of the relation of Islamic and national law is the subject of frequent public discussion, and in Indonesia several political parties have grown up around this issue. Another problem is the relation between Islamic law and the customary law of a country, as has been noted in China and Indonesia in particular. This will inevitably continue to be a problem as Islam spreads throughout the rest of the world.

SECTS IN ISLAM

From the beginning, the basic sources of Islam have been the Quran and the Sunnah. Muslims have always looked to the Quran as their guide and have prayed and fasted and made pilgrimages as the Prophet did. For the details governing their lives, Muslims have relied upon their reason in applying the principles of the Quran and the Sunnah, and this has been the cause of the different schools of law, the various tendencies, and the sects which are found in Islam.

Followers of the Hanafi school of law tend toward rationalism, such as is found among the Mutazilities; the Shafii school follows the moderate theology of the Asharites; the Malikites are predestinationist; and the Hanbalites tend to be literal in their interpretation of theology. These are theological tendencies, but not sectarian differences.

The two major sects in Islam are the Sunnis and the Shias, whose distinctive characteristics have been discussed at length in earlier chapters in this book. Among the Shias the three leading sects are the Ithna Ashariya, the Sabiya, and the Zaidis. The Ithna Ashariya is the major group among the Shias, found primarily in Iraq and Iran; they accept the twelve Imams. The Sabiya, sometimes called the Seveners because they broke away over the claim that Isma'il was the seventh Imam, are also known as the Ismailis. They have divided into several sects, of which the best known is the group which follows the Agha Khan, found in Pakistan, India, Iran, Syria, and East Africa. The Zaidis, now found in Yemen, are a small Shia sect which has drawn closer to the Sunnis over the years.

The Kharijites, who rebelled against Ali, were originally Shia and have been somewhat influenced by Sunni thought. They are found in Oman and Muscat, and in North Africa where they are known as Ibadis.

More than ninety per cent of the Muslims of the world are Sunnis, followers of the Sunnah. The only sects of any importance among the Sunnis are the Wahhabis, the reformist sect of Arabia, and the Qadiani sect of Pakistan which is generally looked upon as somewhat heretical—although its Lahori branch is not always so regarded. The various tendencies among the Sunnis have often led to differences in point of view, but not to the creation of new sects. The most widely accepted theological position is that of the Asharites. The rationalism of the Mu'tazilites at one time almost led to the formation of a recognizable sect, but today the rationalist point of view is only one of several tendencies among the Sunnis. Differences between the firmly orthodox and the modern reformist have not created a sectarian division.

The numerous Sufi orders cannot be classed as separate sects because they are made up of people who consider themselves to be Sunnis or Shias as well as Sufis. Sufi orders have been banned by the government of Turkey, but Sufism continues there as a powerful factor in the Islamic life of the country; both intellectuals and common people study the writings of their famous Sufis and continue their personal Sufi disciplines. The Sufi orders continue to be an important factor in Africa, though their influence in Egypt is declining. There is still, however, a strong interest in Sufi writings among the intellectuals in Egypt. The Shias have pronounced Sufi tendencies which have influenced the devotional life in Iran and Iraq as well as Pakistan and India. The Sufism of Pakistan and India has sometimes been influenced by the mysticism of Hinduism, leading on occasion to pantheistic tendencies there. In Indonesia, as we have seen, Sufism plays a major role in the devotional life of the Muslims, both as organized orders among the common people and as a study and discipline among the intellectuals. Only in China do we find that Sufism has not been an important factor in the Muslim community.

Sufism has been especially susceptible to the influences of Greek, Iranian, and Indian thought which have sometimes led it to excesses and fanaticism which were contrary to the real spirit of Islam. Some Sufis even denounced the Pillars of Islam and taught that union with God is the aim of Islam, a pantheistic doctrine which is heretical. Other Sufis have followed the teachings of Ghazali, combining the rituals of Islam with deep religious feeling. Such Sufis have made, and are making today, a valuable contribution to the religious life of the Muslim world.

Characteristic of Islamic Practices

Muslims are exhorted to follow the straight path of Islam in every detail of their daily lives, guided by the Quran, by the example of the life of the Prophet, and by the Hadith. The life of a Muslim should illustrate the teachings and example of the Prophet.

When a Muslim baby is born, it is recommended that some one should whisper the call to prayer in his ear, "God is Most Great.. there is no God other than Allah.. Muhammad is the Messenger of God... Welcome prayer.. Welcome good fortune... God is Most Great When the baby is one week old it is suggested that the parents sacrifice a sheep—one sheep for a girl and two for a boy—and distribute the meat among the poor. A baby should be given a good name on the seventh day. It is also recommended that boys should be circumcised, and girls also, for the sake of cleanliness. The parents are urged to teach the children how to pray so that by the age of nine they should know everything about the prayers, including the proper ablutions to be done before prayers.

The ablutions before prayer simply require the washing of the hands up to the wrist, washing the face and the head—a part of it is sufficient—and washing the feet up to the ankle. After any pollution or sexual intercourse, a Muslim must take an obligatory bath; in case there is no water, a symbolic action is necessary.

Muslims are required to pray five times a day, with two prostrations in the early morning before sunrise, four a little before midday, four in the afternoon when the shadow of a thing is as tall as the thing itself, three after sunset, and four about one hour later. Each prayer takes not more than five minutes, though it may be lengthened with optional prayers. It is recommended that the prayers be performed collectively, or at least with one companion. In case a person is travelling, two prayers can be performed together and shortened by half. Shias customarily carry a small tablet made of the clay from Karbala which they place on the ground and touch with their forehead as they prostrate themselves in prayer.

All Muslims should attend the Friday midday prayer in the mosque and listen attentively to the address given by an Imam. Women may also go to the mosque, but they must pray behind the men. In practice, women either gather at a separate place in the mosque or do not attend the collective prayers at all.

At the two major festivals, the Id al-Fitr at the end of the Ramadan fast and the Id-ul-Adha—or Id-ul-Qurban—at the end of the pilgrimage, Muslims are urged to perform additional congregational prayers, preferably in the open air, and to listen to the special address by the Imam. Before the prayers at the end of Ramadan they are urged to contribute food to the needy so no one may be hungry that day, and after the pilgrimage prayers they are exhorted to sacrifice a sheep, a cow, or a camel and distribute the meat to the needy. There is no restriction on association between men and women in the Islamic community, the only reservation in the instructions being that there must be no occasion for misconduct. Thus, a woman must not meet a man alone, nor should a woman travel alone. She must protect her body decently but her face need not be covered. The practice of purdah, of veiling the face in public, which is followed in many Islamic countries, is only an exaggeration of the instructions enjoining modesty which has been deeprooted in Islamic communities by long centuries of ignorance.

When a young man wishes to marry he is allowed to see his prospective wife in order to assure the success of the marriage. The girl is protected by her parents, but they must ask her consent before giving her in marriage. If she is a widow, the consent must be explicit, and if she is a virgin tacit consent by silence is suffiecent. The bridegroom must pay a dowry to the bride, which may be only a token. Two male witnesses are necessary for the marriage contract. A celebration after the marriage is recommended, but it should not be extravagant.

The husband must provide maintenance for the wife and children. Divorce is permitted only as a last resort. In case differences arise between a husband and his wife, relatives of both parties should serve as a committee of arbitration. Since divorce is a serious event "by which the throne of God is shaken," in the words of the Prophet, it must be delayed by two stages before it becomes final, and during that time the wife must receive maintenance. A wife can also ask for a divorce on the grounds of cruel treatment, sexual defect, contagious disease, and like conditions which make the marriage intolerable.

Polygamy is neither forbidden nor required. It may be called a necessary evil. If a man needs a son and his wife does not give birth to a male, for example, he might take a second wife. The question is still a subject of controversy among Muslim jurists, but there is general agreement that more than one wife is not permitted for the purpose of satisfying one's lust. Muta, a temporary marriage which may be terminated after even one day upon payment of a gift, is permitted among the Shias. It was originally permitted by the Prophet, but later the permission was abrogated, according to the Sunnis. The Shia still maintain that there was no abrogation, but even those who claim that the permission continues are against the prevalent practice, which does not differ much from prostitution. Adultery is forbidden; if the evidence is sufficient, the prescribed penalty is flogging with eighty lashes or stoning to death if the offender is married.

In case of death a man inherits from his wife or a wife inherits from her husband. The laws of inheritance are given in considerable detail but they follow the general principle that a man inherits twice as much as a woman. This is because the man must bear the responsibility for maintenance of his wife and must provide dowry for the marriage, while a woman who marries will receive both dowry and maintenance.

A dead person must be bathed and given ablution before burial and the community must pray for him. The prayer for a dead person is an obligation of the whole community. If it is neglected, the whole community is sinful, but if one person performs the prayer, the community is considered to have performed its duty. It is recommended that neighbours of the bereaved family should prepare food to be offered to the mourners and their visitors. It is also recommended that relatives should visit the grave from time to time to put flowers on it and to pray for the departed soul. Women, however, are urged not to go to the graveyard to pray for the deceased, since they are too sensitive.

Concerning food, Muslims are permitted to eat anything that is not explicitly forbidden. It is related that the Prophet said, "What God permits in His Book is permitted, and what He forbids is forbidden, and what is not mentioned is in favour, therefore take His favour. God does not forget." According to the Quran, Muslims are forbidden to eat a corpse, blood, pork, a pagan sacrifice, suffocated animals, animals killed other than by slaughtering, animals which died from a fall, animals killed by other animals, remnants of food eaten by a beast, food offered as a sacrifice to idols. All fish which live in the sea may be eaten, according to the ninety-sixth verse of the fifth Surah. All animals which live in the water and on land, such as frogs, crocodiles, turtles, and the like, are forbidden as food. Of land animals, it is permitted to eat camels, cows, sheep, horses, and the like. It is forbidden to eat donkeys; beasts with claws such as lions, tigers, wolves, and bears; birds with talons, such as hawks and falcons; animals which the Prophet ordered killed, such as snakes, mice, crows; creatures which the Prophet forbade killing, such as ants and bees; animals judged to be dirty, and animals which live on dirt. In deciding what food can be eaten and what is forbidden Muslim jurisprudence accepts as guides the Quran, the Hadith, what the Prophet ordered to be killed and what he forbade killing, and the foods which are abhorrent to human feeling.

The verses of the Quran make it clear that all kinds of drinks are permitted except wine. Wine is forbidden because it is intoxicating. On this point the Holy Quran is so clear that no other interpretation is possible. Thus, however small the quantity may be, the drinking of wine is absolutely forbidden. By wine is meant the fermented juice of grapes. As to other fermented drinks, there is a difference of opinion among Muslim jurists. Some maintain that juices extracted from fruits other than grapes, such as apples or dates, are permitted. They base their opinion on some Traditions which say that Muhammad sometimes fermented dates for one or two days.

A Muslim is forbidden to steal, and if he steals a certain amount deliberately the punishment prescribed is the cutting off of the hands. A Muslim must not gamble nor participate in lotteries. He must not deceive concerning measures or weights; he must not break a promise or go back on his word. He is forbidden to pay or receive interest when borrowing or lending money, but a debtor may present a token of gratitude to the creditor.

These requirements and prohibitions, mentioned here only in general outline, are representative of the rules found in the Quran and Traditions which govern the lives of all Muslims.

Islamic Society

To understand the role of Islam in society one must first realize that Islam is a universal religion in which all Muslims are brothers, regardless of differences in homeland, race, colour, or rank. This brotherhood does not divide the world into Muslims and non-Muslims, for Muslims must be friendly toward non-Muslims so long as they are friendly, so long as they do not attack Islam. Islam has retained its unity and universal characteristics in the midst of such diverse cultures as those of Arabia, Greece, Rome, and Iran in ancient times, and later in the cultures of Africa, Egypt, Turkey, Central Asia, India, China, and Southeast Asia. Once more the universalism of Islam is being shown as it comes into contact with the new culture of the W/est.

In this interplay between Islam and the various cultures of the world it should be remembered that Islam has no master organization which requires conformity or organizes missionary programmes. The interplay is a spontaneous movement on the part of individual Muslims who seek to follow the straight path of Islam. These Muslims recognize no distinction between the religious and the secular; they try to follow in their social life the rules revealed to them in the Quran and the Sunnah and interpreted in Islamic law. For Islam, the present world is but a transitory existence to be followed by the Eternal World which is better by far, "And verily the latter portion will be better for thee than the former" (Surah XCIII, 4). This does not mean that we must neglect this world; on the contrary, Islam warns us against neglecting it, for the Quran says, "But seek the abode of the Hereafter in that which Allah has given thee and neglect not thy portion of the world, and be thou kind even as Allah has been kind to thee, and seek not corruption in the earth; lo! Allah loves not corrupters" (Surah XXVIII, 77). Islam recognizes the importance of life in the community in this world, but it warns the Muslim against considering this world as the end of existence. Moral and religious values must be seen to be higher than material values.

The importance of social justice is constantly emphasized in Islam through the obligation of zakat and the distribution of gifts at the times of the great festivals. In the older Islamic countries this has been the origin of waqfs for all kinds of service to the community. The teachings concerning zakat stress the principle that the ownership of wealth is a privilege, not a right, and one which imposes obligations to the community. In the Traditions the Prophet exhorts us to give our servants the same food we eat and the same clothes we wear.

In Islam the merit of a person depends upon his deeds, not upon his words, nor his ancestors, nor his rank in the community. The Quran says, "there is nothing for the person but what he has done" (Surah LIII, 39) and again, "The highest among you is the most pious" (Surah XLIX, 13). The only recognized difference in rank in Islam is that which is merited by religious devotion and insight. Such recognition is accorded on the basis of deeds, not on the basis of office. Islam has no ordained clergy, no religious hierarchy with authority over their fellow Muslims. The ulama, the Shaikh, Mullah, Imam, Ahund, Mufti, Mujtahid, Hatib—all are only men like the others in the Muslim community, men who perform special services and are respected and elevated only on the basis of the Quranic principle that the highest is the most pious.

Slavery was customary at the time that Islam was revealed, but Islam prepared the grounds for its elimination. It encourages the emancipation of slaves by giving them the possibility of purchasing their freedom, it urges that part of zakat be given to slaves to help them free themselves, and it offers the possibility of atonement for certain sins, such as having sexual intercourse during fasting days, by releasing slaves.

Women are given equality with men, in principle, for the Quran says, "Whoever, male or female, who is a believer, performs good actions, they will enter into Paradise" (Surah IV, 124), and again, "Men have reward for what they do, and women have reward for what they do" (Surah IV, 32). But we cannot deny that in general men are superior to women and consequently men have authority over women. The Quran says, "Men have authority over women" (Surah IV, 14).

With the rise of nationalism in the modern world, the relation of nationalism to Islam has become a problem which is frequently discussed. Many people think that since Islam is universal it must be against nationalism, but this is not the case. Universalism can begin with national loyalty, for nationalism is simply the result of the organization of a group of people in one political body, regardless of their differences in religion. Islam does not prohibit such political organizations so long as they do not jeopardize the essentials of Islamic teachings. Nationalism can unite or divide, and when it is guided by the universal principles of Islam it can lead men to unity rather than to divisions. In this regard it should be noted that the demand for the Caliphate, in the political sense, has greatly lessened in modern times. Pan-Islamism in our day is not a movement for one super-government over all Muslims, but for cooperation between Islamic nations.

Jihad, holy war, has sometimes been misunderstood as meaning that Muslims must declare war on non-Muslims until they accept Islam. This mistake arises from a misreading of the Quran without knowing the context of the verses and the circumstances in which they were revealed.

The verses which call for war against unbelievers were revealed when pagans were still putting obstacles in the way of the activities of Muhammad even after opportunities for reconciliation had been given. War in Islam is only legitimate when it is declared in defense of religion, property, and prestige. The Quran says, 'Fight in the way of God those who wage war on you, and do not commit aggression. God does not like aggressors" (Surah II, 190).

Islam does not approve of hostility toward other religions. Rather, it proclaims freedom of religion and forbids coercion in religion. During his lifetime, Muhammad himself was very kind toward his neighbours and friends of other beliefs, Jews as well as Christians. He even married a Jewish woman, Safijah, and a Christian slave, Marie, who was given him by the ruler of Egypt. When the Emperor of Abyssinia died, Muhammad prayed for him in recognition of his help given to the Muslims who took refuge there in the early days of Islam.

Islamic society has been greatly influenced, and the spread of Islam has been aided, by the educational opportunities offered through the mosques and religious leaders. The Prophet encouraged education by appointing many of his Companions as teachers in Arabia when Islam spread throughout the country. It was ruled that a poor man could marry a woman with a dowry of teaching her a chapter of the Quran. As Islam spread to other lands, centres of study grew up at Baghdad, Kufa, and many other cities of the Muslim world.

The system of education was simple, without organized programme or ceremony. Any pupil could approach a teacher and stay with him as long as he' continued to learn; then he might go on to other teachers, or receive a license to be a teacher himself. In the family the parents educated their children. The teachers did not form a special class but were at the same time landowners, merchants, or government officials. This system continues today in most Muslim countries.

In addition, there have been in most countries the madrassas associated with the mosques, and special schools of higher learning. The oldest Islamic university is the Al Azhar in Cairo, founded in the fourth century (tenth century AD). Other centres for higher Islamic studies today are found at Fez in Morocco, at Zaitouna University in Tunisia, at Medina, at Istanbul and Ankara in Turkey, at Baghdad and Karbala in Iraq, at Tehran in Iran, at Lahore in Pakistan, at Lucknow and at Alighar and Usmania Universities in India, and at Jogjakarta in Indonesia. In some of these centres the Islamic studies are associated with government-supported universities; there are also government universities in other countries which offer special courses in Islam, as is the case on Taiwan. Instruction in Islam is given in local languages at the lower levels, but for higher studies a good knowledge of Arabic is necessary and mastery of Persian and Turkish is required for any extensive research.

Since art and music flourish in times of peace and prospenty, there was little time for them in the early days of the Prophet. Muhammad, however, approved of the music known in his day. He forbade the art which was prevalent in his time, consisting chiefly of human figures, since it was symbolic of idols and would have spread paganism. Because of that, the literal-minded jurists deduced that Islam opposed art and music, which is not correct. The better deduction would have been that we must be careful of the consequences of any kind of art. Art for art's sake is unknown in Islam. As long as art is useful as a means of heightening religion and morality, it is permitted; but if it leads to immorality, it is forbidden.

LATEST DEVELOPMENTS IN ISLAM

When the Mu'tazilite, or rational, movement was suppressed and the political organization of the Muslim world disintegrated, the Muslim people lost their vitality. They neglected the study of the Quran and the Traditions which are the original sources of Islam and instead adopted the teachings of the scholars. They thought that ijtihad was forbidden and that they must only imitate the four schools of law. Instead of making use of reason, they accepted the four schools of law as complete and unchanging and turned to mysticism and belief in the supernatural powers of saints, dead and alive. That gave rise to the worship of the graves of saints which is found today in all Islamic countries from North Africa to Indonesia.

The Wahhabi movement in Arabia was a reaction against the worship of saints, but it made use of force rather than arguments, and failed to establish a general reform. After the French occupied Egypt many scholars studied in Europe and a renaissance was started which culminated in the work of the great scholar, Muhammad Abduh, who brought new ideas to the people of Egypt. At about the same time the Muslims of India, led by such men as Sir Sayyid Ahmad Khan, who founded Alighar University, became conscious of their cultural importance and their national existence. Within the past half-century the greater ease of communication and travel has brought the peoples of the Muslim world into closer contact with each other and with the cultures of the rest of the world and made them aware of the need for a new evaluation of the ideas of the jurists and thinkers of the middle ages. This is the period in which much of the Muslim world has attained political independence and the people have been preoccupied with political and international problems.

Today the Muslims of Morocco, Tunisia, Egypt, the Levant, Turkey, Iraq, Iran, Pakistan, India, and Indonesia are vitally concerned with problems associated with the establishment of their new, independent governments. At the same time, the Muslims of Algeria and much of Africa, of the Soviet Union and of China, are struggling with political controls which are not encouraging to Islam and are often inimical. These political problems have been faced at the time when the impact of Western culture in the Muslim world has been most pronounced. More than anything else, Islam today needs a period of peace in order that favorable conditions may develop for the growth of Islamic thought.

Since the time of Ibn Khaldun, more than five centuries ago, no great thinker has arisen in the Muslim world. Now more than ever there is a need for a time of peace and intellectual freedom in which devout thinkers can interpret the Quran in the light of the progress of human knowledge. The rituals will remain as they are, the fundamentals will remain unchanged, but the understanding of Islam will be illuminated anew for our time.

At the present time, there are four major tendencies in the Islamic world—orthodoxy, reform, Sufism, and Shia. The increase in commumcation and in education is bringing to the followers of each tendency a better understanding of the others. Significant progress is being made in Cairo in encouraging better understanding and reconciliation between Shia and Sunni. Orthodoxy is becoming less reactionary and the reformers less intolerant. The Sufi orders are declining in influence at the same time that the devotional and mystical teachings of the Sufi masters are being studied more sympathetically by intellectuals. In Turkey, Egypt, and Indonesia in particular there are many evidences of a new vitality and interest in Islamic thought. Many books are being published, many students are engaged in Islamic studies, new mosques are being built.

Islam spread originally along the trade routes through North Africa, Iran, Central Asia, Indonesia, and China. As Muslim traders settled along those routes they married and established families which often became the nucleus for a new Muslim community. In spite of the diversities of cultures, they maintained the unity of Islam through the centuries. Today, with trade routes easily followed around the world, it is inevitable that the same process will be repeated and Islam will spread to new regions where it has not been known.

In this discussion of the unity and variety of Islam we have seen that divergences from the essential unity of Islam have occurred only when there is ignorance among the common people—a low level of education. It is the task of the present generation to provide training in the essentials of Islam, to know Islam deeply, for out of that knowledge of the straight path of Islam will come the unity of belief and practice which has been revealed to mankind in the Quran and the Sunnah.

Origins

Islam means submission to Allah (God). Islam was revealed to the Prophet Muhammad who lived from 570 CE to 632 CE in Mecca in modern-day Saudi Arabia. Muhammad was called to prophethood when God dictated the Quran to him through the archangel Gabriel. Although he gained a small following in his tribe, Muhammad was initially persecuted for his beliefs. In 622 CE he fled to Yathrib, now called Medina, where the first Muslim political community was formed. Enlisting the help of nomadic Arab clans, Muhammad returned to Mecca, stripping the city of all signs of pagan belief. He was generous to those he defeated, however, and many converted to Islam. Two years later, in front of the Kaaba in Mecca, he declared Islam the religion of the people, saying he had fulfilled his mission and that he left behind him the Book of Allah and a set of clear commandments.

History and Spread

By the time of Muhammad's death, many people of the Arabian Peninsula had begun to follow Islam. A series of caliphs and dynasties led the Muslim community after Muhammad's death, creating an Islamic empire that expanded as far as modern-day Pakistan in the east, Spain in the north, and North Africa to the south. This was a period of great intellectual, cultural and spiritual vitality. In Spain, Islamic civilisation lasted until 1492 when the Christian monarchs regained power. After the collapse of the Empire, Islam remained the dominant religion in most Middle Eastern countries and significant pockets throughout North Africa and Asia.

In Australia

The history of Islam in Australia pre-dates European settlement. From 1650, Muslim fisherman from South East Asia communicated and traded with Aborigines from Australia's north. Some inter-marriage occurred. In the 1860s, some 3000 camel drivers-with camels-came from Afghanistan and the Indian sub-continent. This group contributed to the exploration of the Australian outback, working on both the railway line between Port Augusta and Alice Springs, and the Overland Telegraph Line from Adelaide to Darwin, which connected Australia to London via India. Since the late 1960s there have been a number of significant Muslim migrations into Australia, most notably from Turkey and Lebanon. In the 1990s, refugees and migrants from the Horn of Africa, Afghanistan, Iran, Iraq, Bosnia-Herzegovina, Albania, Indonesia and Malaysia have all made their home in Australia.

Some Islamic societies in Australia are affiliated with AFIC (The Australian Federation of Islamic Councils), which does not control the individual societies but gives a public voice and face to Islam, both in state and federal politics and matters of community representation. Between 1991 and 1996, the Muslim community grew by 36 per cent (approx. 53 000). In 1996, there were over 280,000 Muslims in Australia, belonging to over 70 ethnic groups (ABS).

Key Movements

Islam is divided into two main sects, the Sunni and the Shia. This division arose over the order of caliph succession in the first century of the Islamic calendar. Shiites believe that the true authority and leadership of Muslims after Muhammad's son-in-law, Ali, continued through a line of imams (religious teachers). Sunnis uphold the supremacy of the caliphs, the line of rulers elected by the people and mandated to guard the prophetic legacy in the administration of community affairs. This gave rise to the development of Sharia law.

Shiites constitute less than 10 per cent of world's Muslims, and possess many internal divisions. The largest contemporary Shia group are the Ithnaasharis, or Travellers. Shiites are a majority in Iran. Sunni Muslims constitute 90% of the world's Muslims and are considered the orthodox face of Islam. There are various mystic strands of Islam, such as Sufism and the Ibadites of Oman, East Africa and Algeria. These are not, strictly speaking, sectarian divisions.

Organisational Structure

Muslims do not require an intermediary between themselves and God. Imams-religious teachers and leaders of prayer in the mosques-do, however, play a significant role. They are often formally educated in matters of religion and jurisprudence, and systems exist for settling questions of law and religious observance. The al-Azahr, a Islamic university in Cairo, is conventionally regarded as the highest authority in Sunni Islam. The Shia developed a hierarchy in line with their beliefs in the succession of rule; in Iran, this finds expression in the system of ayatollahs (senior interpreters and arbiters of religious law).

Mosques are not denominational and are run on a number of models depending on the mosque's governing constitution. Some are ethnically-based.

Key Beliefs

- Muslims hold six articles of belief
- There is only one God without limit, called Allah.
- Muhammad received the Quran as a copy of the eternal Quran which is inscribed in heaven.
- God created heavenly beings called angels to serve God and they are opposed by evil spirits.
- God sent his prophets to the earth at their appointed times, and the Prophet Muhammad was the last and greatest messenger of God.
- There will be a last day of world history called the Day of Judgement. Good and evil will be weighed in the balance. The wicked will be punished and the just will enjoy eternal life in Paradise.
- Everything in the universe has a predetermined course. Nothing happens without the will or knowledge of God.

The sunna is a collection of traditions, moral sayings and anecdotes (hadiths) of Muhammad. It embodies all the elaborations of Quranic teaching.

The practice of religious faith is also built on the five pillars of Islam:

- Shahadah (declaration of faith): "I bear witness that there is no god, but God; I bear witness that Muhammad is the prophet of God." By reciting this, one enters Islamic faith.
- Salaah (prayer): Muslims are required to pray five times a day, washing themselves before prayer and facing in the direction of Mecca while praying.
- Zakat (charity): Muslims are required to give away a percentage of their earnings to those less fortunate, regardless of their religion.
- Saum (fasting): Muslims fast for one lunar month each year, a period called Ramadan. During this time, Muslims reflect on their behaviour and strive to purify their thoughts.
- Hajj (pilgrimage): If it is financially possible, Muslims are required to travel to Mecca once in their lifetime.

- Ijma means 'the agreement of Islam.' It is an important mechanism for resolving theological conflicts because it is embodies a sense of past community in present action.
- Sharia is the sacred law of Islam, based on the divine revelations contained in the Quran and sunna.
- Dietary requirements. Animals have souls and so need to be slaughtered in a special way. This is the meaning of halal (permitted).

Key Festivals

- Ramadan: Celebrates the gift of the Quran. During the month of Ramadan, Muslims must fast between sunrise and sunset.
- Eid-al-Fitr: The festival for the first day after Ramadan.
- Dhu Al-Hijja: The month of pilgrimage during which all Muslims, at least once in their life, should try to make the pilgrimage to Mecca.
- Eid-al-adha: The Festival of Sacrifice which occurs 70 days after Eid-al-Fitr. It commemorates Abraham's willingness to sacrifice his son for God. Every family who can afford it must slaughter an animal and distribute the meat among relatives, neighbours and the poor.
- The first day of Muharram: The Islamic New Year begins on the day Muhammad left Mecca to travel to Medina.
- The twelfth day of Rabi I: Celebrates the birth of the prophet.
- Mirajun Nabi: Commemorates the prophet's journey from Mecca to the heavens.

6

Islamic Faith

The Religion of Peace

Islam is a religion of peace. This is evident even from the name "Islam" itself. ("Islam" is an Arabic word.) The word "Islam" and the Arabic word for peace, "salam" both come from the same root, "salima". Muslims are taught to greet each other by saying "salamun alaykum--peace be upon you." The daily prayers also end with the same sentence. In Islam, one of the names by which God is known is "Salam" which means peace.

However, one must realize that peace can never be achieved in vacuum. It is intertwined with justice. One can have peace only on basis of justice. "Justice" means putting everything in its rightful place. If one starts putting things in the wrong places, then he disrupts the social harmony and disturbs peace. Islam seeks to promote peace on two levels:

Peace within One's Self: A person can achieve inner peace by creating harmony and balance between his main emotions (desire and anger) and his spiritual self. In other words, between his emotions and his conscience.

Human's spiritual power or conscience is not a static phenomenon: it has the ability of growth as well as decadence. God swears by the soul of human being and says, "He inspired to it to understand what is good and what is evil. Prosperous in the person who purifies it, and failed is he who seduces it." (Quran; chp. 91, verse 10).

Peace With Others: Islam very strongly emphasizes on the rights which people have over each other. It seeks to perserve peace in society by training and urging its followers to fulfill the rights of each other. In Islam, salvation is not possible by just fulfilling the rights of God; one has to fulfill the rights of other human beings also.

Unfortnately, because of the Middle Eastern events of the last three decades, Islam has been branded by the media as a religion of violence. In recent years, the word "Islamic" has become one of the adjectives of "terrorism." In this backdrop, firstly, one must realize that the events in the Middle East can be fairly and fully understood only in the light of the post-WWI history of that region, in particular the promises given by the British to the Arabs.

Secondly, no fair-minded person would allow himself to blame the religion of Islam for the wrong-doings of those who call themselves as Muslims. It is just like saying that the Catholic Church promotes violence and terrorism because of the Irish Republican Army's activites!

1. Unity of God

The Islamic creed is that THERE IS NO GOD SAVE ALLAH AND THAT MUHAMMAD IS HIS PROPHET. (LA ILAAHA ILLA-ALLAH MUHAMMADUR-RASOOLILLAH).

Muslims believe that Allah is ONE. He was neither begotten nor does He beget. He has no Partner. He is the Beginning and He is the End. He is Omniscient and Omnipresent.

The Quran says that He is closer to man than his jugular vein yet He cannot be encompassed by human intellect.

See the following verses of the Quran:

II:115	II:163	II:255	VI:101	VII:7	XXIII:91-92
XXXVII:4-5		XXXVIII:65-68			
CXII:1-4					

Imam Ali says in a supplication:

"Oh God, verily I ask Thee by Thy Name, in the name of Allah, the All-merciful, the All-compassionate, O the Possessor of Majesty and Splendour, the Living, the Self-subsistent, the Eternal, there is no God other than Thou, Oh He of Whom no one knows what He is, or how He is, or Where He is, or in respect of what He is, And yet, we know that He is."

2. Justice of God

Allah is Just. In XCV:8, the Quran says "Is not Allah the most conclusive of all judges?"

Again in XXI:47 "And we have provided a Just balance for the Day of Judgement. No soul shall be dealt with unjustly in any way. (Any good deed or evil deed) though it be as small as a grain of the mustard seed, will be brought forth by Us (in testimony). We suffice as the best of reckoners."

The Sunni School of thought subscribes to the view that nothing is good or evil per se. What God commanded us to do became good by virtue of His command. What he forbade became evil. The Shias believe that there is intrinsic good or evil in things. God commanded us to do the good things and forbade the evil. God acts according to a purpose or design. Human reason cannot comprehend this design or purpose in its entirety though man must always strive to understand as much as he can.

Compulsion or Freedom?

The various schools of thought are divided.

i. Mutazzilas believe that man is totally free and God exercises no power over his action. Those who subscribe to this view are also known as Qadariyyas.

ii. Mujabbira school of thought believe that man has no freedom and is only a tool in the hands of God.

iii. The Asharia school of thought to which most Sunnis subscribe believe that though man has no free will, he will earn the reward of his good deeds. The Sunni scholar Al-Ghazzalli sums up this doctrine as follows: "No act of any individual, even though it be done purely for his benefit, is independent of the will of Allah for its existence. There does not occur in either the physical or the extra-terrestrial world the twinkle of an eye, the hint of a thought, or the most sudden glance except by the Decree of Allah, of His Power, Desire, and Will. This includes evil and good, benefit and harm, success and failures, sin and righteousness, obedience and disobedience, polytheism and true belief."

iv. The Shias believe that there is neither total compulsion nor total freedom. The true position is the one in-between. They maintain that Allah has fore-knowledge of human action but does not compel man to any particular course of action.

See Quran:

II:284	IV:79	VI:17	IX:51	X:107	XI:6
XI:56	XXVII:62	XXX:60	XXXIX:52-54		XLII:30

3. Prophethood

God created mankind to serve Him (LI:56). He endowed man with faculties and freedom of action and out of His Grace (LUTF) and Justice sent Prophets to instruct and guide mankind. No nation or community was left without such guidance. (X:47 and XVI:36).

Some of these prophets were sent with Divine Revelation, scripture and miracles. The first Prophet was Adam and the last was Muhammad, the Seal of Prophets (XXX:40).

While Quran mentions only twenty-five most prominent of the prophets it also states that there were many more whose names have not been revealed in the Quran. (XL:78). Muslims believe that there have been 124,000 prophets. Amongst those specifically mentioned are Adam, Enoch, Noah, Abraham, Ishmael, Issac, Lot, Jacob, Joseph, Job, Moses, Aaron, Ezekiel, David, Solomon, Jonah, Zachariah, John the Baptist, Jesus and Muhammad. Five of these prophets brought new codes of law. These were Noah, Abraham, Moses, Jesus and Muhammad. These are called the "ulu l-azm" prophets meaning those of great constancy.

Quran mentions five divine books.

a. The Book of Abraham, sometimes referred as the Booklet (LXXXVII:19).

b. The Psalms given to David (IV:63 and XVII:55).

c. The Torah granted to Moses (II:87, III:3 & 4, VI:91 & 154).

d. The Evangel or the Gospel revealed to Jesus (V:46).

e. The Quran revealed to Muhammad.

A Muslim must believe in all the Holy Books. (II:4 & 285). He must also believe in all the prophets. (IV:152).

The Shiahs also believe that all the prophets were infallible and sinless. Not all the Sunnis subscribe to this belief.

4. Resurrection

The world will come to an end on the Day of the Rising (Qiyamah), the day of final human accountability. All men will be resurrected and presented before God Who will decide their fate according to their deeds. The good will be rewarded with paradise (jannah) and the evil will be punished with hell (jahannam). (XXII:6-9 & 1-2; III:185; VI:62). The dominant factor in the administration of His Justice by Allah will be His Mercy (VI:12).

5. Imaamah

Only the Shiahs believe in the institution of Imaamah. Literally "imaam" means a leader. In Shiah belief an Imaam is the person appointed by God and introduced by the Prophet and then by each preceding Imaam by explicit designation (nass) to lead the Muslim community, interpret and protect the religion and the law (shariah), and guide the community in all affairs. An Imaam is first and foremost the Representative of God and the successor of the Prophet. He must be sinless and possess divine knowledge of both the exoteric and the esoteric meaning of the verses of the Quran. There are many Shiah sects e.g. the Zaidis, the Ismailis etc. The principal sect is the Travellers (Ithnasharis).

NOTE: In these Notes, unless specifically stated otherwise, references to the Shiahs and Shiah beliefs, should be construed as references to the Shiah Ithnasheriyya school of thought. The Travellers believe that the Prophet was succeeded by twelve Imaams. These are:

---

1. Ali ibne Abu Talib — Died 40 A.H./659 A.D

He was the Prophet`s son-in-law, having married his daughter Fatimah.

2. Hassan ibne Ali — Died 50 A.H./669 A.D.
3. Hussain ibne Ali — Died 61 A.H./680 A.D.
4. Ali ibne Hussain — Died 95 A.H./712 A.D.

5. Muhammad ibne Ali	Died 114 A.H./732 A.D.
6. Jafar ibne Muhammad	Died 148 A.H./765 A.D.
7. Musa ibne Jafar	Died 183 A.H./799 A.D.
8. Ali ibne Musa	Died 203 A.H./817 A.D.
9. Muhammad ibne Ali	Died 220 A.H./835 A.D.
10. Ali ibne Muhammad	Died 254 A.H./868 A.D.
11. Hassan ibne Ali	Died 260 A.H./872 A.D.
12. Muhammad ibne Hassan	Born 256 A.H./868 A.D.

On the death of his father in 260 A.H. the twelfth Imam went into occultation (Gaybah), appearing only to a few leading Shiahs. Until 329 A.H./939 A.D. he performed the functions of the Imaam through representatives appointed by himself. He then went into major occultation which will continue until the day God grants him permission to manifest himself.

The Sunni View

The Sunnis use the term Imaam synonymously with the term khalifah. A khalifah may be elected, or nominated by his predecessor, or selected by a committee, or may acquire power through military force. A khalifah need not be sinless. It is lawful for a person of inferior qualities to be made a khalifah while persons of superior qualities are present.

DEVELOPMENT OF JURISPRUDENCE AND THEOLOGY

A. The Shiah School

During their life time the Imaams remained the chief exponents of the shariah, the Islamic law. Many of the Imaams, when the political atmosphere permitted, held theological classes and also taught other sciences. Since the major occultation of the twelfth Imaam the Shias have, as commanded not only by him but also most of the preceding Imaams, sought guidance from mujtahids and followed the institution of taqleed.

Taqleed literally means to follow or to imitate someone. In Islamic jurisprudence it means to follow a mujtahid in matters pertaining to law. (XXI:7 and IX:124)

Taqleed applies only to matters of shariah. There is no taqleed in matters of beliefs (the articles of faith). A Muslim must seek to attain conviction of their truth through reflection and rational examination. A mujtahid must be a person learned in all the Islamic sciences. At any given time there would normally be a number of persons qualified as mujtahids and it is not uncommon to have two members of the same family in taqleed of two different mujtahids.

Any Muslim can address any question of law to any mujtahid, whether or not he is in the taqleed of that mujtahid and the mujtahid would issue a fatwaa giving his opinion on that subject. This would invariably be by way of a statement of the law which in the opinion of the mujtahid is the correct legal position. The fatwaa would be binding on all the persons in the taqleed of that mujtahid. A mujtahid is so called because he does ijtehaad which term means to strive for deriving the laws of the shariah from its sources which are:

1. the Quran;
2. the sunnah which mean the traditions (ahadees) and the practice of the Prophet and the Imaams;
3. reasoning (aql);
4. consensus of the mujtahids (ijmaa).

B. The Sunni School

The ruling khalifah invariably assumed the mantle of the chief exponent of the shariah.

For nearly a hundred years following the death of the Prophet the State retained absolute control over authentication, collection and publication of the sayings (ahadees) of the Prophet. A few unscrupulous khalifahs did not hesitate to use this power to legitimise their misdeeds by arranging to have apocryphal ahadees produced. After the Banu Abbas came into power in 132 A.H. (750 A.D.), the formation of the Sunni community was formalised. Although there are many sects and sub-sects in the sunni school of thought, the four main sects are-

1. The Hanafis, founded by Imaam Abu Hanifa an-Nu'maan ibne Thabit (died 150 A.H./769 A.D.). He is a scholar greatly respected not only by his followers but also the other sunnis.
2. The Malikis, founded by Imaam Abu Abdullah Malik ibne Anas (died 179 A.H./797 A.D).

3. The Shafeis, founded by Imaam Abu Abdullah Muhammad ibne Idris al-Shafei (died 204 A.H/819 A.D.)
4. The Hanbalis, founded by Imaam Ahmed ibne Muhammad ibne Hanbal (died 241 A.H./855 A.D.)

Although there are many irreconcilable differences in the four Sunni schools, in the main, however, they agree on the fundamental bases of their doctrines and laws. Each claims to have derived them from the following four sources:

1. The Quran;
2. The Sunnah of the Holy Prophet and at times the Sunnah of the first four khalifahs;
3. The Ijmaa (consensus among the companions of the Prophet or of the religious leaders or among the followers);
4. The Qiyas (deduction of legal prescriptions from the Quran and the sunnah through rational analogy).

The extent of the acceptance of the theological and legal doctrines of any of the above four sunni schools depended largely on the inclination of the ruler of the time. For example, although Abu Hanifa himself did not gain great popularity with the khalifah, his successor Abu Yusuf became a powerful figure in the court and held office of the Chief Kadhi. The khalifah, however, always continued to remain the final arbiter in the exposition of the law and the jurists were relegated to an advisory role.

Since the abolition of the institution of khilafah following the fall of the Ottoman Empire the sunni schools have not developed as fast as they need to so as to keep pace with the social, economic, political and scientific development. Some Sunni sects have recognized the need for ijtehaad, a few appear to concentrate on ijmaa as the main instrument for reform.

In addition to their differences in jurisprudence, the Sunnis and the Shiahs hold divergent theological views on various aspects of the articles of beliefs e.g. human freedom of action and the Justice of God, whether God has a corporeal form. Some sunni sects believe in anthropomorphism.

The Shiahs and the Sunnis, however, agree on the following fundamental beliefs:

1. That Allah is One and has no partners;
2. That Muhammad is the last Prophet of God;
3. That there will be Resurrection and Judgement.

Acts of Worship

The Arabic term used for Acts of worship is Ibaadah. This does not mean worship. It means service. To serve God in the manner in which He has commanded his creatures to serve Him is Ibaadah. The term would include all acts of piety as well as the mandatory acts of worship. The mandatory acts of worship accepted by both the Sunnis and the Shiahs are:

1. Salaah (The Daily Prayers)

Every Muslim, from the time he or she attains puberty must perform the salaah. Except for a woman in menstruation, no person is excused from this act of worship.

Before a person begins his salaah he must perform the ritual ablution in the prescribed form. The object is symbolic preparation for the salaah and not, as often believed, cleanliness. A person has to be clean to perform the ablution (wudhoo). Then he stands facing Mecca and declares his intention to pray for gaining proximity to Allah. With this declaration he enters the formal state of salaah in which he remains until the completion of his prayers.

A salaah consists of a number of units called rakaahs. Each unit (rakaah) consists of:

i. recitation of the opening chapter and one other chapter of the Quran while in the standing position,

ii. the bowing down (rukoo) and glorifying God in that position and

iii. two prostrations each called a sajdaah in which again God is glorified. Then the second rakaah would commence.

The morning prayers to be performed between the dawn and sunrise have two rakaahs, the mid-day prayers four rakaahs, the sunset three and the evening four.

The prayers are ended by affirmation that Allah is One and has no partners and that Muhammad is His servant and messenger. Salutations are offered to the Prophet, all the righteous souls and all who are engaged in prayers.

Salaah is regarded as not only a ritual act of worship but a communion with the Maker. It is the most important form of ibaadah and sickness (other than insanity), age or infirmity is no excuse for not performing prayers.

Lapsed prayers constitute a debt to God and are a first charge on a Muslim's time and conscience. In the event of a person having died without having said any of his lapsed prayers, the eldest son, or if the deceased is not survived by a son, his heir must say or pay someone to say the lapsed prayers of the deceased.

Seyyid Hossein Nasr writes in his Ideals and Realities of Islam:

> *"In the canonical prayers man stands before God as the representative of all creatures. He prays for and in the name of all beings."*

Amongst the many sayings of the Prophet on the subject are:

> *"Salaah is the spiritual ascension of the faithful where he communes with Allah."*
>
> *"The good deeds wipe out the evil deeds of a man. The salaah and patience (sabr) are the best of deeds."*

Salaah is a spiritual activity where the person performing it is totally immersed, mentally and physically, in the remembrance of God. (XXIX:45, XXII:34 & 35, XXVII:1-3, XX:6-7 and 14, IX:71, LXXIV:38-48, VI:71 & 72, XV:98 & 99, XI:114 & 225).

2. Saum (Fasting)

The second act of worship is fasting in the month of Ramadhaan, the 9th month of the Islamic calendar. This is obligatory upon every mature Muslim except the sick, the traveller, a woman during her menstruation period and those infirm by age.

Fasting involves refraining from eating, drinking and sexual activity from the beginning of the nautical dawn to sunset. But these are not the sole objectives. Fasting is a conscious obedience of Allah's command. It is the human being's struggle to dedicate a whole month to activities which please his Maker. "It is the means", says Nasr, "by which man pulls the reins of his animal desires and realizes that he is more than an animal."

Fasting also begins with a declaration of intent to fast for the attainment of proximity to Allah. (II:184, 185, 187)

It is incumbent upon a Muslim to know why he prays and why he fasts. Imaam Ali says, "One who knows not why he prays or why he fasts, his prayers and fasts are little more than meaningless physical exertions, hunger and thirst."

3. Hajj (Pilgrimage To Mecca).

Every Muslim who has attained puberty and has sufficient means not only to undertake a journey to Mecca but also for the subsistence of his dependants during his absence, must once in his life time perform pilgrimage.

Kaaba is the edifice which was presented to God as a gift by His Prophets Abraham and Ishmael.

The rites for the pilgrimage begin on the 8th of the eleventh month and culminate into the Idd of Sacrifice on the 10th. (II:158, 196-203; III:97; V:3; XXII 26:33).

A Muslim's journey to the House of God, and there seeking his Maker's forgiveness through expression of repentance and the performance of all the rituals attending pilgrimage, is a spiritual experience so overwhelming that the pilgrim's very soul appears to undergo a purification.

The pilgrimage has another philosophical aspect.

In the Quran, like in the Old Testament, there is the story of Abraham having been commanded to sacrifice his son. The Quran, however, states that the son was Ishmael.

The father communicates the message to the young lad who had just attained puberty. The lad exhorts the father to comply with the divine command adding, "God willing, you shall find me amongst the patient ones."

Unbeknown to the mother, the father and the son travel to the planes of Arafaa, a short distance from Mecca. There they spend the night in prayers. The following afternoon they travel to the town of Meena where the sacrifice was to take place. They spend the night on the outskirts of the town. The following morning they enter Meena.

On the way to the appointed place, the Satan tries thrice to lure them into abandoning the enterprise, but each time the father and the son chase him away by throwing pebbles at him.

When they get to the place of sacrifice, the father blindfolds his son saying that he did not wish the lad to see the anguish on the father's face. He then blindfolds himself for, as he reasoned, how could any father watch his son die ?

God saves Ishmael by substituting a ram and sends His salutations to Abraham for his act of obedience. God also promises Abraham to immortalize the event. (II:125-127; III:96-97; XXXVII:101-111).

The mother, on learning what had happened, screams and falls unconscious at the thought of what might have happened had Allah not intervened to save her beloved son. Shortly afterwards she dies and is buried close to Kaaba. Her burial place is treated as being included in the hallowed ground around which the pilgrim circumambulates.

Every pilgrim takes the same route which Abraham and Ishmael had taken. He too spends the first night, as they did, in Arafaa and the second night outside Meena. He too symbolically stones the satan at the three places in Meena.

While of-course the visit to the House of Allah has its own great spirituality, the pilgrim also must reflect upon the rituals which appear to enshrine family values, parents' love for their off-spring, the vanquishing of the satan, the one within man's heart, by symbolically stoning him and above all the willingness to make sacrifices for the pleasure of God.

4. Zakah (The Wealth Tax)

Zakah, which literally means purity or purification, is a wealth tax of a small percentage (usually 2.5%) for the benefit of the needy in the society. It is regarded as a debt to God and must be distributed for the pleasure of Allah to the less fortunate amongst one's relatives, and the orphans, and the needy, and the wayfarers, and the beggars, and for the freeing of slaves. (II: 2-3, II-43, II:177, IX:11, XXII:41, IX:71, III:91, XIV:91, XXIV:22, XXVI:9, XIV:35-37, XXII:26)

There are innumerable traditions of the Prophet insisting upon zakah being paid by every Muslim. Imaam Jafar Sadiq said that the one who does not give zakah can not expect his salaah to be accepted by Allah. The Doctrine Of Five Pillars:

> *Many Sunni theologians, instead of enumerating the Articles of Faith and Acts of Worship separately, state that belief in God and the Prophet as affirmed in the creed (the Kalemah), together with the foregoing four acts of worship constitute the Five Pillars of Faith.*

The Shiahs list the five Articles of Faith as the roots of religion (Usool-e-Deen) and the Acts of Worship as the branches of religion (Furoo-e-Deen). In addition to the above acts of worship the Shiahs believe in the following acts of worship (The sunnis regard them as mandatory acts of piety):

5. Jihad Struggle Or Striving:

There are two kinds of jihad, the major jihad and the minor jihad.

The Major Jihad: (Jihad Al-Akbar)

This is the struggle against one's inner self (nafs) to subjugate and control one's passions and carnal desires. The base self (nafs-e-ammara) must be controlled by the conscience (nafs-e-lawwama), and only when one succeeds in this struggle does one attain the perfect self, the self at peace with itself (nafs-e-mutmainna). To those who attain this state, the God says:

> *" O the soul at peace, return to your Lord, pleased with His good pleasure AND enter into the company of My true servants. Enter the Garden !." (LXXXIX:27-30).*

The Minor Jihad (Jihad Al-Asghar)

This means to struggle for Islam. Not for extension of boundaries, not for personal glory, not for the glory of any tribe, community or nation, but for the defence of Islam and the protection of its values. Such a struggle can take many forms, through the use of pen, through the use of tongue or through the use of the sword. This last form is often referred to in the Quran as Qitaal (warfare).

In the Shiah theology, a general qitaal can be declared only by an Imaam. A mujtahid has no authority to summon Muslims to a jihad involving qitaal.

6. Amr Bi L-Ma-Aroof (Directing others towards Good)

It is an act of worship for a Muslim to advise and direct others to the doing of good deeds for the pleasure of Allah.

7. Nahy 'An Al Munkir (Directing others away from Evil)

Similarly it is the duty of every Muslim to advise others against committing sins. (III:103, 109, 113; VII:199; IX:71, 112; XXII:41; XXI:17.)

8. Khums (The One-fifth Tax)

Only the Shiahs believe in this additional tax and they regard it as a major obligation of every Shiah Muslim. It was instituted by God as a token of regard for the Prophet and his family. (VII:1:41; XXXIII:27; LIX:6-9).

It is a 20% tax on all earnings after deduction of house-hold and commercial expenses.

Khums is paid to the mujtahid and is divided into two equal portions. One half of all receipts of khums by the mujtahid is the portion belonging to the Imaam in occultation and the mujtahid spends this portion in educational, social and economic projects for the betterment of the Shiah community. First priority is accorded to the community from which the khums was received. The second half is distributed amongst the poor and deserving descendants of the Prophet (the sayyids) each of whom may receive only up to a year's subsistence.

OTHER ACTS OF PIETY

Theocentricity: Islam does not have the concept of secularism. All human activities must be either in accordance of the law (the shariah) or the prescribed code of conduct. An act which accords with either is an act of piety.

A Muslim's must consider his life on this earth as a journey from his Maker to his Maker and must strive to gain the pleasure of his Maker. "Give glad tidings to the steadfast who say........`We are from Allah and to Him we return'. Such are they upon whom are blessings from their Lord, and mercy. Such are the rightly guided." (II:155-157).

The purpose of every creation, other than humans) is to serve mankind (XXXI:20; XLV:13; LXVII:5). Man, who has been created of the best structure (XCV:4), must serve none other than Allah.(LI:56-58). It will be beneath the dignity and status of man to worship any being, thing or power other than Allah.

The doctrine of the Unity of God is not just an article of faith. It is an important factor in man's comprehension of himself and his raison d'etre. God the One, the Indivisible must be his sole Guide in his journey on this earth.

The sixth Imaam explaining the Unity of God said, " The true ibaadah is for the human being to ensure that the essence of the unity of God lies between his intent and his deed.

The Prophet has said, "Man's every action must incline towards Allah".

The Islamic ethical code is too vast and extensive to permit a full discussion in this course. We shall, therefore, confine ourselves to a cursory glance at a few aspects of the code of conduct.

Pursuit of Knowledge: Islam regards ignorance as impure (najasah) and the acquisition of knowledge as a great act of piety. "One who has knowledge can never be equal to the one who is ignorant" (XXXIX:9).

The Prophet has said:

"It is the duty of every Muslim male and every Muslim female to seek knowledge".

"Seek knowledge even if you have to travel as far as China for it."

"Sitting an hour in a learned gathering is better than a thousand nights spent in performance of (optional) salaah, and better than engaging in a battle for the sake of God on thousand occasions. If one leaves one's house with the intention of gaining knowledge, for every step that he takes God shall bestow upon him the reward reserved for a prophet."

Parents: Respect for, and obedience and kindness to, parents are enjoined upon Muslims. Obedience is, however, excused where the parents require injustice to be perpetrated. (XVII:23, XXIX:8, XXXI:14, XLVI:15-18).

The Prophet has said:

"It is an act of worship to look at either parent with affection and kindness".

"Allah is pleased when one has pleased his parents, and Allah is angry when one has angered either parent".

"Paradise lies under the feet of your mother".

Charity: Quran enjoins the spending of one's wealth in the cause of Allah, for the poor, the needy, the freeing of slaves, the curing of the sick and other good causes. Charity is a precondition to the attainment of piety. (II:195, 215, 245, 254, 261, 262-273; III:92; XXXVI:47; LVII:10, 11; LXIV:15-18)

There are innumerable traditions of the Prophet and the Imaams on the merits of charity. In one of these it is said, "If you have nothing to give, give a kind word or even just an affectionate smile." Dissemination of knowledge by a scholar is an act of charity. So is the visiting of a sick.

Caring for the bereaved is also a great act of piety. There is a tradition which requires the extended family or the community to feed the immediate family of the deceased for at least three days after the death has occurred and to offer them solace and comfort.

Resisting Oppression

Imaam Ali has said:

" To suffer oppression passively is as bad as to commit oppression".

"He who makes no effort to alleviate the suffering of an oppressed one is an oppressor".

Justice: A Muslim is required to act with justice in all his dealings with other human beings and in all circumstances. (IV:58, 105, 135; VII:29; XVI:90).

In IV:135 the Quran says:

"O You who believe, be staunch in justice.......though it may be against your interests, or the interests of your parents or near relatives, and whether you are dealing with a rich person or a poor person. Remember Allah is nearer to them both in compassion. Therefore do not follow your low desires."

Lewdness And Indecencies:

These are totally forbidden. (XVI:90)

Idle Chatter, Slander and Infringement of Privacy:

These are totally forbidden. (XLIX:11 & 12)

The Freeing of Slaves:

This is not only an act of piety but is also prescribed as the primary penalty for certain wilful acts or omissions e.g. failure to fast or repay a lapsed fast, infringement of any regulation required to be observed during pilgrimage etc.

Liberation of slaves was also highly recommended as an atonement for various sins.

Ill treatment of slaves and servants is also forbidden.

It is highly recommended that zakaah and other alms be spent for liberating slaves. (XXIV:33; IX:60; II:177; XC:12, 13).

Reasoning And Reflection:

"Will they not reflect and ponder on the Quran or are there locks on their intellect ?" (XLVII:24)

"Say unto them, O Muhammad: I exhort you unto one thing only. That you awake for Allah's sake, by two or singly, and then reflect." (XXXIV:46)

"In the creation of heavens and earth and in the difference between night and day are tokens for men of understanding. These are those who remember Allah, standing, sitting, and reclining, and consider the creation of the heavens and the earth, (and then cry out): Our Lord! Thou hast not created this in vain. Glory be to Thee !" (III:190-191).

The eighth Imaam has said:

"Worship does not lie in engaging oneself in saying prayers endlessly or in fasting copiously, but in engaging oneself in the contemplation of the works of Allah."

The Prophet has said, "Allah has endowed man with the most precious gift, the reason. The slumber of a man of reason is better than the movement of the ignorant." Other Good Deeds:

1. Respect for the elders.
2. Respect for teachers and scholars.

   The Fourth Imaam has said, " Your teacher has the following rights. Firstly, total respect from you. Secondly that you listen attentively when he speaks. Thirdly, that you never raise your voice in his presence".
3. Hospitality.
4. The keeping of promises, adhering to contracts and covenants, and repayment of debts. All these are mandatory. In V:1 God says, " O you who believe, fulfil your undertakings".
5. The forgiving of any debt owed to one by a person unable to repay.

Women in Islam

Islam does not accept that the first woman was created of any inferior composition (IV:1) or that it was Eve who fell to the promptings of Satan in disobeying God. Both were equally to blame. (VII:20-21).

Women play an important role and are equal partners of men.

"The women are raiment (comfort, embellishment and protection) for you and you are raiment for them." (II:187; IV:1).

As a daughter, she is to be shown greater affection than a son. The Prophet commands that a daughter must receive twice as much love and affection as a son.

As a wife, the woman has no obligation to provide for her husband or the children out her income or wealth. The husband has this responsibility. What a woman earns, or receives by way of inheritance or gift, is her own property over which she has sole control.

It is injustice for the husband to require the wife to do the house-hold chores. It is for the parties to agree on the division of labour.

The wife, however, is under a duty to obey the lawful and just commands of her husband.

As a mother the woman occupies a unique position. She is placed upon an almost divine pedestal. She must be obeyed (save where obedience would lead to injustice), revered and her feelings never hurt.

The Prophet has said that while both parents must be obeyed and respected, the father's place is three rungs below that of the mother.

The woman is the pivot of the family, and Islam holds the family as being the most important unit of the society. From the moment of conception to birth and up to the attainment of puberty, it is the mother who shapes the mind, the thinking and the behaviour of that future member of the society. The Prophet repeatedly emphasised the importance of the upbringing of children and the role of the mother. He is reported to have said:

> *"It is better to bring up your children so that they have good manners and morals than to spend your wealth for the pleasure of Allah."*

There are also several traditions of the Prophet and the Imaams about the treatment and conduct of pregnant mothers.

Dress

The Quran commands both men and women to `lower their gaze and be modest'.

The women have been further commanded `not to display their ornaments except what appears thereof and to wear their head-coverings over their bosom and not to display their ornaments except to their husband (and other members of their family within the prohibited degree of marriage e.g. a son, father, brother, uncles excluding uncles by marriage etc.)'. (XXIV:30 & 31). Again in XXXIII:59 God says:

"O Prophet, tell your wives and your daughters and the women of the believers that they let down upon them their over-garments. This will be more proper. They will be known and will therefore not be given trouble."

The above verses have been interpreted by some jurists as requiring a veiled face and body and others as requiring a scarf over the head to conceal the hair (an essential ornament) and the rest of the body, except the face, the hands and the feet, to be covered by a loose fitting outer garment. In different cultures different forms of women`s dress, or veil or "purdah" have evolved.

The Quranic object clearly appears to be protection of women from molestation and disrespect, and not their treatment as inferior beings.

Marriage

Marriage is a solemn contract between a man and a woman, each giving his or her consent freely and without any duress, to become life partners and enjoy the rights conferred and fulfil the obligations imposed by the shariah.

The basic requirements are free consent, the mahr (dowry) and the recitation of the marriage formula (the aqd) in the prescribed form and perfect Arabic.

The mahr is the giving or a promise to give any sum of money to the bride and/or to fulfil any condition or obligation that the bride may impose.

The parties may recite the aqd themselves or appoint agents to do so on their behalf.

According to some Shiah jurists the bride may, in the mahr, confer upon herself a right to divorce, or provide for the division of property of property in the event of divorce or any other condition to reserve for herself any right or benefit which under the shariah she would not normally enjoy.

The relationship between husband and wife must be founded upon love and mutual tolerance:

"And of His (God's) signs is that He has created for you mates from amongst yourselves so that you might find

comfort and solace in them, and He has ordained between you love and mercy." (XXX:21)

There are many traditions and sayings on this subject. Two are given below:

1. May Allah bless the man who lays the foundation of his relations with his wifeon goodness. (Imaam Jafar Sadiq)
2. A man must honour and love his wife. (The Prophet)

Temporary Marriages (Mutaa): The Shiah law also permits temporary marriages. It has the same rights and obligations as a permanent marriage except that the marriage will terminate by effluxion of time, and, if the parties so agree, the relationship may be for companionship only without consummation.

Polygamy: A marriage with up to four wives is permitted. There are, however, strict conditions as to equal and just treatment of all the wives.

Divorce

Islam permits divorce where the marriage has irreparably broken down. But first there must be a process of reconciliation in which the elders of the two families as well as of the community must strive to get the parties to reconcile.

The Prophet has said that of all the permissible things divorce is the most detestable to Allah.

Political Science: Sovereignty belongs to God. The ruler, whether a king or an elected or nominated representative, can only rule as His vicegerent and in accordance with His laws. (XLII:38; XXII:41).

When Imaam Ali was finally elected the khalifah he endeavoured to establish an Islamic government but alas he was not permitted to rule for long.

However, during the five years of Ali's reign he wrote several letters to his Governors and Commanders restating the principles of governance in Islam. These letters and instructions have been compiled into a book called `Nahjul Balaagah', English translations of which are available.

The most famous of these documents is Ali's letter to his Governor in Egypt, Maalik Ashtar, which deals with a variety of subjects including administration, judiciary, treatment of non-Muslims, the army and the conduct of a ruler or his representative.

In the preamble of the letter Ali says:

"This is what Allah's servant Ali has ordered Malik ibne al-Harith al-Ashtar when he appointed him Governor of Egypt, for the collection of its (Egypt's) revenues, fighting against its enemies, seeking the good of its people and making its cities properous."

The Quran and Modern Science

The French author Maurice Bucaille has written a book entitled `La Bible, le Coran et la Science', which has been translated into English.

In this book the author writes:

"The relationship between the Quran and science is a priori a surprise, especially when it turns out to be one of harmony and not of discord........The totally erroneous statements made about Islam in the West are sometimes the result of ignorance and some times of systematic denigration."

The author then proceeds to take various scientific subjects and give Quranic references which fully accord with the modern scientific conclusions. While it is not proposed to deal with the subject in any detail in this course, it might be interesting to give here a few of the scientific subjects dealt with by Bucaille and the corresponding Quranic verses cited by him:

The sky:	(L:6; XIII:2; XLV:13; X:5).
The Planets:	(XXIV:35; XXXVII:6).
Celestial organization:	(XXXVI:40; XXXV:13; LI:47).
Conquest of space:	(LV:33; XV:14 & 15).
The earth:	(II:22; XX:53 & 54).
The water cycle:	(XXX:48; VII:57; XXV:48 & 49).
Origin of life in water:	(XXI:30; XX:53).
Vegetable and animal reproduction:	(XX:53; XII:3; LIII:45 & 46).

Animal communities:	(VI:38).
Bees:	(XVI:68 & 69).
Spiders:	(XXIX:41).
Human reproduction:	(LXXXII: 6-8; XVI:4; LXXV:37; XXIII:13; XXII:5; XXIII:14; LIII:45 & 46; XXXV:11).

Islamic Jurisprudence

This too is a subject beyond the scope of this course. The main sources of Islamic Jurisprudence are the Quran and the sunnah, and encompasses inheritance, marriage, divorce, paternity, waqfs (trusts), contracts, penal laws, evidence and procedure.

Islamic Culture?

Culture has been defined as,

"the totality of socially transmitted behaviour patterns, arts, beliefs, institutions, and all other products of human work and thought characteristic of a community or a population. It is the set of shared beliefs, attitudes, values, and behavioural patterns of a group or organisation." (Readers Digest Universal Dictionary)

Religion on the other hand is "the expression of man's belief in and reverence for God or gods who created the Universe and Govern it."

It is as naive to think that any religion encompasses the totality of culture as it is to think that any culture is solely the product of a religion. Islam like many other religions claims to be universal accommodating within its fold the cultures of all its adherents provided that the bounds of the religious laws are not transgressed.

Islam has broad parameters of rules and regulations and within these parameters an African can remain as much a Muslim as a Pakistani or a Bangladeshi or an English-man or Scots-man or an American or Chinese or any individual from any country anywhere in the world.

Nevertheless there is a difference of opinion on whether Islam has its own distinct culture. Scholars are divided on whether there is a central cultural theme in Islam.

Some vehemently argue that there is such a central theme. Others maintain that because of the universality of Islam it is wrong to insist upon a common cultural theme.

This latter school of thought argue that culture is an historical heritage of a nation, people or society in the fields of art, architecture, dress, cuisine, language, literature and other cultural norms and pursuits.

Islam, on the other hand, consists of beliefs, acts of worship, a code of conduct and jurisprudence. So long as the culture of a society lies within the parameters of Islamic beliefs, acts of worship, code of conduct and the shariah, that culture would be acceptable in Islam.

Many an artist, architect, poet, author and chef has, upon acceptance of Islam, adjusted himself/herself so as conform to the Islamic requirements.

Muslims in Great Britain

There is a substantial Muslim community in Great Britain and at times there occur conflicts between them and other communities.

It is wrong to link racism with religion. Racism is an attitude of hostility based upon racial prejudice. This is often exploited by unscrupulous politicians and community leaders for their own ends.

Unfortunately, both the victims and the perpetrators of racial prejudice tend to foster the image of it being the result of the diversity in religious beliefs.

This often rallies support for the victim community and provides the perpetrators with the mantle of defending their faith.

At the same time there is amongst the indigenous population a fear, nurtured by irresponsible media, that Islam poses a threat to their community.

If a solution is not found, and found soon, the Muslim communities could be driven to extreme ethnicity with the future generation growing up as pariahs in their own country.

Consideration must be given to promoting a better understanding of Islam in the indigenous population. For this both the communities will need to strive hard.

Islam is a tolerant religion. It accepts Christianity and Judaism as sister faiths and respects other religions as well. The Muslims are enjoined to respect churches, synagogues and other places of worship.

There is a need to ensure that each side is enriched by the values of the religion of the other through amicable inter-action without anyone from either side losing his identity.

To ensure harmony efforts must be made to create a community of British Muslims rather than a community, or a number of communities, of Muslims in Britain.

7

Islamic Beliefs

1. Monotheism: The Oneness of Allah (Tawhid)

Allah, or God, is the centre of Muslim belief. Whereas certain religions focus on individuals, like Christianity focuses on Jesus (peace be upon him), Islam focuses solely on Allah. Although Muslims respect the divine prophets, the prophets-including Prophet Muhammad (peace be upon him and his family)-are still only servants of Allah.

The Quran itself speaks of the oneness of God: "Allah has borne witness that there is no God but Him-and the angels, and those with knowledge also witness this. He is always standing firm on justice. There is no God but Him, the Mighty, the Wise." (3:18)

The oneness of Allah is not only a philosophical argument but is an affirmation that all human beings declared before their souls came into their bodies:

[Remember] when your Lord brought forth the children of Adam from their loins and made them testify over themselves, saying, "Am I not your Lord?" They said, "Yes! We testify," lest you should say on the Day of Resurrection, "Verily, we were unaware of this." (7:172)

Such was the covenant that Allah made with all people at the time of creation regardless of whether these same people now claim to believe in God or not. At that time, they proclaimed His majesty, His sovereignty, His power, and His absolute oneness and transcendence.

Likewise, all people today, regardless of their origins, are naturally inclined towards the idea that God is one and without partner. The Quran tells Prophet Muhammad (peace be upon him):

Set your face to the true religion [Islamic monotheism], the natural inclination (fitra) with which Allah has created mankind. [Let there be] no change in what Allah has made; that is the straight religion, but most people do not understand. (30:30)

Describing God

One of the shortest chapters of the Quran, "The Oneness of God", ummarizes the nature of God in five verses:

In the name of Allah, the most Gracious, the Most Merciful

Say, He is Allah, the One

Allah, the Eternal

He begets not, nor was He begotten

And there is nothing at all comparable to Him.

The most fundamental Islamic teachings about God are contained in these verses, i.e. that there is only one God Who is eternal, unique, and has no blood relation to any human beings. Different prophets also gave their own descriptions of God which are also related in the Quran. Prophet Abraham (peace be upon him) says: "My Lord is He Who gives life and causes death." (2:258) After him, Moses (peace be upon him), when confronting the Pharaoh, says: "Our Lord is He Who gave each thing its form and nature then guided it aright." (20:50) These two verses both describe Allah in His relation to human beings, but of course Allah's being extends far beyond His relation to mankind.

Imam 'Ali (peace be upon him) has also described Him thus:

He who assigns to Him different conditions does not believe in His oneness, nor does he who likens Him grasp His reality. He who illustrates Him does not signify Him; he who points at Him and imagines Him does not mean Him. Everything that is known through itself has been created, and everything that exists by virtue of other things is the effect of a cause. He works, but not with the help of instruments; He fixes measures, but not with the activities of thinking; He is rich, but not by acquisition. Time does not keep company with Him, and implements do not help Him. His being precedes time, His existence precedes non-existence, and His eternity precedes beginning. By His creating the senses, it is known that He has no senses. By the contraries in various matters, it is known that He has no contrary, and by the similarity between things it is known that there is nothing similar to Him. He has made light the contrary of darkness, brightness that of gloom, dryness that of moisture, and heat that of cold. He produces affection among inimical things.... He is not confined by limits nor counted by numbers. Material parts can surround things of their own kind, and organs can point out things similar to themselves.... Through them, the Creator manifests Himself to the intelligence, and through them He is guarded from the sight of the eyes.... He has not begotten anyone lest He be regarded as having been born. He has not been begotten, otherwise He would be contained within limits. He is too high to have sons.... Understanding cannot think of Him so as to give Him shape....

Allah expresses His own eternity and perpetuity Himself: "Every thing on earth shall perish, but the face of Allah will remain, full of majesty and honour." (55:26-27)

THE 99 NAMES OF ALLAH

"And to Allah belong the most beautiful names, so call on Him by them." (7:180) Islamic tradition says that Allah has many different names representing different aspects of His being, and 99 of them are commonly recited together:

English	Arabic
The Merciful	ar-rahim
The Beneficent	ar-rahmaan
The Sovereign	al-malik
The Holy	al-quddus
The Peace	as-salaam
The Guardian of Faith	al-mumin

The Protector	al-muhaymin
The Mighty	al-'aziz
The Compellor	al-jabbar
The Majestic	al-mutakabbir
The Creator	al-khaaliq
The Evolver	al-baari'
The Fashioner	al-musawwir
The Forgiver	al-ghaffar
The Subduer	al-qahhar
The Bestower	al-wahhab
The Provider	ar-razzaq
The Opener	al-fattah
The Knowing	al-'alim
The Constrictor	al-qaabid
The Abaser	al-khaafid
The Expander	al-baasit
The Honorer	al-muizz
The Exalter	ar-raafi'
The Hearing	as-sami'
The Dishonorer	al-mudhill
The Judge	al-hakam
The Seeing	al-basir
The Subtle	al-latif
The Kind	al-halim
The Just	al-'adl
The Aware	al-khabir
The All-Forgiving	al-ghafur
The Great	al-'azim
The High	al-'aliy
The Appreciative	ash-shakur
The Preserver	al-hafiz
The Immense	al-kabir
The Reckoner	al-hasib
The Maintainer	al-muqit
The Generous	al-karim
The Majestic	al-jalil

The Responsive	al-mujib
The Wise	al-hakim
The Watchful	ar-raqib
The All-Surrounding	al-waasi'
The Glorious	al-majid
The Loving	al-wadud
The Witness	ash-shahid
The Resurrector	al-baaith
The Truth	al-haqq
The Trustee	al-wakil
The Strong	al-qawi
The Firm	al-matin
The Praiseworthy	al-hamid
The Guardian	al-wali
The Originator	al-mubdi
The Reckoner	al-muhsi
The Giver of Life	al-muhyi
The Restorer	al-muid
The Creator of Death	al-mumit
The Living	al-hayy
The Self-Subsisting	al-qayyum
The Finder	al-waajid
The Noble	al-maajid
The Unique	al-waahid
The One	al-ahad
The Eternal	as-samad
The Able	al-qadir
The Powerful	al-muqtadir
The Expediter	al-muqaddim
The Delayer	al-muakhkhir
The First	al-awwal
The Last	al-aakhir
The Manifest	az-zaahir
The Hidden	al-baatin
The Governor	al-waali
The Exalted	al-muta'ali

The Source of Goodness	al-barr
The Acceptor of Repentance	at-tawwab
The Avenger	al-muntaqim
The Pardoner	al-'afuw
The Compassionate	ar-rauf
The Owner of Soverignty	maalik al-mulk
The Lord of Majesty Bounty	dhul jalaali wal-ikraam and
The Equitable	al-muqsit
The Gatherer	al-jaami'
The Self-Sufficient	al-ghani
The Enricher	al-mughni
The Preventer	al-mani'
The Distresser	ad-darr
The Benefitor	an-naafi'
The Light	an-nur
The Guide	al-haadi
The Incomparable	al-badi'
The Everlasting	al-baaqi
The Inheritor	al-waarith
The Guide to the Right Path	ar-rashid
The Patient	as-sabur

2. Divine Justice ('adl)

Anyone who believes in Islamic monotheism must believe in the Almighty's justice. Because Allah is just, He never wrongs His creatures, for injustice is an evil deed while He is far from doing evil. Because He is omniscient, He does not neglect anything, and because He is self-sufficient, He has no cause to wrong others. Since He owns everything, He does not need the actions of anyone. His wisdom also transcends the universe.

Thus, unlike some human beings, He has no cause for injustice:

> *"He is always standing firm on justice. There is no God but Him, the Mighty, the Wise." (3:18)*
>
> *"And your Lord does not deal unjustly with anyone." (18:49)*

"We did not wrong them, but they wronged themselves." (16:118)

Just as Allah encourages human beings to emulate some of His attributes, such as being patient and forgiving, He also tells us to follow the way of justice. "Say: 'My Lord has enjoined upon me justice.'" (7:29) Although common people may falter in this area, none of the prophets of God or their successors ever committed any act of injustice.

Allah's justice embraces the entire universe. Whoever ponders over the existence of the universe and the order therein will not only observe the spread of Allah's justice over His entire creation but also each of its signs apparent in all aspects of nature--from the physical world to the biological world, and from the microcosmos to the macrocosmos. The justice of God is particularly visible in the fate and destiny of human beings, and in their freedom of choice.

Although Allah's justice encompasses everything, people should pray to Allah to treat them not with His justice but rather with His mercy, for if He treated people solely with His justice and punished them immediately for all of their sins, humanity would have perished a long time ago.

Predestination or Free Will?

The question of man's predestination or freedom of choice has preoccupied mankind throughout the ages and continues to be discussed by Islamic philosophers and scholars. Ultimately, two schools of thought regarding this question have emerged. One, called the Compulsionists, holds that human beings have no freedom of choice whatsoever in life. Every decision people make, every word people say has been predestined since the time of creation. If someone is faithful, it is not he who decides to embrace the faith; if someone is unfaithful, it is not he who rejects the faith. All has been written.

The second school of thought, the Free Will school, declares that human beings are masters of their own acts. This notion is in concordance with the Quran, which states: "None will be wronged in anything, nor will you be requited anything except that which you used to do," (36:54) as well as: "The truth is from your Lord. So whomever wills, let him believe, and whoever wills, let him disbelieve." (18:29) From these two verses, it is clear that human beings have the freedom to act but must bear the moral responsibilities for their own actions. Furthermore, the acknowledgement of divine justice itself forces people to accept that their every action is not predestined.

The beginning of guidance is always from Allah, but the beginning of man's destruction is in his own erroneous opinions. "Whatever good reaches you is from Allah, but whatever evil befalls you is from yourself." (4:79)

3. Prophethood (Nubuwwa)

The prophets were the people who received divine revelation. Allah has sent numerous prophets and messengers to humankind since the dawn of history. These prophets were of two types: "local" and "universal." While the local prophets were sent with specific messages to specific groups of people, the universal prophets were sent with messages and books for all of humankind. There were only five universal prophets, and their names were Noah, Abraham, Moses, Jesus, and Muhammad (may the peace of Allah be upon all of them).

A unique characteristic of all the prophets and messengers is that they were infallible-that is, they never committed any sin. The easiest way to see this is to consider that these people were the examples sent for humanity to follow, and so if they committed errors, people would be obliged to follow their errors, thereby making the prophets and messengers untrustable. Infallibility means protection, and, in Islamic terminology, means the spiritual grace of Allah enabling a person to abstain from sins by his own free will. This power of infallibility and sinlessness does not make a person incapable of committing sins; rather, he refrains from sins and mistakes by his own power and will.

Infallibility is essential since the job of the prophets and messengers is not only to convey the divine scriptures of Allah but also to lead and guide humanity towards the right path. Therefore, they have to be role models and perfect examples for mankind. This has basis in both the Quran and conventional wisdom; the Quran mentions infallibility 13 times. Allah says to the Satan: "Certainly you shall have no authority over My servants except those who follow you and go astray." (15:42) The Satan then says to Allah: "By Your might, then I will surely mislead them all, except Your chosen servants among them [the messengers and imams]."(38:82)

Not only did Prophet Muhammad (peace be upon him and his family) not commit any sins, but he was also never harsh to human beings or animals. Allah says: "And by the mercy of Allah you dealt with them [people] gently, and had you been severe and harsh-hearted, they would have broken away from you." (3:158)

In most societies, people with bad records would be ineligible to be presidential, governmental, or mayoral candidates since they would be expected to lead society and be good examples of righteousness and honesty. Unfortunately, as a campaign of distorting the image of the prophets of God, many distorted stories exist today, such as the stories in the present-day version of the Old Testament accusing Prophet David (peace be upon him) of adultery with Baathsheba, Prophet Noah (peace be upon him) getting drunk, Prophet Lot (peace be upon him) committing incest, and Prophet Moses (peace be upon him) committing adultery with the Ethiopian women. These are examples of the ethical wrongdoings and moral weaknesses that the enemies of Allah tried to ascribe to His pure messengers.

The Holy Quran speaks of the sins attributed to certain prophets such as Adam (peace be upon him). These verses should not be understood literally in the sense that Adam was committing a sin; allegorical verses are common in the Quran. Adam (peace be upon him) did not disobey the obligatory commands of Allah; the command that he did not honour was a recommended command, and, therefore, in the Islamic law, he cannot be considered to have committed a sin.

Although Allah preordained who the prophets were going to be, the prophets nonetheless had to strive for this position. The foremost example of this testing that the prophets had to endure can be seen in the life of Prophet Abraham (peace be upon him), the father of the prophets. Abraham (peace be upon him) was born into an idolatrous society, but by the purity of his nature he recognized that the idols his people worshipped were capable of nothing, neither harm nor good. So one day, when no one was present, he smashed all of them but the largest, and when the people came to him and asked who had destroyed their gods, he told them to ask the remaining statue if they really believed that their stone idols had power.

Although the people realized at that point that their idols were powerless, they didn't know how to respond, so out of shame and anger they cast Abraham (peace be upon him) into a huge fire. But Allah protected Abraham (peace be upon him) from the fire and confounded the plots of the polytheists.

After being tortured for and then saved by his faith in Allah, Abraham (peace be upon him) still had to undergo the hardest test of obedience to Allah-the direct order, from Allah, to sacrifice his son Ishmael.

This order came to him in a dream, and although sadness overwhelmed him, he was a strong believer in Allah and did not question it. Ishmael too accepted the command of Allah unquestioningly and allowed his father to lead him to a mountaintop to be sacrificed. His only request was that his father place him face down so that his father would not see his expression as he was being killed.

Abraham (peace be upon him) raised his blade, still ready to comply with the command of Allah. But just then came the revelation that this had only been a test, that God would not order Abraham (peace be upon him) to sacrifice his son, and that Abraham (peace be upon him) could sacrifice a sheep in his stead. This event is commemorated every year on a holiday called the Feast of Sacrifice ('eid al-adhaa) on which animals are killed and the meat distributed to the poor.

After passing these tests, Abraham (peace be upon him) became the leader of humankind as well as the father of the prophets of the three main monotheistic religions-Judaism, Christianity, and Islam. Although Allah sent prophets to every group of people on the earth, the Quran only mentions the names of 25 of them.

The first of them was Adam (peace be upon him), the father of humanity, and the last of them and the seal of the prophets was Prophet Muhammad (peace be upon him and his family).

Why did Allah send different Prophets and different Religions?

The way of Allah is one, and because the final messenger, Prophet Muhammad (peace be upon him and his family), has come, there should be no dispute as to what is the right way to follow.

However, throughout history, different messengers with slightly different messages were sent to different peoples because the religious needs of humanity were growing and developing just as the human race was itself growing and developing, and also because different civilizations needed different types of guidance. Nevertheless, the source and basic message behind them was the same-namely, Allah the Exalted and Glorious.

Allah sent Moses (peace be upon him) with the Torah as a light and guidance for the Children of Israel (the Jews) along with many other prophets such as David, Solomon, and so on (peace be upon them). 1,500 years after Moses, Allah sent Jesus (peace be upon him), the son of Mary (peace be upon her), confirming the Torah and bringing the Gospel which has also been likened to guidance and light.

Finally, 600 years after Jesus (peace be upon him), Allah sent Prophet Muhammad (peace be upon him and his family) with the Quran to confirm all the messages before him and to complete the revelation of religion to mankind.

Since all the Judeo-Christian-Islamic prophets were sent sequentially, the question arises as to why Judaism, Christianity, and Islam now exist as separate religions.

The answer is that the followers of these religions, particularly Judaism and Christianity, corrupted the original teachings given to them and ended up making sects of their own rather than following the pure word of God. But as the Quran says:

For each of you, We have made a Law and a clear way. If Allah had willed, He would have made you one nation but that He may test you in what He has given you. So strive as a race in good deeds. Your return is to Allah; then He will inform you about that which you used to differ. (5:48)

The Life of Prophet Muhammad (Peace be Upon Him and His Family)

In 6th-century CE Arabia, the majority of people were pagans. They lived in tribes, each with its own leader. Some were farmers, others traders, but many reared camels and raided other tribes for booty. It was into this society, in CE 570, that Prophet Muhammad (peace be upon him and his family) was born in Mecca. His parents died and he was looked after first by his grandfather and then by his uncle. As he grew up, Prophet Muhammad (peace be upon him and his family) became known as Prophet Muhammad (peace be upon him and his family) al-Amin, 'the trustworthy'. He worked for a wealthy older widow, Khadija, who, impressed with his honesty, asked him to marry her. He was twenty-five, and they remained married until her death twenty-five years later.

Prophet Muhammad (peace be upon him and his family) often used to go from the bustle of Mecca for periods of reflection in a cave outside the city. During one such time, when he was forty years old, he heard the voice of the angel Jibril giving him a command:

> *Recite in the Name of your Lord who creates, Creates man from a clot. Recite! Your Lord is the Most Bountiful, Who taught the use of the pen, Taught humankind that which they knew not. (96:1-5)*

Prophet Muhammad (peace be upon him and his family) repeated the words until he had learned them by heart. He rushed home and related his experience to his wife, who comforted and reassured him. Khadija and the Prophet's young cousin 'Ali (peace be upon him) were the first people to understand and accept that Allah had chosen 'the trustworthy one' to deliver his final guidance.

Prophet Muhammad (peace be upon him and his family) continued to receive revelations for over twenty years.

As time passed, it became clear to ever-increasing numbers of people that Prophet Muhammad (peace be upon him and his family) was indeed a Messenger of Allah. The least receptive were those powerful Makkans who trafficked in idols and slaves and benefited most from idol worship and the pilgrim trade. They treated Prophet Muhammad (peace be upon him and his family) with derision. Despite this, he continued to deliver the revelations of Allah's mercy and justice, which were welcomed by the poor and oppressed.

The Prophet (peace be upon him and his family), his family, and followers were driven from Mecca. For three years they sheltered in a valley outside the city in conditions of hardship and hunger. Narrowly escaping assassination in Mecca, the Prophet (peace be upon him and his family) traveled to Medina in CE 622. The migration from Mecca to Medina, known as the Hijrah, became the starting point of the Muslim calendar.

Prophet Muhammad (peace be upon him and his family) was very well received in Medina where he became head of what was to become the first Islamic state. In CE 630, Prophet Muhammad (peace be upon him and his family) and his followers entered Mecca. At the Kaaba, Prophet Muhammad (peace be upon him and his family) cleared the hundreds of idols from inside and proclaimed that truth had come and falsehood had vanished. He was 63 when he died, and by the time of his death the majority of people in Arabia had accepted Islam as their way of life.

The final verse of the Quran to be revealed to Prophet Muhammad (peace be upon him and his family), a few days before his death, was this: "Today I [Allah] have perfected for you your religion, completed my favour upon you, and have chosen for you Islam as your religion." (5:3)

4. Succession to the Prophet Muhammad (Peace be Upon Him and His Family) (Imama)

All of the prophets and messengers of God had successors, and just as Allah appointed His prophets and messengers for the guidance of mankind, He also appointed successors to the prophets and messengers as a matter of necessity. Abraham (peace be upon him) was succeeded by two of his sons, Isaac and Ishmael (peace be upon them), while Moses (peace be upon him) was succeeded by his brother Aaron (peace be upon him) and Jesus (peace be upon him) by two prophets whom the Quran mentions in the chapter called "Ya Sin". (36:13-14) Likewise, Prophet Muhammad (peace be upon him and his family) was succeeded by twelve distinguished successors, one after another. These successors were called imams and were appointed by Allah, not by humankind. The right to ordain imams belongs only to Almighty Allah, and the Quran speaks about this in many verses:

> *"And remember when your Lord said to the angels, 'Verily I am going to place a successor (khalifa)." (2:30)*
>
> *Allah addressed Prophet David (peace be upon him) as such: "O David! Verily We have placed you as a successor on earth." (38:26) "And remember when the Lord of Abraham tried him with certain commands which he fulfilled; Allah said to him, 'Verily I am going to make you a leader (imam) of mankind.'" (2:124)*
>
> *Allah also attributes the right of appointing leaders to Himself: "We made from among them leaders, giving guidance under Our command." (32:24)*

During his lifetime, Prophet Muhammad (peace be upon him and his family) specifically mentioned the names of the leaders that would come after him, that there would be twelve of them, and that all of them would be descended from a particular Arab tribe called Quraysh.

The twelve successors to Prophet Muhammad (peace be upon him and his family) are as follows:

Imam 'Ali ibn Abi Talib (600-661) Imam 'Ali (peace be upon him) was the Prophet's cousin and son-in-law and the one about whom he said: "I am the city of knowledge and 'Ali is its gate." He also said, "Whoever considers me his leader, 'Ali is also his leader." 110,000 people heard the Prophet (peace be upon him and his family) say this at a place called Ghadir Khum. Muslims and non-Muslims alike recognized Imam 'Ali (peace be upon him) for his wisdom, bravery, and justice. Many of his sayings and speeches have been preserved in a book called The Peak of Eloquence (Nahj al-Balagha). He was assassinated by members of a fringe movement while he was praying.

Fatima az-Zahra (562-580) Although not one of the successors, Fatima al-Zahra (peace be upon her) is included in this list because of her high status and importance. Fatima al-Zahra (peace be upon her) was the daughter of the beloved Prophet of Islam (peace be upon him and his family) from his respected wife Khadija. She was born in Mecca on the twentieth day of Jumaada al-Thaani (the sixth month of the Islamic calendar). Although he had several children, Fatima was his favourite, for she was carrying the light of the message of the Prophet (peace be upon him and his family) to the generations to come through her offspring. A chapter of the Quran was revealed about her:

> *Verily We have granted you [Prophet Muhammad] al-kawthar. Therefore, turn in prayer to your Lord and sacrifice for Him. And he who makes you angry-he will be cut off from offspring.*

She and her father had a mutual attachment; 'Aisha, one of the wives of the Prophet (peace be upon him and his family), has said: "I never saw a person who so resembled her father in speech, movements, and gestures more than Fatima, and once she goes to visit her father, he stands, takes her hand, kisses it, and places her in his own seat." Fatima was so emotionally and spiritually close to her father that he declared: "Fatima is part of me. Whoever angers her angers me, and she is the mother of her father." Fatima proved to be the best daughter to her father, mother for her four children (Hasan, Husain, Zaynab, and Um Kalthoum), and the ideal wife for her husband Imam 'Ali (peace be upon him). She was the perfect example of a virtuous, righteous lady in Islam. She set many examples in her social and political life. As a result of the conflict over power after the demise of the Holy Prophet (peace be upon him and his family), Fatima al-Zahra (peace be upon her) died at the age of 18 years.

Imam Hasan ibn 'Ali (625-670)

Imam Husain ibn 'Ali (626-680): Imam Husain (peace be upon him) revolted against the tyrant of his time, Yazid the son of Muawiyah. He left his hometown of Medina to go to the city of Mecca and then with 72 of his followers and close family members to Iraq where he was brutally massacred on the day of Ashura in the city of Karbala, 60 miles to the south of Baghdad. Imam Husain (peace be upon him) stood for truth, sacrificed himself for truth and justice, and fought corruption and aggression. The battle of Karbala represents the battle between truth and falsehood, good versus evil, and justice versus aggression, oppression, and tyranny. Therefore, he became the beacon of light for all free people in this universe, shook the foundations of the Muslim nation with his martyrdom, and steered the consciousness of the Muslim people at that time. Hundreds of revolutions and revolts followed his martyrdom until the corrupt empire of Bani Umayyah collapsed. Imam Husain (peace be upon him) still plays a very significant role in the life of the Muslims in their endeavour to fight injustice and deviation in all societies.

Imam 'Ali Ibn al-Husain (659-713)

Imam Muhammad Al-Baqir (676-733)

Imam Jafar as-Sadiq (702-765): Imam Jafar al-Sadiq (peace be upon him) was the son of Muhammad al-Baqir (peace be upon him) and was the sixth imam of the school of the ahl al-bayt. He was born on the seventeenth day of Rabi' al-Awwal (the third month of the Islamic calendar) in the city of Medina. He learned from his father the sciences of religion and the teachings of Islam and became the authority of jurisprudents, scholars, and preachers after the martyrdom of his father.

He made the mosque of Medina a university from which to spread Islamic ideology and graduated hundreds of scholars versed in Islamic sciences and prophetic traditions.

Scholars and preachers gave their testimonies acknowledging his great standing and abundant knowledge. One of them, Sibt al-Jawzi has said, "Never have I seen scholars less knowledgeable in the presence of a man like al-Sadiq." The men of knowledge and piety saw in Imam Jafar al-Sadiq (peace be upon him) a leader, a scholar, and an unmatched educator. He was also a great social personality and an effective political force in the leading political circles.

Imam al-Sadiq (peace be upon him) taught two of the leaders of the other Islamic schools of jurisprudence: Abu Hanifa (Nu'man ibn Thabit) and Malik ibn Anas. Imam al-Sadiq (peace be upon him) uttered thousands of hadith (Prophetic traditions) regarding every facet of life.

He extensively discussed Islamic ethics, mannerisms, integrity, goodness of character, and acts of worship in addition to jurisprudence and debated with leaders of other schools of thought.

Imam al-Sadiq (peace be upon him) was poisoned by the caliph of his time and was buried in the cemetery of al-Baqi' in Medina.

Imam Musa al-Kazim (746-799)

Imam 'Ali ar-Rida (765-818)

Imam Muhammad al-Jawad (811-835)

Imam 'Ali al-Hadi (827-868)

Imam Hasan al-Askari (846-874)

Imam Muhammad al-Mahdi (869-present): Imam al-Mahdi is the last of the imams of the people on earth, and with him the line of succession to the Holy Prophet (peace be upon him and his family) ends. Because of the necessity of having a representative from Allah present on the earth, he still-by the will of Allah-lives in this world, but he does not live in public view. He will, however, reappear towards the end of human civilization at a time when the world has been filled with evil and injustice to restore order and make justice prevail.

These imams were the authorities of Allah among mankind. Like the Holy Prophet (peace be upon him and his family), they were all special personalities in matters of knowledge, forbearance, morality, and justice.

The Family of the Prophet (Ahl al-Bayt)

The ahl al-bayt are the immediately family of the Prophet Muhammad (peace be upon him and his family), namely: his daughter Fatima al-Zahra; his cousin, son-in-law, and first successor Imam 'Ali; and his grandchildren Hasan and Husain (peace be upon them). The purity of these five is spoken of in the Quran: "Allah only wishes to remove all uncleanliness from you, O People of the House (ahl al-bayt), and to make you as pure as possible." (33:33) Like the prophets and the prophets' successors, these five were infallible, free from all sin or error.

Near the end of his life, Prophet Muhammad (peace be upon him) said: "It is probable that I will be called soon, and I will respond. So I leave behind me among you two weighty things: the Book of Allah [the Quran], and my Ahl al-Bayt. Verily, Allah, the Merciful, the Aware, has informed me that these two will never be separated from each other until they meet me at the fountain in Heaven called Kawthar." The Prophet (peace be upon him and his family) has also said: "The parable of my ahl al-bayt is similar to that of Noah's ark. Whoever embarks on it will certainly be rescued, but whoever opposes the boarding of it will surely be drowned." The necessity of taking hold of both things that the Prophet (peace be upon him and his family) left behind cannot be overemphasized; those who choose to follow the Quran but not the guidance of the ahl al-bayt will invariably go astray.

As a rule, the prophets of Allah did not ask any reward for the pain and suffering they endured while attempting to guide mankind. In fact, this refusal to accept compensation can be seen as the mark of a prophet: "Obey those who ask no reward from you and who have themselves received guidance." (36:21) However, by the command of Allah, Prophet Muhammad (peace be upon him and his family) made one slight exception; although he refused to accept anything for himself, he was commanded to say: "I do not ask you for any reward except love for my relatives [the ahl al-bayt]." (42:23) Love for the Prophet's ahl al-bayt does not benefit the Prophet himself (peace be upon him and his family) so much as it does the one who approaches them with kindness and loyalty and in return derives knowledge, guidance, and blessings from Allah.

Imam 'Ali (peace be upon him) has spoken about the ahl al-bayt:

> *We, the ahl al-bayt, possess the doors of wisdom and light of governance. Beware that the paths of religion are one and its highways are straight. He who follows them achieves and secures the aim and objective. And he who stands away from them goes astray and incurs repentance.*

The example of the descendants of Muhammad-peace and blessing of Allah be upon him and his descendants-is like that of stars in the sky. When one star sets another one rises.

We are lights of the heavens and the earth and the ships of salvation. We are the repository of knowledge, and towards us is the homecoming of all matters. Through our Mahdi (the final successor to the Prophet) all arguments shall be refuted, and he is the seal of the imams, the deliverer of the ummah (the Muslim nation), and the extremity of the light. Happy are those who hold onto our handle and are brought together upon our love.

5. The Day of Judgement and the Resurrection (Qiyamat)

Approximately 1,200 verses of the Quran speak of life after death and the Day of Resurrection, as do a vast number of sayings related from Prophet Muhammad and his successors (peace be upon all of them). This number reveals the importance and significance of life after death and emphasizes that the life of the human being does not end at death but in fact continues afterwards towards a new life-indeed, its true life. Allah placed human beings on the earth to test them, and so different people live for different lengths of time before they die and their souls are separated from their bodies. Their souls then live on, facing the grave and the questioning therein. After that, the souls return to their bodies which will be resurrected on the Day of Judgement, on which day they will receive whatever they deserve according to their beliefs and deeds in life.

Some people will go to Heaven, also called the Garden, or the Paradise. Others will go to Hell, oftentimes called the Fire. And a select few will be brought into a state of nearness to God. Both Heaven and Hell have different levels; the worst of people will be in the lowest depths of Hell, while the best of them will be in the highest parts of Heaven.

Death and Life after Death

And they ask you concerning the spirit. Say: "The spirit, it is one of the things, the knowledge of which is only with my Lord, and of knowledge, you mankind have been given only a little. (17:85)

Although humanity has been permitted to know only a little about life after death right now, the Holy Quran still reveals some of the secrets surrounding the soul. The Quran says:

> *It is Allah who takes away the souls at the time of their death, and those that die not during their sleep. He keeps those souls for which He has ordained death and sends the rest for a term appointed. Verily, in this are signs for people who think deeply. (39:42)*

The soul will be buried along with the body in the grave. It could get permission from Allah to depart from the grave, but it must go back to it again. Each individual, if faithful, faces two paradises after death, or if he is unfaithful and a sinner, two hells. One of them is for the souls before the Day of Judgement, and the second is the permanent abode.

Once Prophet Jesus (peace be upon him) sent two messengers to the city of Antioch to call for monotheism and the worshipping of Allah. One of the men of that town embraced the faith and followed them, so the king of the land ordered that righteous man to be killed. When he died, he said: "Verily I have believed in your Lord. So listen to me. It was said to him when the disbelievers killed him, 'Enter paradise.' He said, Would that my people knew what my Lord Allah has forgiven me for and made me one of the honoured ones.'" (36:25-27) The paradise that he had entered was of the kind, called barzakh, that the soul lives in before the Day of Judgement; on the Day of Judgement everyone will know the fate of everyone else, and there will be no need, as above, to tell others.

The descriptions of both types of hellfire are very vivid and painful: "Evil torment encompassed Pharaoh's people-the fire: they are exposed to it morning and afternoon, and on the day when the Hour will be established." (40:46)

Islam teaches that the parting of the soul is accompanied with severe pain. The moment of death has been described:

Nay! When the soul reaches the collarbone, and it will be said, "Who can cure him and save him from death?" and he, the dying person, will conclude that it is the time of departing, and he is shrouded; the drive on that day will be to your Lord. (75:26-30)

Remember that the two recording angels receive each human being after attaining the age of puberty, one sitting on the right and one on the left, to note his actions. Not a word does he utter but there is a watcher sitting by him to record it. And the stupor of death will come in truth; this is what you have been avoiding. And the trumpet will be blown; that will be the day whereof warning had been given, and every person will come forth with an angel to drive him and an angel to bear witness. It will be said to the sinners: "Indeed, you were heedless of this.

Now We have removed your covering, and sharp is your sight this day." (50:17-22)

But for the true believers, the departure of the soul will be peaceful:

It will be said to the pious: "O you in complete rest and satisfaction, come back to your Lord well-please yourself and well-pleasing unto Him. Enter then among my honoured servants, and enter my Paradise." (89:27-30)

REPENTANCE AND FORGIVENESS

Repentance is the giving up of sin and is the best way of expressing regret for having committed one. It involves both sincerely regretting having committed the particular sin and then resolving never to do it again. Repentance is the source of and means to success: "Turn to Allah, O Believers, that you may be successful." (24:31) No matter how grievous a person's sin may be, the forgiveness of Allah is greater, and no one should be ashamed to turn towards Allah in repentance because Allah can erase the sins of whomever He pleases.

Say: "O My servants who have transgressed against themselves, despair not of the mercy of Allah; verily, Allah forgives all sins. Verily, He is the Forgiving, the Merciful. (39:53)

Tell My servants that I am the Forgiving, the Merciful. (15:49)

Will they not turn to Allah and ask His forgiveness? Allah is the Forgiving, the Merciful. (5:74)

Your Lord is full of forgiveness for mankind in spite of their wrongdoing. (13:6)

Despite His ability to destroy mankind if he so willed, the main characteristics of Allah are forgiveness and mercifulness, and for this reason Muslims begin nearly every action, speech, or endeavour with the words, "In the name of Allah, the most Merciful, the most Compassionate."

Repentance is of benefit both now and during the Hereafter. Prophet Muhammad (peace be upon him and his family) has narrated that repenting brings an increase of wealth, protection from danger, and an easing of hardships and difficulties.

Furthermore, it has been said that the fastest way to attain nearness to Allah is to humble the self before Allah and admit to wrongdoing. The benefits of repentance for the next life are obvious-entrance into Paradise and safety from the Hellfire.

Repentance will be accepted up until the moment of death. Prophet Muhammad (peace be upon him and his family) once said that if a person seeks repentance one year before dying, Allah will accept it. Even if a person seeks repentance one day before dying, Allah will accept it. Then he pointed to his throat and said that even if someone seeks repentance before his soul reaches here, Allah will accept it.

Nonetheless, repentance should be done as soon as possible and should not be delayed; this point has been emphasized again and again in the Islamic tradition. Imam 'Ali says: "How numerous are the procrastinators who postpone [repenting and doing good deeds] until death overtakes them!"

Repentance should be done in secrecy and privacy. People can establish a direct link to Allah while seeking repentance without the necessity of a third person interfering and in fact should not let others know about their sins. Prophet Muhammad (peace be upon him and his family) once told Imam 'Ali (peace be upon him): "O 'Ali, blessed is he whom Allah looks upon while he is weeping for the sin that none is aware of except Allah."

In addition to not revealing his own sins, every person must conceal the faults of his brother or sister in religion to preserve that person's honour and society. That person's faults may be dealt with personally and privately but must not be spread among society.

A person who sincerely repents is loved by Allah and is as if he or she had never committed any sins at all. Imam al-Baqir (peace be upon him) has said: "He who repents of his sins is as one who has not any burden of sin." But repentance must be sincere; Allah knows who sincerely regrets misdeeds and who is just saying words. A person came to Imam 'Ali (peace be upon him) and said, "Astaghfirullah, I seek Allah's forgiveness," and the Imam (peace be upon him) replied:

Do you know what asking Allah's forgiveness is? It is a word that stands on six supports. The first is to repent over the past. The second is to make a firm determination never to revert to it. The third is to discharge all the rights of people so that you may meet Allah quite clean with nothing to account for. The fourth is to fulfill every obligation which you ignored in the past so that you may now be just with it. The fifth is to aim at the flesh grown as a result of unlawful earning so that you may melt it by grief of repentance till the skin touches the bone and a new flesh grows between them. And the sixth is to make the body taste the pain of obedience as you previously made it taste the sweetness of disobedience. On such an occasion, you may say, "I seek Allah's forgiveness."

RELIGIOUS TEXTS

The Quran

The Quran is the last in a series of divine books revealed by Allah to mankind through the prophets. The Holy Quran was revealed to Prophet Muhammad (peace be upon him and his family) over a period of 23 years and consists of 114 chapters arranged from longest to shortest. Its length compares to that of the New Testament. The revelations were written down by a group of people appointed by the Prophet (peace be upon him and his family) and, after his death, first compiled by Imam 'Ali (peace be upon him).

The Quran sheds light on many different aspects of life-legal, moral, social, political, economic, philosophical, mystical, and scientific-and also contains stories of previous prophets. "We have sent down to you the Book as an exposition of everything-a guidance, a mercy, and glad tidings for those who have submitted themselves to Allah as Muslims." (16:89) Less rigid than poetry but more beautiful than prose, its peculiar music transcends all other forms of writing. It speaks only the truth, and its directives are universal for all places and times. In reality, it is the completion of the earlier revelations, such as the Old and New Testaments, and is the only divine revelation to exist in its original unchanged form: "Verily, it is We Who have sent down the Quran, and surely We will guard it from corruption." (15:9) From the time of the Prophet (peace be upon him and his family) until today, not one word of the Quran has been edited, altered, added, omitted, lost, distorted, or otherwise changed.

The Quran plays an important role in Muslim life. It constantly reminds Muslims of their duties, rights, obligations, and destiny. Muslims are asked to study, memorize, ponder, and reflect on the Quran and then to implement its teachings. The chapters of the Quran contain the supreme divine wisdom which is meant for all seekers of truth-ordinary people, scholars, specialists, old, young, Muslims, and non-Muslims. It addresses all mankind; specific verses even clarify this fact by beginning with the words, "O mankind!" The Quran satisfies people with its symphony of words, its science, its narrations and intellectual discourse, and fascinates them with its richness and depth.

Science and the Quran

Many scientific facts and realities are present in the Quran, which is the only religious book not to contradict science. Creation is described on the embryological and cosmological levels:

"And indeed We created man out of an extract of clay. Thereafter, We made him as mixed drops of the male and female fluids and lodged him in a safe lodging (womb of the mother). Then We made the mixed drops into a clot (a piece of thick coagulated blood). Then We made the clot into a little lump of flesh. Then We made out of that little lump of flesh bones. Then We clothed the bones with flesh. And then We brought it forth as another creation. So blessed be Allah, the best of creators." (23:12-14)

A careful comparison of this verse with the actual details of embryological development will reveal no contradictions. The creation of life, the earth, and the universe is also described in a way that parallels modern scientific theory:

"Do not those who disbelieve know that the heavens and the earth were joined together as one united piece, then We parted them? And We have made from water every living thing. Will they then not believe? And We have placed on the earth firm mountains, lest it should shake with them, and We placed therein broad highways for them to pass through that they may be guided, and We have made the heaven a roof, safe, and well-guarded. Yet they turn away from its signs. And He it is Who has created the night and the day, and the sun and the moon, each in an orbit floating" (21:30-33)

Human beings are asked to ponder the creation of the universe and consider their role therein: Verily, in the creation of the heavens and the earth, and in the alternation of night and day there are indeed signs for men of understanding-those who remember Allah always, standing, sitting, and lying down on their sides, and think deeply about the creation of the heavens and the earth, saying, "O Lord! You have not created all this without purpose! Glory be to You! Give us salvation from the torment of the fire." (3:190)

Are you more difficult to create or the heavens above? (79:27)

Many of the chapters are named after cosmological objects such as "The Star" and "The Sun", the latter of which begins:

By the sun and its brightness, and by the moon as it follows it, and by the day as it shows up in the sun's brightness, and by the night as it conceals it, and by the heavens and Him who built it, and by the earth and Him who spread it....

Although the people of the Prophet's time knew nothing about the lifetimes or mechanisms of the sun and stars, the Quran refers to the fact that stars exist for a fixed period of time: And the sun runs on its fixed course for a term appointed. That is the decree of the Almighty, the Omniscient. And the moon, We have measured for it mansions to traverse till it returns like the old dried curved date-stalk. It is not for the sun to overtake the moon, nor does the night outstrip the day. They all swim each in an orbit. (36:38)

Even the expansion of the universe is alluded to: "With power did We construct the heavens; verily, We are able to expand the vastness of space thereof." (51:47)

The end of this universe, too, is described: And remember the day when We will roll up the heavens like a scroll rolled up for books. As We began the first creation, We shall repeat it. It is a promise binding upon Us. Truly, We shall do it. (21:104)

When the sun has wound around and lost its light and has been overthrown, and when the stars shall fall, and when the mountains shall be made to pass away... And when the seas shall become a blazing far or shall overflow.... (81:1-3,6)

When the Heaven is cleft asunder, and when the stars have fallen and scattered, and when the seas have burst forth.... (82:1-3)

When the Event befalls-and there can be no denying its befalling-it will bring low some, and others it will exalt. When the earth will be shaken with a terrible shaking, and the mountains will be powdered to dust so that they will become floating dust particles.... (56:1-6)

And they ask you concerning the mountains. Say, "My Lord will blast them and scatter them as particles of dust; then He shall leave it as a smooth, level plain. You will see therein nothing crooked or curved." (20:105-107)

The Quran does not contradict science because Allah Who revealed the Quran is the same Allah Who made this creation.

The Qualities of the Quran

And know that this Quran is an adviser who never deceives, a leader who never misleads, and a narrator who never speaks a lie. No one will sit beside this Quran but that when he rises he will achieve one addition or one diminution-addition in his guidance and elimination in his (spiritual) blindness. You should also know that no one will need any thing after (guidance from) the Quran and no one will be free from want before (guidance from) the Quran. Therefore, seek cure from it for your ailments and seek its assistance in your distresses. It contains a cure for the biggest diseases, namely, unbelief, hypocrisy, revolt, and misguidance. Pray to Allah through it and turn to Allah with its love. Do not ask the people through it. There is nothing like it through which the people should turn to Allah, the Sublime.

The Dua, or Supplications to God

Supplications and prayers (*dua*) focus on the idea that human beings are in constant need of God. Even those who reach the peak of wealth, knowledge, strength, and dignity still are in need of God. The word *dua* itself means to call out to God, and *dua* is of equal importance to those inflicted by calamities and hardships and to those living in comfort and abundance. Speaking with Allah through *dua* defends against adversity and tribulation and leads to salvation and relief.

Islam encourages its followers to offer *dua* constantly, either using their own words, directly from the heart, or else repeating some of the beautiful words that have been left behind by the Prophet (peace be upon him and his family) and his successors (peace be upon them).

Allah has guaranteed His servants that He will answer their prayers:

When My servants ask you concerning Me, I am indeed close to them. I listen to the prayer of every suppliant when he calls upon Me. Let them also with a will listen to My call and believe in Me that they walk in the right way. (2:186)

And your Lord says, "Call on me, I will answer your prayer." (40:60)

Dua Kumail

A man named Kumail ibn Ziyad once asked Imam 'Ali (peace be upon him) for a way to approach Allah. In response, Imam 'Ali (peace be upon him) gave him this prayer and told him to recite it every day, if he could, or else once a week, or even once a year-and if reciting it once a year was too difficult, then to recite it at least once in his lifetime. Muslims usually recite it once a week together on Thursday night:

In the name of Allah, the Beneficent, the Merciful

O Allah, I ask You by Your Mercy which embraces all things,

By Your Strength, through which You dominate all things, towards which all things are humble, and before which all things are lowly;

By Your Invincibility, through which You overwhelm all things;

By Your Might, which nothing can resist;

By Your Greatness, which has filled all things;

By Your Power, which towers over all things;

By Your Face, which subsists after annihilation of all things;

By Your Names, which have filled the foundations of all things;

By Your Knowledge, which encompasses all things; and

By the Light of Your Face, through which all things are illumined!

O Light! O All-Holy!

O First of the first and Last of the Last!

O Allah, forgive me the sins which tear apart safeguards!

O Allah, forgive me the sins which bring down adversities!

O Allah, forgive me the sins which alter blessings!

O Allah, forgive me the sins which hold back supplication!

O Allah, forgive me the sins which dash all hopes!

O Allah, forgive me the sins which bring about tribulation!

O Allah, forgive me ever sin I have committed and every mistake I have made!

O Allah, verily I seek nearness to You through remembrance of You, I seek intercession from You with Yourself, and I ask You through Your Munificence, to bring me nearer to Your Mercy, to bless me with gratitude to You and to inspire me with Your remembrance....

8

Other Islamic Issues

Leadership of the Muslims after Prophet Muhammad (Peace be Upon Him and His Family)

The Quran emphasizes the role and significance of leadership in Islam. Allah states: "And remember the day on which we will call together all human beings with their leaders (imams)." (17:71)

Therefore, Prophet Muhammad (peace be upon him and his family) was very keen on appointing a successor after himself by the command of his Lord. Allah commands the Prophet (peace be upon him and his family): "O Prophet! Proclaim what has been revealed to you from your Lord [the succession of Imam 'Ali], for if you do not, you will not have conveyed His message, and Allah will protect you from the people." (5:67)

This event has been remembered as the event of Ghadir Khum, which was the name of a place intersecting Mecca and Medina, and occurred when the Prophet (peace be upon him and his family)was concluding his Hajj rites and heading back with 110,000 companions. When he received the command of Allah, he immediately appointed Imam 'Ali (peace be upon him) as his successor after his death. In approval, the Quran says: "This day, I have perfected your religion for you, completed my favour on you, and have chosen for you Islam as your religion." (5:3)

All the companions of the Prophet (peace be upon him and his family) paid allegiance to Imam 'Ali (peace be upon him) and accepted him as the first caliph after the Holy Prophet (peace be upon him and his family).

However, only 70 days after this monumental incident, the Prophet Muhammad (peace be upon him and his family) left this life, and the first setback to his teachings occurred when the Muslims did not honour their allegiance to Allah to accept Imam 'Ali (peace be upon him) as the first caliph. Confusion and disarray overtook the Muslims regarding who should succeed the Prophet (peace be upon him and his family) as leader of the Muslim community. In a hasty meeting at Saqifa Bani Saida in Medina, Abu Bakr assumed leadership (632-634), followed by 'Umar ibn al-Khattab (634-644), 'Uthman ibn 'Affan (644-656), and finally 'Ali ibn Abi Talib (656-661).

After the khilafa of 'Ali (peace be upon him), two dynasties followed--the Umayyids and the Abbasids--before massive political changes overtook the Islamic world.

Social Life in Islam

Islam places tremendous emphasis on the social aspect of life. The Islamic practices have not only spiritual dimensions but also social ones. For example, Islam encourages people to perform their daily prayers in congregation; Prophet Muhammad (peace be upon him and his family) has said: "One prayer of a man in congregation is worthier than his forty years of prayers at home alone." Praying in congregation strengthens the ties between people by giving them the opportunity to interact with each other and discuss their issues in a holy place. Once a blind man came to the Prophet (peace be upon him and his family) and said that there was no one to take him to the mosque to attend the congregational prayer.

Prophet Muhammad (peace be upon him and his family) told him to stretch a thread from his house to the mosque and use it to go to the mosque to attend the congregational prayer. Similarly, fasting has many social aspects: it causes Muslims to feel the starvation and the agony of the poor and deprived in society and encourages them to extend their hands in help towards them. The Hajj undoubtedly is the largest religious and social convention bringing millions of people from around the globe into one arena to strengthen their ties, develop their skills, and exchange ideas and opinions as to how to improve their situations. Khums and zakaat (charity) also play an important social role in Islam by causing Muslims to think that they themselves are responsible for bridging the gap between the rich and the poor as well as for sharing their own wealth with the needy and disadvantaged in society. Enjoining the good and forbidding the evil is a social responsibility which falls on the shoulders of each and every individual in the Islamic society to promote goodness, kindness, peace and justice and to fight oppression, corruption, and evil. Therefore, Islam is truly a social religion.

Marriage and Family Life

Another aspect of Islamic sociality is marriage and establishing families. Islam encourages its followers to get married and avoid celibacy; Prophet Muhammad (peace be upon him and his family) has said: "The person who marries gains half of his faith; then he must fear of Allah for the next remaining half." In another saying, the Holy Prophet has said: "He who wishes to be clean and purified when he meets Allah should marry and have a spouse."

The Quran describes the union between man and woman:

"And among His signs is that he created for you spouses from among yourselves that you may dwell in tranquility with them, and He has put love and mercy between your hearts. Verily, in that are signs for those who reflect." (30:21)

This verse establishes the three pillars of a successful marriage. First, it should provide emotional and social shelter ("dwell in tranquility") whereby the husband and the wife find stability and financial, spiritual, emotional, and social security. The second pillar of a successful marriage is the love between the spouses. Marriage which is not based on love is apt to fail at any time. And the third pillar is the mercy between the spouses which leads to mutual understanding, appreciation, respect, and care for each other.

Although heavily discouraged, divorce is permissible in Islam. It exists as a safety valve for a failed marriage which has no possibility of progress or development. Allah does not want a couple to remain in misery and sustain emotional, physical, and financial damage. Thus, Allah explains the laws and rules of divorce in a chapter of the Quran called "Divorce."

Islam encourages reconciliation between the spouses, and their families and friends have the responsibility to help them with this as much as possible, but if this process ultimately fails then the last resort is divorce. After divorce, there is a waiting period for women to consider their life and the fate of their children. Most people go back to their spouses sometime during this waiting period, but if it elapses and the two people show no interest in returning to each other, then the divorce will be finalized.

Part of Islamic social life is to have regard for kinship; he who wishes his sustenance to be increased and his death day to be delayed should pay attention to his kinsfolk. Kindness and respect for one's parents holds a high place in Islam:

The Lord has decreed that you worship none but Him, and that you be kind to your parents, whether one or both of them attains old age in your life. Say not to them a word of contempt nor repel them, but address them in terms of honour, and out of kindness lower to them the wing of humility and say, "My Lord, bestow on them Thy mercy, even as they cherished me in childhood." (23:24)

Respect and kindness towards parents is as important as worship. Imam al-Sadiq (peace be upon him) has said: "He who glares at his parents with wrathful eyes, although they have been unjust to him, Allah will not accept his prayers unless he repents." Respecting one's mother is particularly important; the Prophet (peace be upon him and his family) said: "Treat kindly your mother. Treat kindly your mother. Treat kindly your mother, and be kind to your father."

Imam al-Sadiq (peace be upon him) has narrated: He who wishes Allah, Almighty and Glorious, to lighten the agonies of death should have regard for his kinship and treat his parents with goodness. Then Allah will make the agonies of death easy for him, and he will not be stricken by poverty in his life at all.

In general, human beings should all serve one another whether they are related or not. Prophet Muhammad (peace be upon him and his family) has said: "He who decreases a grief out of the agonies for his Muslim brother, Allah will decrease for him a grief out of the agonies of the hereafter." He (peace be upon him and his family) also said: "People are the dependants of Allah for sustenance. So the most beloved person with Allah is the one who is helpful to the dependents of Allah and makes the family members of a house happy." As a social responsibility, Islam also encourages its followers to help the needy; Imam al-Sadiq (peace be upon him) has said:

Whoever satiates a hungry believer so that the one is satisfied fully, neither a human being among people nor a near-stationed angel nor a divine messenger knows how great his reward is in the Hereafter except Allah, the Lord of the Worlds.

And

Feeding a hungry Muslim is among the means of forgiveness.

Even those who are not indigent should still be helped in any way possible: "He who is referred to by his Muslim brother [to borrow] but does not give him a loan, Allah will forbid him from entering Paradise on the day when the righteous will be recompensed."

Women in Islam

Islam equalizes men and women on the following issues: creation, religious obligations, honour and dignity. However, there are natural differences in the peculiarities of each gender. The female as a mother differs in her personality and peculiarities from the man as a father. For each one of them, there is a specified message in life.

The Holy Quran declares that men and women are born equal. It gives women such rights as owning property, engaging in businesses, choosing a husband, claiming inheritance, receiving education, and being treated with respect. An entire chapter of the Quran (chapter 4) discusses women's' rights in the society. It starts by addressing people: "O Mankind! Be dutiful to your Lord Who created you from a single soul, and He created its mate out of it, and from them both He created many men and women."

Some of the verses equalizing men and women are as follows:

There is a share for men and a share for women from what is left by parents and those nearest related, whether the property be small or large (5:7)

O You who believe, you are forbidden to inherit women against their will, and you should not treat them with harshness, and live with them honourably. If you dislike them, it may be that you dislike a thing and that Allah brings through it a great deal of good. (4:19)

For men there is reward for what they have earned, and for women there is reward for what they have earned. (4:32)

Whoever works righteousness, whether male or female, while he or she is a true believer, verily to him We will give a good life in this world, with respect, contentment, and lawful provision, and We shall certainly pay them a reward in proportion to the best of what they used to do. (16:97)

Islam grants women full political, financial, social, and educational rights in society. Women have the right to vote in Islam, and to participate in the democratic process. "O Prophet! When believing women come to you to give you political and religious allegiance... then accept their allegiance, and ask Allah to forgive them; verily, Allah is Oft-Forgiving, most Mericiful." (60:12) Women should also have the full right to choose their own husbands without pressure or intimidation. Arranged marriages in the sense of women being dragged into marriages that they are unaware of or dislike are unlawful in Islam.

Women have the right to participate in the educational and cultural activities as well as religious and spiritual endeavours. No field is closed to women unless it interferes with their dignity, respect, and chastity in society. Therefore, Islam does forbid women to display their attractions and physical appearance in society and calls for modesty and conservatism in their behaviour and dress, as well as loyalty to the family, ideals which Islam also enjoins upon men as well. Women are instructed to cover modestly which includes covering the hair as well as the rest of the body except the hands and the face.

HUMAN RIGHTS IN ISLAM

Islam has laid down fundamental, universal rights for humanity which are to be observed and respected in all circumstances. These rights are those which were specified and granted by Allah and apply to all human beings, not just

Muslims. An integral part of the Islamic faith is to accept, recognize, and enforce these human rights. The verdict in the Quran is unequivocal for those who fail to do so: "Those who do not judge by what God has sent down are the disbelievers." (5:44)

The rights guaranteed by Islam and the Quran include: the right to life, the right to safety, respect for women's honour and dignity, the right to a basic standard of life, the right to individual freedom, the right to justice, and the inherent equality of human beings.

Mosques (Masjid)

Mosques are places of worship used by Muslims. Islam encourages people to perform their prayers in mosques and also encourages people to participate in building mosques. Prophet Muhammad (peace be upon him and his family) has said: "Whoever builds a mosque, Allah will build for him a house in Paradise." The mosque plays a vital role in Muslim life; in addition to the five daily congregational prayers and the recommended prayers, the mosque also accommodates Muslims during the Friday noon prayers and on the 'eid holidays. Therefore, the mosque is considered a sacred place, and it should not be sold or defiled, and men and women who are ritually impure may not enter.

The first mosque built by Prophet Muhammad (peace be upon him and his family) was called Kaaba and was located in the outskirts in the city of Medina, while the first house of worship built on earth was al-masjid al-haram, the sacred mosque in Mecca. This mosque is the holiest of the mosques, the second holiest being the Prophet's Mosque in Medina which was built after the Prophet's migration from Mecca to Medina.

Mosques have many distinctive features. There are the musallah, or prayer hall; the minbar, or pulpit, where the preacher or imam stands to deliver his sermon; the mihrab, the niche which faces the direction of the Kaaba in Makka (al-qiblah); and also there are minarets and domes from which the call to prayers is raised.

Before entering mosques, the shoes must be removed, and women should be dressed conservatively (this includes covering the head). Neither men nor women should carry on loud conversations inside. Mosques belong to Allah, not to specific individuals, families, communities, or tribes: "And the mosques are for Allah alone, so invoke not anyone along with Allah." (72:18) And Allah encourages people to construct and fill mosques: "The mosques of Allah shall be maintained only by those who believe in Allah and the last day, perform prayers, and give zakaat and fear none but Allah. It is they who surely are on true guidance." (9:18) Hence, barring people from conducting their worshipping in the mosque is considered a grave sin in Islam: "And who is more unjust than those who forbid that Allah's name be glorified and mentioned much in Allah's mosques and strive for their ruin?" (2:114)

Allah exists everywhere and throughout all time, and the Quran states: "To Allah belong the East and the West, so wherever you turn your face there is the face of Allah." (2:115) Nevertheless, as a sign of unity Muslims are instructed to face the qiblah, the direction of the Kaaba in Mecca, during prayer.

Islamic Law and Punishment

Before speaking of the law and punishment in Islam, many premises must be introduced regarding Islamic jurisprudence. Islamic ideology stipulates that Allah is the main source of Islamic law. These laws were revealed to all divine messengers in different eras and geographical places in accordance with the intellectual progress of the various societies, and reached their perfection through the Holy Quran which carries a universal message for mankind. Therefore, the Islamic law is not bound by time and place and is designed to cater to the different needs of the human race until eternity.

The Islamic law of punishment is based on prevention, not retribution-meaning that Islam cares to prevent criminal acts before they happen and disrupt the peace of society. These laws are dynamic, everlasting, and not bound by individualistic interests. They take into consideration the general interest of society. Allah speaks about the punishment of the criminals by saying: "O you who believe, the law of equality in punishment is prescribed for you in case of murder, but if the killer is forgiven by the relatives of the killed against blood money, then adhering to it with fairness and payment of the blood money to the heir should be made in fairness. This is an alleviation and a mercy from your Lord." (2:178) Although Islam tries to combat crime and terror with full seriousness, it leave room for mercy and forgiveness, emphasizing the human nature of people and that they should learn mercy and forgiveness from their Lord.

However, Islam has to be introduced as a whole to the people, and to incorporate Islam in all aspects of life, not only in the judicial system. Islam invites the rulers and the subjects alike to spread social justice, equality, and distribution of wealth in society. Once every individual in society has adequate food, shelter, clothing, and opportunities for work, education, and marriage and the gap between the haves and the have-nots has been bridged-then if an individual or group of people tries to jeopardize the safety and security of society and terrorize the people, then in this case Islam would stand firmly in their face and the law of punishment would be exercised.

RELIGION

Religion refers to the beliefs and a series of practical and moral instructions that the prophets have related on behalf of Allah to guide and lead human beings.

Believing in these tenets and performing these instructions result in man's prosperity and happiness in this world and in the world Hereafter.

So if we abide by religion and follow the orders of Allah and the Prophet (SA), we will become prosperous not only in this short life, but also in the everlasting and endless world Hereafter.

We are aware that a happy and prosperous person is one who has a true objective in his life and who does not live in misdeed and aberration. He possesses a good and praiseworthy demeanour and performs good deeds and has a confident, strong, and peaceful heart in this turbulent world.

The religion of Allah directs us towards this happiness and prosperity. Without religion, there would be no prosperity and bliss. Religious tenets are like secret police in the heart of man and always accompany him. They keep man away from moral wickedness and force him to be virtuous.

Belief is the strongest and most solid refuge in which man never confronts fear and anguish in the ups and downs of life. The worshippers of Allah never lose their courage in any circumstances and never feel disdain and inferior, for they see themselves connected to the infinite might of the Creator of the world and under all circumstances, they remember Allah and seek refuge with Allah; they possess a confident, strong, and peaceful heart.

Religion commands us to have a praiseworthy behaviour and to perform good and decent deeds as far as we can.

Therefore, religion is divided into three parts:

(1) Beliefs;

(2) Ethics; and

(3) Commandments.

This brief account should be elaborated to be acceptable to the honourable readers.

1. Beliefs

If we use our commonsense and conscience, we realize that this world of existence with its wonderful order could not be created by itself and this astonishing order of the world of creation could not be achieved without an organizer. Undoubtedly, there is a Creator Who has created this vast and magnificent world with His infinite capability and knowledge and who has established the world of creation with exact order by the invariable and unchangeable rules that He has set up throughout the world of existence. Nothing has been created uselessly and extravagantly. No creature falls outside the purview of the laws of Allah that govern the world.

Can it be believed that such a compassionate Allah with all the grace and blessings that He has toward His creatures would leave man, the masterpiece creation, on his own? And that He would leave human beings to man's wisdom which is mostly victim of carnal desires and is, as a result, faced with aberration and misery? The reply to this question is self-evident.

Consequently, Allah must send instructions to human beings by prophets-who are free from any kind of sin and error-to lead men to happiness and prosperity by following them.

We realize that in this world, the signs and valuable benefits of adherence to religious principles do not become completely evident. Neither the righteous are rewarded, nor the criminals and oppressors are punished for their deeds.

From this, we understand that another world must exist where people's deeds are closely investigated, so that if one has done a charitable act, he would be rewarded or if he has committed an indecent deed, he would be castigated. Religion encourages people with these tenets and other rightful beliefs, which will later be thoroughly discussed in this book, and warns them of paganism and ignorance.

2. Ethics

Religion decrees that we adopt praiseworthy qualities in life, have a good nature, and accomplish ourselves with good and commendable attributes. We must be conscientious, benevolent, philanthropic, kind, faithful, good-natured, pleasing to meet, and just.

We must defend our own rights. We must !lot transgress our own limits and rights and should not encroach upon the property, reputation, and lives of people. In search of knowledge and civility, we must not spare any effort for self-sacrifice and self-denial whatsoever. Finally, we must have equality and moderation in all affairs of life.

3. Commandments

Religion decrees that we perform acts that are beneficial to ourselves and to our society during our life and refrain from acts that cause corruption and immorality. It also teaches us to engage in reciting salat (prayers), observing sawm (fasting), and performing similar other duties which are signs of servitude and obedience towards Allah.

These are the laws and instructions the religion offers and invites us to perform. As it is evident, some of them are doctrinal, others ethical, and some others practical. As mentioned before, acceptance and performance of these principles is the only means of happiness and prosperity, for we are aware that man should be nothing but realistic and should live with good ethics and praiseworthy deeds.

IS IT NECESSARY FOR MAN TO FOLLOW A RELIGION?

The foremost question that comes up here is "what is the relation of men's lives with religion and piety?" Is it not possible for a human society to continue its humanitarian existence without religion and faith in Allah? Is it not that a religious person is one who proves Allah's existence and performs specific acts for His satisfaction?

It is possible that in the society, according to the laws enacted by human beings, the duty of each member of the society determines the benefit and the loss. In this case, the laws of men replace religious laws and there will be no need for religion. But with little attention and deliberation on Islamic commandments and regulations, the opposite of this is proved, for Islam has not been concerned only with praying to and praising Allah, rather it has enacted comprehensive instructions and specific regulations for all individual and social positions of man. Islam has considered the vast world of humanity in an astonishing manner and has enacted suitable regulations in accordance with man's individual and social actions and otherwise. Finally, Islam has provided and guaranteed the happiness and prosperity of the members of social community in every respect and to the maximum extent possible. Every just person acknowledges that the laws sprang from man's limited thoughts and knowledge cannot equal those of religion. This power of the Almighty Allah has described the religion of Islam in the Holy Quran. As examples, we will cite few verses here:

> *"Surely the (true) religion with Allah is Islam, and those to whom the Book had been given did not show opposition but after knowledge had come to them, out of envy among themselves: and whoever disbelieves in the communications of Allah then surely Allah is quick in reckoning (3:19)."*

The religion towards which all prophets have invited people consists of theism and submission to Allah's orders. Though the religious scholars specified right through wrong, they did not accept what was rightful due to their prejudice and animosity. Each scholar adopted a specific course of action; as a result, different religions came into existence on earth. In fact, this category of people did not believe in the Divine verses. Allah will soon retribute their deeds.

"And whoever desires a religion other than Islam, it shall not be accepted from him and in the Hereafter he shall be one of the losers (3:85)."

"O you who believe! enter into submission one and all, and do not follow the footsteps of Shaytan (satan); surely he is your open enemy (2:208)."

"And fulfil the covenant of Allah when you have made a covenant, and do not break the oaths after making them fast, and you have indeed made Allah a surety for you; surely Allah knows what you do (16:91)."

The purpose of this verse is to indicate that any Muslim who makes a promise to Allah or to people must keep it and must not breach it.

"Call to the way of your Lord with wisdom and goodly exhortation, and have debates with them in the best manner; surely your Lord best knows those who go astray from His path, and He knows best those who follow the right way (16:125)."

This refers to the fact that to promote religion, a Muslim must converse with people according to their understanding and in a way that is beneficial to them. However, if he fails to guide a person through logic and advice then he must debate in the best manner, which is one of the means of proving something, to guide him towards truth.

"And when the Quran is recited, then listen to it and remain silent, that mercy may be shown to you (7:204)."

"O you who believe! Obey Allah and obey the Prophet and those in authority from among you; then if you quarrel about anything, refer it to Allah and the Prophet, if you believe in Allah and the Last Day; this is better and very good in the end (4:59)."

This verse means that in an Islamic society, disputes can only be settled by the Quran and the Hadith of the Prophet (SA). Every difference must be settled by these two factors. If a Muslim settles differences by the logic of reason, this is due to the fact that the Quran has accepted the rule of logic.

"Thus, it is due to mercy from Allah that you deal with them gently, and had you been rough, hard-hearted, they would certainly have dispersed from around you; pardon them therefore and ask pardon for them, and take counsel with them in the affair; so when you have decided, then place your trust in Allah; surely Allah loves those who trust (3:159)."

Good behaviour, benevolence, and taking counsel in the affairs result in fellowship and kindness. Members of the society must respect their leader to be influenced by him. Allah orders the honourable leader of the Muslims to be benevolent and to take counsel.

But since it is possible that people may make mistakes in their decisions, Allah orders the leader to be independent in his decision after taking counsel and to have trust in Allah, because no one can oppose Allah's will.

In like manner, the Almighty Allah introduces Judaism and Christianity with their Divine books of Tawrat (Old Testament) and the Injil (Bible) and their social precepts and provisions as:

"And how do they make you a judge and they have the Tawrat wherein is Allah's judgement... Surely We revealed Tawrat in which was guidance and light; with it the prophets who submitted themselves (to Allah) judged (matters) for those who were Jews, and the masters of divine knowledge and the doctors... And We sent after them in their footsteps 'Isa (Jesus), son of Maryam (Mary)... and We gave him the Injil in which was guidance and light, and verifying what was before it of Tawrat... And the followers of the Injil should have judged by what Allah revealed in it... And We have revealed to you the Book with the truth, verifying what is before it of the Book and a guardian over it, therefore judge between them by what Allah has revealed...(5:43-48)."

Tawrat and Injil which are now in the hands of the Jews and Christians emphasize this point, because the Tawrat contains many legal and judicial provisions and apparently the Injil confirms and certifies the religious laws of Tawrat.

Conclusion

From the aforementioned statement, it becomes evident that religion as viewed by the Quran is the same as the method of living from which man cannot escape. The difference between religion and a social law is that religion is descended by the Almighty Allah, whereas social laws spring from people's minds. In other words, religion unites man's social life with his worship and obedience of the Almighty Allah, while no attempt at such unity is made by social laws.

QURAN'S TEACHINGS ABOUT THE CREATOR OF THE WORLD

The Existence of the Creator

"... Is there doubt about Allah, the Maker of the heavens and the earth... (14:10)?"

Explanation: In daylight, everything is visible. We can see ourselves, others, houses, city, desert, mountains, jungle, and sea. But when the darkness of night prevails, all these bright and evident things lose their brightness. Then we realize that this brightness did not belong to them, rather it was due to the sun which illuminated them by a kind of contact. The sun is bright and, with its reflection, makes the earth and all that is on it bright and visible. If these objects had a brightness of their own, they would never lose it.

Human beings and other living beings perceive objects by their eyes, ears, and senses. They em bark on activities by their hands, feet, and other internal and external organs. After a while, however, they lose their senses and motions and no longer show any movement or activity and apparently die.

By witnessing this scene, we come to the conclusion that the intellect, determination, and movement of these living beings are not due to their posture and figure, rather they spring from their soul and psyche. When their soul goes out they lose their livelihood and activity.

For example, if seeing and hearing were done only by the eyes and ears, these activities would continue so long as these two organs existed, but this is not the case at all. In like manner, if the undoubted existence and genesis of the vast world of existence, of which we are a part and can never doubt its existence, sprang from and belonged to itself, it would never lose them. In spite of this, we see that the components of the world lose their existence vitality one after another and are incessantly in the state of change and transformation. They replace one condition by another and assume another shape.

For this reason, one must decisively judge that the existence and genesis of all living things originate from something else which is their Creator and Generator. As soon as the Creator cuts off relation of creation with something, that object plunges into annihilation and obliteration and becomes invisible.

That Infinite Existence, which is the support of the world of creation and the Preserver of people, is Allah.

There is no annihilation and obliteration for Allah; otherwise, like all other living beings, His existence would not have been from itself and would have been dependent on others.

Quran and Tawhid

If with a pure nature and peaceful heart, man glances at the world of existence, he will see proofs and signs for the pure existence of the Creator in its nooks and corners. He will find evidences from every place to back up this truth. In this world, everything that man faces is either a phenomenon created by Allah or possesses a characteristic endowed by Allah or is a system that runs and governs everything by Allah's command. Man is one such being and his entire body attests this fact. Neither does man's existence belong to himself nor are the traits that he manifests based on his will. Man has neither devised the plan of life that he takes up from the beginning of his life, nor can he consider this system based on chance and accident and, therefore, cut off. Man cannot attribute his existence and the system of his existence to the environment in which he came into being. This is because the existence of the above-mentioned environment and the system that governs it are not made by that environment and have not evolved by chance and accident.

Thus man has no choice but to prove an origin for the world of creation. This origin creates and fosters things. It gives life to every being and leads it in the path of survival to its specific perfection by a particular system. When man sees that the creation of objects is related and a unified system exists in the world, he is forced to accept that the source of creation and manager of its system is no one except Allah.

The Holy Quran states:

"If there had been in them any gods except Allah, they would both have certainly been in a state of disorder... (21:22)."

Explanation: If many gods governed the world and, as idolaters say, different gods ran various parts of the world, then the earth, heavens, seas, and jungles would each have a god for its own. As a result of the differences among such gods, various systems would be established in the world, so that inevitably the world would face corruption and annihilation. However, we see that all components of the world have complete relation and harmony with one another and comprise a system. Thus, it must be said that there is no partner for the Providence and Creator of the world.

Some might assume that since the supposed gods are wise and aware that their differences lead the world toward annihilation and corruption, they never differ with each other. But this is a depraved assumption because Allah, Who governs the world of existence or a part of it and Whose activity and motion are for the system of creation, performs no mental activity like us.

From the first day that our eyes open upon the world of creation and view the system at work in it, we acquire mental impressions from this system. These constitute our knowledge. Then as we work to provide our basic needs, we coordinate our action with our mental impressions to make it correspond to the prevalent system of creation. For example, we eat to satisfy our hunger. To quench our thirst, we drink water. To be relieved from cold and heat, we wear suitable clothes, because we realize that these exigencies are satisfied by such means in the world order.

Thus our action (in this view) in contingent upon and subsequent to our thoughts and our thoughts depend upon and are subsequent to the world order. Therefore, our actions are two stages subsequent to the world order. But for Allah Who governs the world or a part of it, the external world order is an action. It is not rational to believe that His actions occur due to premeditations on the system.

The Almighty Allah Possesses All Attributes of Perfection

What is perfection? A house is perfect when it provides for all the needs of a family's living such as enough rooms to serve as a living room, a guesthouse, a kitchen for making food, a bathroom, and other rooms. If it lacks these utilities, it is proportionately deficient.

Why Doesn't Man Accept this Truth at Times?

This fact is evident for man without the least speculation and there is no doubt in it, but that at times man becomes so entangled with the conflicts of life that he uses all the power of his wisdom for vital struggles. He spends all his time probing life, therefore, he has no time to spend on these kinds of thoughts. As a result, he becomes heedless of this fact or enchanted by nature's charming outward appearances and indulges in voluptuousness and pleasure. Since adherence to these facts precludes materialistic unrestrainedness, such a man naturally refuses to accept this fact and its like and is intolerant of it.

The Holy Quran has paid greater attention, in different ways, and has presented evidences for the creation of the creatures and the system prevalent and dominant among them. This is because most people, especially those who are infatuated by nature's charming appearances and who find prosperity in voluptuousness and worldly pleasures, are unable to think philosophically and to investigate subtle logical theories due to their fondness of material and perceptible things.

In any case, man is a part of the world of creation and is not free from want of its other components and the general and particular systems that govern it. He can consider the world of creation and the system prevalent in it at any time to find out the existence of the Creator and Lord of the world. The Almighty Allah states:

> *"Most surely in the heavens and the earth there are signs for the believers. And in your (own) creation and in what He spreads abroad of animals there are signs*

for a people that are sure, and (in) the variation of the night and the day, and (in) what Allah sends down of sustenance from the cloud, then gives life thereby to the earth after its death, and (in) the changing of the winds, there are signs for a people who understand (45:3-5)."

Explanation: In the Holy Quran, many verses invite people to think about the creation of the heavens, the sun, the moon, the stars, the earth, mountains, seas, plants, animals, and human beings. The Quran also mentions the astonishing system that governs each of these kinds. Truly, the mechanism of creation and the system that leads different activities of the world towards the goals of creation and the causes for existence are very astonishing and wonderful. The seed of wheat or the kernel of almond, planted on the earth, respectively turn into a clustered shrub or a fruit-bearing tree.

From the moment they are planted deeply in the heart of the earth, they rip up, produce green tips, and strike their white roots into the heart of the earth. To attain their final goal, vast and enormous systems, whose magnitude and vastness astound the intellect, begin to operate. The stars in the skies, the bright sun, the luminous moon, and the earth all with their rotation, movement, and potential power along with the mysterious powers in the seed or kernel, the four seasons of the year, the atmospheric conditions, the clouds, rains, winds, and days and nights all contribute to the growing of a seed into a shrub of wheat. Like nurses, these factors foster this new phenomenon and turn it from one hand to another until it reaches the last stage of its growth and development.

Likewise, the coming into existence of a human infant is much more complex than the bud of a plant or other phenomena, because it is the product of millions or rather billions of years of complex and systematic activity of the mechanism of creation. Man's daily life, in addition to external connections with the world of creation, springs from an astonishing system within his being which has amused the perceptive minds of the scientists of the world engaged for many centuries in observation of its outward things. Each day another layer is removed from its secrets, but still their knowledge about the unknown is rather insignificant.

If a human being possesses what is needful in the system of being of a normal man, he is perfect. But if he lacks one of them, for instance, if he does not have a hand, foot, or an eye, he is deficient in that respect.

From what has been said, the attribute of perfection is that which meets some of the needs of existence and obviates deficiency. For example, the epithet of knowledge obviates the darkness of ignorance and elucidates what is known to the scholar. Also power enables a powerful person to attain his ends and satisfy his demands and makes him competent to do so. Other epithets are life, comprehension, etc.

Our conscience judges that the Creator of the world (He, from whom the existence of the world and creatures originate and who meets any need that could be conceived and grants every blessing and perfection) possesses all attributes of perfection, because from a realistic point of view, it can never be assumed that anyone possessing an attribute can prevent others from having it. The Almighty Allah names all attributes of His perfection and declares Himself Immaculate and Pure from any fault and deficiency:

"And your Lord is the Self-sufficient One, the Lord of Mercy... (6:133)."

Allah states:

"Allah-there is no god but He; His are the very best names (20:8)."

(Allah is Living, Wise, Clear-sighted, Hearing, Mighty, Creator, and Free from want.) Thus the Almighty Allah possesses all epithets of perfection and His Holy Presence is Pure and Immaculate. Because if He had deficiency, He would be dependent in that respect and a superior god would have to provide His needs.

"...Glory be to Him and exalted be He above what they associate (with Him) (30:40)."

The Power and Knowledge of Allah

Observation of the interconnected components of this magnificent world, its astonishing usual revolution, its dazzling minute and interrelated systems which are at work here and there, as a result of which various phenomena move in an utmost orderly manner towards a specific goal and a particular destination, informs any wise man that the existence and survival of the world of existence and all that is associated with it originate from an Immortal One and Power. This Immortal One has created the world and all its inhabitants with His Boundless Might and Infinite Knowledge. Having placed His creatures in the cradle of nurturing, He leads them to an ideal perfection by His blessing. He has an immortal life and is Omnipotent and Omniscient. The Almighty Allah states:

"His is the kingdom of the heavens and the earth; He gives life and causes death; and He has power over all things. He is the First and the Last and the Ascendant (over all) and the Knower of hidden things, and He is Cognizant of all things (57:2-3)."

Allah also states:

"...And Allah's is the kingdom of the heavens and the earth and what is between them; He creates what He pleases; and Allah has power over all things (5:17)."

Explanation: When we say that such and such a person has the ability to purchase a car, we mean that he has whatever is needed (enough money) to do so. If we say that such and such a person is able to lift a weight of about 60 kilogrammes, we mean that he has the strength to lift a weight of 60 kilogrammes.

On the whole, possessing capability and power over some matter is contingent upon the availability of its requirements. Since the requirements of any phenomenon in the world of existence can be met through the Divine power of the Almighty Allah, it can be said that He is Mighty and Powerful over all things and His Holy Existence is the main source of existence. He also states:

"Does He not know who He created...(67:14)?"

That is to say, since in his creation and existence, each creature relies upon the Infinite Entity of the Almighty Allah there can never be any barrier and isolation between that creature and Allah. Nor can that creature be concealed from Him because He is Knowledgeable and Aware of ins and outs of everything.

Justice

The Almighty Allah is Just and Righteous, for justice is one of the attributes of perfection. Allah possesses all attributes of perfection. He, in His words, has repeatedly praised justice and has reproached injustice and cruelty. He commands people to do justice and prohibits them from injustice. How would it be possible for Allah to possess attributes that He considers indecent or to lack whatever He considers good and decent? The Almighty Allah states:

"Surely Allah does not do injustice to the weight of a particle...(4:40)."

He also states:

"...And your Lord does not deal unjustly with any one (18:49)."

Allah states:

"...And Allah does not desire injustice for (His) servants (40:31)."

He also states:

"Whatever benefit comes to you (O man !), it is from Allah, and whatever misfortune befalls you, it is from yourself..(4:79)."

Allah also states:

"Who made good everything that He has created...(32:7)."

Thus, any phenomenon, in itself, has been created in an extremely proper manner. Any hideousness, injustice, deficiencies, or shortcomings that are seen in some creatures can only be experienced by way of comparison and in relationship with other beings. F or example, snakes and scorpions are evil and unjust in their relation to man. When compared with flowers, thorns are not so beautiful, but they are all, in their own right, wonderful and thoroughly beautiful creatures.

Indeed the Almighty Allah declares some of man's voluntary deeds religiously bad and evil and orders man to refrain from doing them. They include sins such as polytheism, disobedience of parents, killing the innocent, drinking alcoholic beverages, gambling, and any other acts which are against religious obligations.

These kinds of actions, which are called sins, are evil acts and are not attributed to Allah because they bear the title of opposition to and rejection of obligation (title of negation). If these acts are willingly performed by religiously obligated people, then they will be attributed to these people, thus making them responsible and subject to punishment.

Blessing

When we see an enfeebled needy, we try to meet his demands to the best of our ability. We help a desperately poverty-stricken man or take a blind man's hand in our own and lead him to his destination. We consider these acts as compassion and blessing and thus regard them as praiseworthy deeds.

Actions performed by the Capable and Independent Allah can be nothing but blessings. By granting His innumerable graces, He lets everyone enjoy them. Without being dependent upon anyone else, Allah provides part of the needs of the creatures. Allah states:

"...And if you count Allah's favours, you will not be able to number them...(14:34)."

He also states:

"...My mercy encompasses all things...(7:156)."

Other Attributes of Perfection

"And Your Lord is the Self-sufficient one, the Lord of mercy...(6:133)."

Explanation: Any goodness and beauty existing in the world and any attribute of perfection that can be conceived are favours that the Almighty Allah has bestowed upon His creatures, and through this means satisfied one of the needs of creation. Certainly, if He lacked that perfection, He would be unable to grant favours to others and would have a share in the needs of people. Thus, Allah possesses all attributes of perfection and is endowed with all attributes of perfection, such as, life, knowledge, might, etc., without having received a single aspect of perfection from others and without asking them for help. Attributes of imperfection and causes for need and indigence, such as weakness, ignorance, death, difficulty, etc., will not find a way to His Holy Presence.

NUBUWWAH (PROPHETHOOD)

While independent in every respect, the Almighty Allah, with His immense power, has created the world of existence and its various creatures, allowing them to enjoy His countless blessings.

From the first day of creation till the last day of existence, man and other creatures are fostered by Allah. They are each led toward a known and determined goal with a particular order and system. They proceed towards their ends while being exposed to His noteworthy blessings.

If we study and deliberate upon our lifetime, namely the period of infancy, childhood, youth, and old age, our conscience will testify Allah's complete favours to us. When we become more aware of this matter, our wisdom will undoubtedly judge that the Creator of the world is more compassionate to His creatures than anyone else is.

Due to this compassion and favour, Allah always considers their interests and never consents to the corruption and defect of their affairs without wisdom and expediency. Mankind is one of the creatures of Allah. We know that man's interest and prosperity depend upon his being realistic and benevolent; that is to say, he must possess true beliefs, praiseworthy ethics, and good deeds.

One may say that with his Allah-granted wisdom, man can distinguish between good and bad and can recognize a well from a path.

It should be known, however, that wisdom alone cannot resolve this difficulty and lead man to realism and benevolence. All these indecent characteristics and unjust actions witnessed in the human society are committed by those who possess wisdom and discernment, however, as a result of selfishness, profit-seeking, and voluptuousness, their wisdom has been overcome by their sentiments and they have succumbed to their carnal desires, leading them astray. Therefore, the Almighty Allah must lead and invite us to prosperity through some other ways and through means which can never be overcome by carnal desires and which never make blunders or mistakes in their guidance. This path is nothing but the path of Nubuwwah.

The Logic in Nubuwwah

It becomes evident that since Allah creates everything, its fostering also depends upon Him. In other words, the Almighty Allah is the organizer and leader of the movement of any worldly creature or phenomenon that from the very beginning of existence endeavours for its survival, strives to remove its imperfections, eliminates its needs and shortcomings one after another, makes itself independent and self-sufficient as much as possible, and moves in an orderly manner in its path of survival and existence.

A definite conclusion can be drawn from this concept. That is to say, any one of the various kinds of phenomena of the world has a specific evolutionary process for its survival which is done by its special endeavours. In other words, in the path of their survival, worldly creatures of each particular group have a series of specific functions assigned to them by Allah. As the Holy Quran, with reference to this fact, states:

> *"...Our Lord is He Who gave to everything its creation, then guided it (to its goal) (20:50)."*

This order applies to all components of creation without any exception. It includes the stars, the earth, their components, compositions that generate primary phenomena, plants, and animals.

Man's condition is the same as others, in this universal guidance, but there is a difference between him and others.

The Difference between Man and Other Creatures

The earth has supposedly been created millions of years ago. It employs all its hidden forces and endeavours in the environment of its existence to the extent permitted by opposing forces. It displays the signs of its entity in the field of its rotation and transitional movement, thus maintaining its survival. Unless faced with a stronger opposing force, it will continue this activity and will not fall short of carrying out any of its functions.

For example, from the time an almond tree takes root from a seed until it becomes a fully grown tree, it assumes duties, such as nourishing, developing, etc. (in other words, it performs these duties to pursue the course of its existence.) It will never refrain from carrying them out unless it is precluded by a stronger opposing force. This process also applies to any other phenomenon. But mankind performs his particular activities voluntarily and his actions originate from his thoughts and determination. Many a time, man refrains from a task which is entirely to his interests and which is not hindered by any opposing force and undertakes a task which is entirely disadvantageous to him knowingly and intentionally. Sometimes, he abstains from drinking antidote and sometimes he drinks a cup of poison and kills himself.

It is certainly clear that the divine universal guidance will not be compulsory for a creature born with free will. That is to say, the prophets conveyed the message of the Almighty Allah on good and bad and prosperity and wretchedness to the people and warned believers of Allah's chastisement, but the believers have always been free to adopt any one of them. It is true that, in general, man perceives his good and bad and advantage and disadvantage through his wisdom, but that very wisdom often loses its keenness, follows carnal desires, and makes error. Therefore, in addition to the medium of wisdom, divine guidance should positively be achieved through a different medium, which is entirely inviolable to sin and error. In other words, in addition to the medium of wisdom, the Almighty Allah confirms His orders by another medium.

This medium is the same medium of prophethood by which the Almighty Allah reveals His orders to one of His servants through wahy leading mankind to prosperity. Allah appoints him to communicate His orders to the people and to oblige them to follow the orders through hope, despair, encouragement, and threat.

The Almighty Allah states:

"Surely We have revealed to you as We revealed to Nuh (Noah), and the prophets after him...(4:163)." "(We sent) messengers as the bearers of good news and as warners, so that people should not have a plea against Allah after the (coming of) messengers...(4:165)."

9

Attributes of Prophet

From what was discussed, it becomes clear that the Almighty Allah, with His divine teachings, must have provided some of His servants with intuitive knowledge and laws that guarantee man's prosperity and must have sent them to lead the people.

A person who possesses divine messages is called a "nabi (prophet)" and messenger of Allah and the entire set of messages from Allah which he has brought to the people are called "religion".

It has also become clear that a prophet:

(1) Must be free and immuned from error. In order to communicate what has been revealed to him to the people without error and mistake, he should be immuned from forgetfulness and other mental weaknesses; otherwise, divine guidance will not attain its goal and the general guidance rule will forfeit its applicability and lose its power to influence people.

(2) Must be inviolable to error and sin both in deeds and speech, because sinfulness has no effect in propagation. People do not esteem the speech of a person whose manner and speech are at odds. They even take his deeds for his mendacity and imposture by saying if he meant what he said, he would act accordingly.

By bringing these two aspects together in one phrase, we can say that a prophet must be inviolable to errors and sins to render preaching and propagation effective. In His words, the Almighty Allah, too, refers to this point and states: "The Knower of the unseen! so He does not reveal His secrets to any, except to him whom He chooses as a messenger for surely He makes a guard to march before him and after him, so that He may know that they have truly delivered the messages of their Lord...(72:26-28)."

(3) Must possess moral virtues such as chastity, courage, justice, etc., for these are considered as praiseworthy qualities. Anyone who is immune to any sins and follows religion in a perfect manner will never be blemished by moral vices.

Prophets among People

History indicates that there were prophets among people who responded to the call of Allah; however, the details of their life is not so clear. Only the details of life of Prophet Muhammad (SA) is devoid of ambiguity. The Holy Quran, which is the divine book given to Prophet (SA), contains sublime religious aims, has clarified the call of the prophets in the past and has described their goals and objectives.

The Holy Quran stipulates that many prophets have been, assigned by Allah to lead the people, all of whom consistently invited the people to monotheism and the true religion. As Allah states:

"And We did not send before you any messenger but We revealed to him that there is no god but Me, therefore worship Me (21:25)."

Ululazm Anbiya' (Arch-Prophets) and All Other Prophets

There were five prophets who had divine books and independent teachings. They are referred to as Nuh (Noah) (AS), Ibrahim (Abraham) (AS), Musa (Moses) (AS), 'Isa (Jesus) (AS), and Muhammad (SA) in the following verse:

"He has made plain to you of the religion what He enjoined upon Nuh and that which We have revealed to you, and that which We enjoined upon Ibrahim and Musa and 'Isa that keep to obedience and be not divided therein... (42:13)."

These five prophets, who have books and divine religious laws, are called the Ululazm Anbiya' (arch-prophets). The messengers of Allah, however, were not limited to these five prophets, rather each ummah (people) had a messenger. Many prophets were sent by Allah to lead the people, of whom only the names of less than twenty have been mentioned in the Holy Quran. The Almighty Allah states:

> *"... There are some of them that We have mentioned to you and there are others whom We have not mentioned to you...(40:78)."*

He also states:

> *"And every ummah had a messenger...(10:47)."*

Allah states:

> *"...And (there is) a guide for every people (13:7)."*

Yes, prophets, who came after each of the Ululazm Anbiya' invited people to follow the divine religious laws of the same prophets. Thus, prophetic mission and the call continued until Allah appointed the Prophet Muhammad (SA) ibn Abdillah to bring the previous prophetic missions to perfection and to communicate the latest orders and the most complete divine religious laws. His divine book became the last book and consequently, the religion of Prophet Muhammad (SA) will remain valid until Qiyamah (Resurrection) and his religious laws will remain everlasting.

(1) Prophet Nuh (AS)

Nuh (AS) (prophet Noah) was the first prophet appointed to prophetic mission and sent towards mankind as bearer of divine religious laws and a divine book by Allah, the Merciful.

Nuh (AS) invited the people of those days to monotheism and belief in the Oneness of Allah and asked them to refrain from polytheism and idolatry. As evident from his stories in the Holy Quran, Nuh (AS) seriously struggled to settle class distinctions and to eradicate injustice and cruelty. He notified the people of his teachings by way of reasoning which was something new to the people of those days.

After a long period of suffering with ignorant, stubborn, and unruly people, Nuh (AS) guided only a small group of people. Thus, by means of Nuh's (AS) Deluge, the Almighty Allah annihilated unbelievers and cleansed the earth of their defiled entity. Nuh (AS) and a group of his followers who were saved laid the cornerstone of a religious society over again. This Holy Prophet (SA) is the founder of the religious laws of monotheism and the first divine representative who struggled against cruelty, injustice, and rebellion. Owing to his valuable services rendered to the divine religion, he is allotted a praise and greeting by Allah, a praise which will remain alive and perpetual as long as mankind exists.

"Peace and salutation to Nuh among the nations (37:79)."

(2) Prophet Ibrahim (AS)

A long time elapsed after Nuh. (AS). Although many prophets, such as Hud, Salih, and others also led the people towards Allah and righteousness, the polytheism and idolatry flourished day by day and finally became universal. By His sublime wisdom, the Almighty Allah appointed Ibrahim (AS) (prophet Abraham) as a prophet.

Ibrahim (AS) was a perfect example of a man with innate disposition who searched for truth with his pure and immaculate nature. He found out the oneness of Allah and struggled against polytheism and injustice all his life.

As revealed by the Holy Quran and confirmed by the Hadith of the Imams of Ahl al-Bayt (Members of the Household of the Prophet Muhammad [SA]), Ibrahim (AS) spent his childhood in a cave away from the clamours of people and the tumultuous urban life. He only saw his mother who carried food and water for him from time to time.

One day he came out of his cave and followed his mother to town and paid a visit to his uncle, Adhar, but everything seemed new and interesting to him. Amidst thousands of bewilderments and wonders and with utmost impatience and calmness, his immaculate nature focussed on the creation of things that he saw, trying to find out the secret of their existence and the cause of their creation. He saw idols which Adhar and others carved and worshipped. Ibrahim (AS) asked about their identity, but the explanation he got about their divinity was not convincing. He saw a group of people who worshipped venus, others who worshipped the moon, and yet another group who worshipped the sun. Their divinity was unbelievable to Ibrahim (AS) because each one of them set after a few hours.

After these incidents, Ibrahim (AS), fearlessly, announced his worshipping of the Almighty Allah and his disgust of polytheism and idolatry. He thought of nothing but struggle against idolatry and polytheism. He struggled against idol-worshippers tirelessly and relentlessly and invited them towards monotheism.

Finally, he found a way to the idol-temple and broke the idols. Because of this deed, which people regarded as the greatest crime, Ibrahim (AS) was put to trial. After completion of the formalities, Ibrahim (AS) was thrown into the fire, but Allah saved him and he came out of the fire unharmed.

After a while, Ibrahim (AS) emigrated from his original birthplace, Babylon, to Syria and Palestine and continued his invitation of monotheism there.

In the last days of his life, he was blessed with two children: Ishaq (AS) (Prophet Isaac), the father of Israil (AS) and Isma'il (AS) (Prophet Ishmael), the father of 'Arab Mudar. By the order of Allah, Isma'il (AS), in infancy, and his mother were taken to Hijaz by Ibrahim (AS). They settled around Mount Tuhamah in an arid and barren land without inhabitants. In this manner, Ibrahim (AS) invited the nomadic Arabs to monotheism. Then he built Kaaba and described the rites of Hajj (pilgrimage to Mecca) which remained prevalent among the Arabs until the advent of Islam and the call of Prophet Muhammad (SA).

Ibrahim (AS) was endowed with the innate religion. According to the explicit wording of the Holy Quran, he had a divine book. He was the first person to call the divine religion as "Islam" and it's followers as "Muslims". Indeed, the religions of the world advocating monotheism, such as Judaism, Christianity, and Islam terminate at Ibrahim (AS), because Musa (AS), 'Isa (AS), and Prophet Muhammad (SA), the leaders of the aforementioned three religions, were all the descendants of Ibrahim (AS) and had followed his path of call and invitation to monotheism.

(3) Prophet Musa (AS)

Musa (AS) (Prophet Moses) ibn 'Imran is the third of the Ululazm Anbiya' and is bestowed with a book and shariah (divine religious laws). He was a descendant of Israil (AS) or

Yaqub (AS) (Prophet Jacob). Musa (AS) had a tumultuous life. He was born at a time when the Israelites were living in Egypt among Gipsies in a state of abjectness and servitude and when their sons were beheaded by the order of Firawn (Pharaoh*).

The mother of Musa (AS), according to the order given to her while asleep, placed Musa (AS), in a wooden box and left him in the Nile River. The water carried the box directly to the castle of Firawn.

By the order of Firawn, the box was picked up. When they opened it, they found a baby inside.

Because of the insistence of the queen, Firawn dispensed with killing the child. Since they did not have a son, they adopted him as their own son and put him under the care of a nurse (who was incidentally his own mother)

Up to the early stages of his youth, Musa (AS) lived in the palace of Firawn. Then, after an accidental murder, fearing Firawn, he ran away from Egypt. He went to Madyan and met Prophet Shuayb (Jethro) (AS). He married one of Shuayb's daughters and grazed his sheep for a few years. After a few years, he reminisced his birthplace, took his wife with him, and set out for Egypt, carrying his belongings along. On his way, when he reached Mount Sinai at night, he was assigned to prophetic mission by the Almighty Allah. He was chosen by Allah to invite Firawn to the religion of Tawhid, to liberate the Israelites from the yoke of the Gipsies, and to designate his brother, Harun (Aaron), as his minister. But after he announced his mission and communicated the divine message, Firawn who was an idol-worshipper and who had also introduced himself to the people of Egypt as one of the gods, did not accept Musa's (AS) prophetic mission and refused to grant freedom to the Israelites.

Although for many years Musa (AS) invited people to tawhid and showed many miracles, Firawn and his people showed no reaction other than toughness and moroseness. Finally, by the order of Allah, Musa (AS) emigrated the Israelites and went from Egypt to Sinai desert at night. When they reached the Red sea, Firawn, too, came to know and chased them with his army.

Through a miracle, Musa (AS) split the water of the sea and crossed it along with his people, but Firawn and his army were drowned. After this event, Allah revealed the Tawrat to Musa (AS) and established the Shariah of Musa (AS) among the Israelites.

* In Egypt, kings were called "Pharaohs".

(4) Prophet 'Isa (AS)

Prophet 'Isa (AS) is the fourth of the Ululazm Anbiya' bestowed with a book and shariah. The circumstances of his birth were unusual. His mother, Maryam, a pious virgin, was worshipping Allah (in Jerusalem) when Ruhulqudus or Jibril (Gabriel) descended from heavens, gave her the good tidings of 'Isa's (AS) birth; and by Jibril's breathing on her sleeves, Maryam became pregnant with 'Isa (AS).

After his birth, 'Isa (AS) began to speak in the cradle in defence of his m other against unfair calumnies attributed to her. He also informed the people about his Nubuwwah and divine book (Injil). Later, in his youth, he proceeded to invite the people and revived the shariah of Musa (AS) with minor modifications. He sent missionaries from among his hawaris (disciples) to the surrounding places. After his call was spread among the people, the Jews (his ummah) embarked on killing him, but Allah saved him, and the Jews caught someone else in his place and crucified him.

It should be pointed out here that the Almighty Allah, in the Holy Quran, confirms a divine book called the "Injil" for 'Isa (AS), which was revealed to him. It is different from the Gospels written after 'Isa (AS) about his life and call. Among them, four Gospels compiled by Luke, Mark, Matthew, and John are formally recognized by Christians.

(5) Prophet Muhammad (SA) Ibn 'Abdillah

The biography of our Holy Prophet Muhammad (SA) ibn Abdillah is clearer than those of all prophets preceding him, because as a result of the lapse of time and historical changes, their books, shariahs, and even their personalities have been distorted and their biographies have become ambiguous.

In fact, there are no clear documents other than those imparted to us through the divine book of Islam, viz, Quran and the speeches and statements of Prophet Muhammad (SA) and the Ahl al-Bayt (AS). But there is a clear history on the life of Prophet Muhammad (SA) which describes the characteristics of his life adequately.

The Holy Prophet (SA) of Islam is the last prophet appointed by the Almighty Allah to lead the people of the world.

Fourteen centuries ago, mankind lived in such a condition that nothing was left of Tawhid except nominally and when people had completely deviated from Tawhid and theism. Human manners and justice had died away in their society. Holy Kaaba had turned into an idol-temple and the religion of Ibrahim (AS) had converted into idolatry.

Arabs led a tribal life and even a few of their cities in Hijaz and Yemen and elsewhere were governed in the same tribal manner. The Arabs lived in the meanest and most backward conditions. Instead of culture and civilization, they indulged in unchastity, sensuality, alcoholism, and gambling. They buried their daughters alive. Most people subsisted by Way of theft, banditry, murder, and plundering each other's belongings, livestock, and cattle. Cruelty and bloodshed were regarded as the greatest honours.

In such an environment, the compassionate Allah appointed Prophet Muhammad (SA) to reform and lead the people of the world. Allah revealed the Holy Quran to him, consisting of divine education, theism, the ways of implementation of justice, and beneficial advice. Allah commissioned him to invite people toward humanity and adherence to the truth using that divine authentic Book, Quran.

Prophet Muhammad (SA) was born in the city of Mecca in 570 AD (53 years before Hijrah) in the noblest and most honourable Arab family.

Muhammad's (SA) father died before he was born. He lost h is mother when he was six years old. After two years, his grandfather (Abdul Muttalib), who was his guardian, died. Then the Prophet (SA) was put under the guardianship of his kind uncle, Abu Talib (the father of the Leader of the Faithful, 'Ali [AS]).

Abu Talib held him den just like one of his own children. Until a few months before Hijrah, he always did his best for the protection and support of Muhammad (SA) and he was never negligent.

The Arabs of Mecca, like other Arabs, indulged in breeding sheep and camels. They sometimes used to trade with neighbouring countries, especially with Syria. They were illiterate people who made no effort to educate their children.

Like all his people, the Prophet (SA), too, had not learnt to read and write, but from the beginning of his life, he was privileged by having a series of praiseworthy attributes. He never worshipped idols, lied, and committed theft and treachery. He guarded against evil, disrespectful, and indecent actions and was wise and efficient. Therefore, he gained considerable popularity among the people within a short period and became known as "Muhammad al-Amin" meaning "Muhammad the trustworthy". The Arabs often entrusted him with their belongings and talked about his honesty and efficiency. When he was about twenty years old, a wealthy lady of Mecca, Khadijah al-Kubra, designated him as her representative in commercial trade. As a result of his truthfulness, honesty, wisdom, and efficiency, she earned a great deal of profit. She was naturally attracted by the personality and magnanimity of the Holy Prophet (SA) more than ever and finally proposed to him for marriage. Afterwards also for years, she continued commercial works with her husband.

Being considered as one of the people, the Holy Prophet (SA) had an ordinary association with people until the age of forty. Of course, he differed from them in that he had a praiseworthy and decent behaviour and guarded against indecent deeds and conducts which had spoiled others. He did not possess cruelty, hard-heartedness, and status consciousness, thus had earned the respect and confidence of people. It was such that when the Arabs were reconstructing the House of Kaaba, a quarrel and dispute arose among the tribes on the erection of Al-Hajar al-Aswad (the Black Stone). The people unanimously chose the Holy Prophet (SA) as an arbitrator. He then ordered the people to spread a cloak to place Al-Hajar al-Aswad within. The nobles of the tribes lifted the sides of the cloak and the Holy Prophet (SA) installed the Al-Hajar al-Aswad in its place, thus bringing the conflict of the people to an end without any massacre and bloodshed.

Before his Al-Bithat al-Nabawiyyah (appointment for prophethood), although the Holy Prophet (SA) worshipped Allah and refrained from idol-worshipping, the people did not bother about him because he did not explicitly struggle against the superstitious beliefs of idolatry. The same applied to those belonging to other religions such as Jews and christians, who lived respectfully among the Arabs without being bothered by them.

THE INCIDENT OF MONK BUHAYRA

While the Holy Prophet (SA) lived with his uncle, Abu Talib, and while he had not yet reached adolescence, Abu Talib set out for Damascus on business and also took the Holy Prophet (SA) along.

It was a massive caravan and a great number of people travelled along with a huge quantity of merchandise until they arrived in Syria and entered the city of Busra. In the vicinity of a monastery, they pitched a tent and took rest. A monk, whose title was "Buhayra", came out of the monastery and invited them to a feast. Everybody accepted Buhayra's invitation and entered the monastery. Leaving his nephew, Muhammad (SA) with his belongings, Abu Talib also attended the feast along with others.

Buhayra asked: "Is everybody present?" Abu Talib replied, "Everybody is here except a youth who is the youngest of all." Buhayra said: "Bring him along as well!" Abu Talib called on the Holy Prophet (SA) who was standing under an olive tree and came to the monk.

Buhayra cast a deep glance at the Holy Prophet (SA) and said: "come a little bit closer, I have something to tell you." Then, he took the Holy Prophet (SA) aside. Abu Talib also went near them.

Buhayra told the Holy Prophet: "I am going to ask you a question and, by swearing on Lat and 'Uzza, would you answer me" (Lat and 'uzza were the names of two idols worshipped by the people of Mecca).

The Holy Prophet (SA) stated: "These two idols are the most hated ones to me".

Buhayra said: "By swearing on Allah, would you tell the truth". The Holy Prophet said: "I always speak the truth and I have never told a lie; you ask your question".

Buhayra asked: "What do you like the most"?

The Holy Prophet (SA) answered: "Loneliness".

Buhayra asked: "What do you look the most at and what do you like to look at"?

The Holy Prophet said: "The sky and the stars within it".

Buhayra asked: "What do you think of"?

The Holy Prophet (SA) remained silent, but Buhayra carefully glanced at his forehead.

Buhayra asked: "When do you sleep and with what thoughts"?

The Holy Prophet stated: "When I fix my eyes upon the sky, I see the stars and I find them in my lap and myself above them".

Buhayra asked: "Do you see dream also"?

He stated: "Whatever I see in dream, the same I see while I am awake."

Buhayra asked: "What do you dream of, as an example"?

The Holy Prophet (SA) kept quiet, Buhayra also kept quiet.

After a while, Buhayra asked: "May I take a look at the centre of your shoulders"?

The Holy Prophet (SA), while standing still, stated: "Come and see."

Buhayra stood up, came closer, and pulled the dress of the Holy Prophet (SA) off his shoulders. A mole appeared. Buhayra took a look and said in a murmuring voice: "He is the very person".

Abu Talib asked: "Which one? What do you mean"?

Buhayra said: "Tell me, what is your relationship with this youth"?

Since Abu Talib loved the Holy Prophet (SA) as one of his own children, he said: "He is my son".

Buhayra said: "No, the father of this youth must have died".

"How do you know"? said Abu Talib; "That is true, this youth is my nephew".

Buhayra told Abu Talib "Listen, this youth will have a very bright and astonishing future. If others see what I have seen and recognize him, they will kill him. Hide and protect him from the enemies".

Abu Talib said: "Tell me, who is he"?

Buhayra replied: "His eyes bear the signs of the eyes of a prominent prophet and a clear mark of prophethood is on his back".

The Story of Monk Nestorius

After a few years, the Holy Prophet, acting as a representative, set out for Damascus once again along with the merchandise belonging to Khadijah al-Kubra. Khadijah sent her servant, Masirah, along with the Holy Prophet (SA) and advised him to fully obey his orders. In this trip, too, when they arrived in Syria, they landed under a tree in the vicinity of the city of Busra. There was a monastery belonging to a monk called "Nestorius" who was acquainted with Masirah.

Nestorius asked Masirah: "Who is the man resting underneath that tree"?

Masirah replied: "He is a person from the family of Quraysh".

The monk said: "under this tree, no one but a prophet from among the prophets of Allah has lodged or can lodge".

He added: "Is there redness in his eyes".

Masirah said: "Yes, his eyes are always like this".

The monk said: "That's it. He is the last prophet of the prophets of Allah. I wish I could find out the day when he will invite the people."

Good Tidings Given by the Jews of Madinah

Many Jewish tribes, having read about the attributes and location of the Holy Prophet (SA) in their books, had left their homeland for Hijaz and taken abode in Madinah and its suburbs, waiting for the advent of the Holy Prophet (SA), the Ummi (unschooled). As they were a group of wealthy and rich people, the Arabs used to disturb them from time to time and robbed them of their belongings. Complaining against the injustice of the Arabs, the Jews told them that they would tolerate their cruelty and robbery until the migration of the Ummi prophet from Mecca to Madinah. They said that on that day, they would have their faith in him and would take vengeance on them. One of the main factors that led to the rapid belief of the people of Madinah in the Holy Prophet (SA) was the memory they had about these news. Finally, they acknowledged their faith, but the Jews refrained from believing in him due to their strong communalism and prejudice.

Quran's Reference to Prophetic Tidings

In His words the Almighty Allah refers to these good tidings in many instances. Regarding the faith of a group of people endowed with a book, the Quran states:

"Those who follow the Apostle-Prophet, the Ummi, whom they find written down with them in the Tawrat and the Injl, (who) enjoins them good and forbids them evil, and makes lawful to them the good things and makes unlawful to them impure things, and removes from them their burden and the shackles which were upon them...(7:157)."

Again, He states:

"And when there came to them a Book from Allah verifying that which they already had, and aforetime they were seeking victory against those who disbelieved-yet when there came to them that (Book) which they had recognized, they disbelieved in it...(2:89)."

From Al-bithat Al-nabawiyyah to the Hijrah

In the gloomy atmosphere of the Arabian Peninsula that can literally be called "the swamp of misery" and the centre of corruption and in a world full of cruelty and injustice, the Almighty Allah appointed His Prophet (SA) as a blessing for the people of the world and ordered him to invite the people to Tawhid and worshipping the One Allah.

He also ordered him to call people to justice, righteousness, and strengthening their social relations. Allah also ordered him to rise in observance of truth and follow the path of the followers of righteousness and to lay the foundation of man's prosperity on the basis of faith, piety, cooperation, and self-sacrifice.

Initially, the Holy Prophet (SA) was charged with the responsibility of inviting the people. Since the environment was full of obstinacy, ruthlessness, and injustice, the Prophet (SA) talked his mission over only with people who were more or less susceptible to conversion. Thus a limited number of people believed in him and (according to narrations) the first man was 'Ali ibn Abi Talib (AS), the son of his uncle and educated by the Prophet (SA) himself, and the first woman was his wife Khadijah al-Kubra (AS).

Then, Muhammad (SA) was commissioned to invite his close relatives and companions (who were about forty people) to his house and described his divine mission. Then, by the order of Allah, the Holy Prophet (SA) proceeded to an overt and public invitation, thus bringing forward the luminous torch of divine guidance from within the house to the arena of the world.

The reaction of the Arabs, especially the people of Mecca, was very severe against this invitation specifically after it was publicized. Unbelievers and polytheists responded negatively, savagely, and in a cruel way to this immaculate and pure invitation without using any proper logic whatsoever.

Sometimes, they called the Holy Prophet (SA) a soothsayer and magician, while at times they called him lunatic and poet and used to make fun of him. Whenever he wanted to invite the people to the newly-grown religion of Islam or wanted to worship Allah, the people used to make noise and disrupt his actions. They threw garbage and thorns on his head and used to beat and abuse him. Sometimes, they stoned him, while at times, they tried to allure him by giving enticing and sweet promises such as of wealth and leadership, so that through these means they could shake up his resolution and determination. But the Holy Prophet (SA) displayed no weakness and withdrawal. Sometimes, he regretted and became sad because of the ignorance and stubbornness of his people. In this regard, Quranic verses were frequently revealed by which the Almighty Allah expressed His consolation to him and ordered him to be patient and forbearing. Sometimes, verses were revealed to prohibit the Holy Prophet (SA) from showing the least willingness to the remarks of the people or from displaying any weakness and leniency.

Those who believed in the Holy Prophet (SA) were severely tortured and punished by the kafirin. In many instances, they died under torture. Sometimes, the matter became so serious that they were tortured to the extreme and then they sought the permission of the Holy Prophet (SA) to start a bloody movement and finalize their destinies. The Holy Prophet (SA) said: "I do not have an order from the Almighty Allah in this respect. You must wait". A group of people took their belongings with them and left their homeland due to the heavy pressure on them.

After a while, things became much harder on the Muslims due to the extreme torture. The Holy Prophet (SA) allowed his disciples to migrate to Ethiopia to be relieved of the torture and harassment of their people for a while. This group of people, led by Jafar ibn Abi Talib, the brother of 'Ali (AS) (Jafar was one of the most trusted friends of the Holy Prophet [SA]), migrated to Ethiopia along with their families.

After being informed of the Hijrah of the Muslims, the Kafirin of Mecca sent two of their experienced men, along with a large number of gifts and souvenirs, to the king of Ethiopia, requesting the extradition of the immigrants of Mecca. But with a speech delivered in the presence of the king of Ethiopia, Jafar ibn Abi Talib explained the entirely illuminating personality of the Holy Prophet (SA) and the sublime principles of Islam for the king, the Christian priests, and top authorities present at the time. He also cited several Quranic verses of Surah (Chapter) Maryam.

The immaculate statements of Jafar ibn Abi Talib were so attractive that the king and the audience started shedding tears. Thus the king rejected the request of the people of Mecca and declined all gifts and souvenirs sent to him. The king issued instructions to provide all means of convenience, peace, and comfort for the immigrant Muslims in every respect.

After this event, the Kafirin of Mecca decided to break their relations with Banu Hashim (family of Hashim) who were the relatives of the Holy Prophet (SA) and his followers. They also decided to totally stop all relations, discourse, and transactions with them. In this respect, they wrote a special agreement, got it signed by everyone, and left it in Kaaba.

Banu Hashim, accompanied by the Holy Prophet (SA), had to inevitably leave Mecca and take refuge in a valley known as "Shib Abi Talib" and lived there almost in utmost hardship and hunger. In this period, no one dared to come out of the Shib. During the days, they had to endure the burning heat and in the nights, they were faced with the wailing of women and children.

After three years, as a result of the obliteration of the agreement and because of the denouncement by the tribes settled around, the unbelievers dispensed with their agreement and Banu Hashim came out of their refuge.

But at that time, Abu Talib, who was the lone supporter of the Holy Prophet (SA), and also Khadijah al-Kubra, the kind wife of the Holy Prophet (SA), died. As a result, things became much harder for the Holy Prophet (SA) and he was unable to appear in public or reveal his identity to anyone, or stay in a specific place. Altogether, he had no life-security.

A Trip to Taif

The year in which the Holy Prophet (SA) and Banu Hashim came out of the Shib Abi Talib, was 13th year after al-Bithat al-Nabawiyyah. The Holy Prophet (SA) made a short trip to Ta'if (a city about 100 kilometres from Mecca) at that time and invited the people of Taif to embrace Islam. But the ignorant people of Ta'if attacked him from every place, abused and stoned him, and at last drove him out of the city.

The Holy Prophet (SA) returned to Mecca from Ta'if and remained there for a while. But since he had no security of his life, he did not appear among the people. Since the circumstances were favourable to exterminate the Holy Prophet (SA), the elders of Mecca assembled in Darun-Nadwah, which was like a consultative assembly and hatched up the final plot in a secret session to exterminate him once and for all. The plot was designed to select one man from each Arab tribe. The selected men were then to rush into the house of the Holy Prophet (SA) collectively and kill him. The purpose of selecting one representative from each tribe was to prevent the relatives of the Holy Prophet (SA) from rising in revenge and from fighting with all those tribes who would direct the murder. Also the participation of one person from Banu Hashim would also keep the mouths of Banu Hashim shut regarding this matter.

This decision was finalized. About forty people from various tribes were nominated to kill the Holy Prophet (SA). They surrounded his house at night, so as to enter it at dawn in order to carry out their plot, but the divine will was above the determination of these people and thwarted their plans. The Almighty Allah sent His revelation to the Holy Prophet (SA), informed him of their intention, and ordered him to come out of Mecca at night itself and set out for Madinah.

The Holy Prophet (SA) informed 'Ali (AS) of the current situation, ordered him to sleep in his place, and gave him his last wills. He left the house at night and seeing Abu Bakr along the way, he took him also along and set out for Madinah.

Some of the dignitaries of Madinah had already met the Holy Prophet (SA) in Mecca and had expressed their faith prior to his Hijrah. They had also made an agreement to support and vindicate the Holy Prophet (SA), if he came to Madinah, just as they would defend their own life and honour.

The Hijrah of the Holy Prophet (SA) to Madinah

The Holy Prophet (SA) reached a cave in Mount Thawr near Mecca and hid there for three days. After three days, he left the cave and continued his journey until he reached Madinah where he was welcomed by the people of Madinah.

On the other side, the infidels of Mecca who had surrounded the house of the Holy Prophet (SA) at night, dashed inside at dawn, and went to his bed with their swords pulled out. They unexpectedly found 'Ali (AS) sleeping in the bed of the Holy Prophet (SA). As soon as they found out that the Holy Prophet (SA) had left Mecca, they began searching for him around Mecca, but after a thorough search they returned with a great disappointment.

The Holy Prophet (SA) stayed in Madinah where the people most willingly converted to Islam and wholeheartedly supported him. The city of Madinah turned into an Islamic city. Until then, this city was called "Yathrib", but after this occurrence, it assumed the name of "Madinat al-Rasul" (the City of Prophet) and became the first Islamic city. Of course, although munafiqin (hypocrites), the Arab minorities of Madinah who formed about one-third of the city's population, being scared of the majority, pretended to be Muslims.

The sun of Islam began shining in the clear sky of Madinah and began shedding its light. In the first place, the state of conflict which had existed for many years between the two main tribes of Aws and Khazraj turned into peace and compromise. The believers of Madinah encircled like butterflies around the candle of prophetic mission. Gradually, the tribes in the territory of Madinah embraced Islam and the divine precepts descended one after the other and were implemented. Everyday one of the roots of corruption and indecent behaviour was eradicated and replaced by piety and justice. Gradually, the followers of Islam, who had remained in Mecca after the Holy Prophet's (SA) Hijrah and were under the harassment and severe torture by the unbelievers, left their homes and fled to Madinah where they were received with warm hospitality by their religious brethren.

Muslims who had remained in Mecca gradually migrated and gathered in Madinah. These people were called muhajirin (immigrants) and the believers in the city of Madinah were called "Ansar"(helpers).

There were many tribes of Jews in Madinah, its suburbs, Khaybar, and Fadak whose information and scholars constantly notified the Arabs of Madinah of the good tidings of the Holy Prophet's (SA) mission. But when these tribes were invited to Islam after the Hijrah, they did not accept this invitation and turned away from Islam. Finally, a non-aggression treaty was signed between the Jews and Muslims with specific terms.

The rapid advancement of Islam seriously annoyed the unbelievers of Mecca and increased their wrath and animosity towards the Holy Prophet (SA) and the followers of Islam. They were after a pretext to disrupt the unity of the followers of Islam. On the other hand, the followers of Islam, too, especially the Muhajirin of Mecca who were quite unhappy with the unbelievers, expected a divine permission to punish the cruel unbelievers for their evil deeds and to liberate their women, innocent children, and helpless old people living under persecution and torture in Mecca.

The Battle of Badr

The first battle between the Muslims and the unbelievers of Mecca took place at Badr (a valley between Mecca and Madinah) in the second year of the Hijrah. In this battle, the number of fully equipped unbelievers was about one thousand. The Muslims were about one-third of them and lacked all necessary war equipment, but divine dispensation afforded the Muslims a bright victory and defeated the unbelievers in the worst possible way.

Suffering heavy casualties and many captives and losing their entire stock of equipment in this battle, the mushrikin (polytheists) ran away to Mecca. It is said that in this battle, seventy unbelievers were killed, out of which almost half of them were killed by the sword of 'Ali (AS). Also seventy people from the unbelievers were taken as captives.

The Battle of Uhud

In the third year of Hijrah, the unbelievers of Mecca, led by Abu Sufyan again rushed towards Madinah with three thousand men (and according to one narration with five thousand men). They confronted the Muslims at Uhud outside Madinah. In this battle, the Holy Prophet (SA). arrayed seven hundred Muslims to face the enemy. In the beginning of the battle, the Muslims had the upper hand again, but after a few hours due to the mistake of some Muslims, the army of Islam was defeated. At this time, the unbelievers attacked from all sides and the Muslims suddenly found themselves surrounded on all sides by the swords of unbelievers.

In this battle, the Muslims sustained heavy losses. Hamzah, the uncle of the Holy Prophet (SA), along with seventy other disciples of the Holy Prophet (SA) who were mostly Ansar were martyred. The forehead of the Holy Prophet (SA) was wounded and one of his front teeth broke. One of the unbelievers who inflicted a blow on the Holy Prophet's (SA) shoulder shouted: "I killed Muhammad". Hearing this, the army of Islam dispersed. Only 'Ali (AS), along with a few men, remained steadfastly near the Holy Prophet (SA). All these were killed but 'Ali (AS) resisted the enemy until the end of the battle and defended the Holy Prophet (SA).

On the last day, those who had fled away from the army of Islam gathered around the Holy Prophet (SA) once more and prepared for battle. But the army of Abu Sufyan, however, considered only that much success as enough, stopped fighting, and set out for Madinah.

After travelling a few kilometres, the army of the unbelievers seriously regretted why they had not pursued the battle to final victory and why they had not taken Muslims' women and children as captives, and plundered their properties. They even got busy with consultation to attack Madinah once again, but received the information that the information that the army of Islam was following them to continue the battle. Having received this information, the unbelievers became intimidated, gave up the idea of returning to Madinah, and hastily set out for Mecca.

Surely what they had heard was true, because the Holy Prophet (SA), by the order of Allah, had mobilized an army from the injured who were led by 'Ali (AS) to follow the enemy.

Although the Muslims sustained heavy casualties in this battle, in fact, it finished to the advantage of Islam and Muslims. The Muslims drew a more important conclusion out of this battle and experienced the inauspicious consequence of violating the order of the Holy Prophet (SA). Having given up the battle, both the confronting sides promised to fight another battle in Badr next year at the same time. The Holy Prophet (SA), with a group of his disciples, went to Badr on time, but the unbelievers refrained from coming.

After this battle, the Muslims became very well prepared and made advancement on all sides in the peninsula except in the region of Mecca and Ta'if.

The Battle of Khandaq

This was the third battle declared by the Arab unbelievers against the Holy Prophet (SA). It was also the last battle under the leadership of the people of Mecca. It was a very severe battle in which the unbelievershad fully equipped themselves with their forces and powers. In the history, this battle is known as the "Battle of Ahzab" and "Khandaq".

After the battle of Uhud, the leaders of Mecca, led by Abu Sufyan, decided to inflict the final blow upon the Holy Prophet (SA) to put off the light of Islam for good. To this end, they instigated the Arab tribes and asked for their cooperation and assistance. In spite of the non-aggression treaty signed by the Jews and Muslims, the Jewish people also had secretly involved themselves with the plot and violated the treaty and signed a cooperation agreement with the unbelievers.

Thus, in the fifth year of Hijrah, a fully mobilized army comprising of Quraysh, various Arab tribes, and Jewish people rushed to Madinah totally equipped.

Having come to know of the intention of the enemy beforehand, the Holy Prophet (SA) consulted his disciples over the matter. After a long discussion, they dug a trench all around the city of Madinah according to the proposal of Salman al-Farisi who was an intimate Companion of the Holy Prophet (SA). They then got fortified within the city. After reaching Madinah, the army of the enemy found no way to enter the city. They inevitably besieged the city and started the battle in that position. The siege and battle continued for sometime.

It was in this battle only that ' Amr ibn 'Abdwudd, a most renowned equestrian and a most famous brave man of Arabia, was killed by the powerful hands of 'Ali (AS). Finally, as a result of wind, cold, the fatigue of the Arab idolaters from the extended duration of the siege, and the difference and separation between the Jews and Arabs, the siege got broken without any result; thus the army of the unbelievers dispersed from around Madinah.

Battle with the Jews-The Battle of Khaybar

After the Battle of Khandaq, originally provoked by the Jews who cooperated with the Arab unbelievers and who had openly breached their treaty with Muslims, the Holy Prophet (SA) proceeded to punish the Jewish tribes in Madinah by the order of Allah. He fought several battles, all of which ended in the victory and triumph of Muslims. The most important of these battles was the Battle of Khaybar. The Jews of Khaybar had several fortifications in hand and a considerable number of belligerents with adequate equipment at their disposal.

In this battle, 'Ali (AS) killed Marhab of Khaybar, the well-known hero of the Jews, and dispersed the Jewish army. Afterwards, he rushed to the Fort of Khaybar, unhinged its door, and entered the fort along with the army of Islam.

He then hoisted the banner of victory on its top. With these very battles which ended in the fifth year of Hijrah, the problem of the Jews of Hijaz came to an end.

Inviting the Rulers and Kings to Islam

The Holy Prophet (SA) settled in Madinah. Gradually, a great number of the Muslims of Mecca, who were under the torture by the unbelievers, relinquished their homes and belongings and migrated to Madinah. Ansar also kept their promise and received them wholeheartedly.

The Holy Prophet (SA) constructed Masjid al-Nabi at Madinah. Other mosques were also built. Missionaries of Islam were sent to the outskirts and treaties were signed with Jewish tribes of Madinah and its suburbs and also with some Arab tribes. Thus Islam began to flourish with its enormous luminosity.

In the 6th year of the Hijrah, the Holy Prophet (SA) sent letters to the rulers and kings such as the King of Iran, Qaysar (Caesar) of Rome, Khedive of Egypt, and Al-Najashi (Negus) of Ethiopia and invited them to embrace Islam.

After some time, the unbelievers of Mecca breached the treaty and, as a result of this, the Holy Prophet (SA) decided to conquer Mecca. In the 8th year of the Hijrah, the Holy Prophet (SA) rushed to Mecca with ten thousand soldiers and conquered Mecca without any fighting and bloodshed. He also toppled and broke many idols placed in Kaaba. People of Mecca accepted Islam.

The Holy Prophet (SA) summoned all the leaders of Mecca, who had in the last 20 years shown their animosity and behaved inhumanely with him and his followers, and pardoned them all with utmost magnanimity and without showing the slightest harshness and moroseness.

The Battle of Hunayn

After the conquest of Mecca, the Holy Prophet (SA) proceeded to clear out the suburbs of the city and fought numerous battles with the Arab idol-worshippers, one of which was the Battle of Hunayn. The Battle of Hunayn was one of the most important battles of the Holy Prophet (SA). It took place in the valley of Hunayn against the tribe of Hawazin. The army of Islam, with twelve thousand soldiers, arrayed in front of the army of Hawazin which was equipped with a few thousand men. A heavy battle took place between them.

In the beginning of the battle, Hawazin severely defeated the Muslims, so much so that everybody ran away, except Ali (AS) who was carrying the banner of Islam and a few others, who fought in front of the Holy Prophet (SA). But after a few hours, initially the Ansar and then other Muslims returned to their bases and defeated the enemy after a very heavy fighting. In this battle, five thousand enemies were taken as captives by the Muslims, but all of them were released by the Muslims at the request of the Holy Prophet (SA). The Holy Prophet (SA) bought the share of the dissatisfied Muslims by paying them money and released their captives.

The Battle of Tabuk

In the 9th year of Hijrah, the Holy Prophet (SA) despatched an army to Tabuk (located at the borders of Hijaz and Damascus) to fight a battle with Rome, because the rumours had spread that the Qaysar of Rome was preparing an army comprised of Romans and Arabs in that area. The Battle of Mutah was previously fought there with Rome, leading to the martyrdom of the commanders of the army of Islam such as Jafar ibn Abi Talib, Zayd ibn Harithah, and 'Abdullah ibn Rawahah. The Holy Prophet (SA), with an army of thirty thousand soldiers, proceeded towards Tabuk, but the people gathering there had dispersed before the arrival of the army of Islam. The Holy Prophet (SA) stayed in Tabuk for three days, cleared out that territory, and then returned to Madinah.

Other Battles

Within ten years of his stay in Madinah, the Holy Prophet (SA) fought almost eighty major and minor battles other than those previously mentioned. The Holy Prophet (SA) personally participated in almost one-fourth of the number of these battles.

In the battles in which he participated, unlike other commanders who remained in shelters and only issued the orders for attacks and killing, the Holy Prophet (SA) himself took part in the battlefield along with other soldiers, but no occasion arose for him to embark upon killing anyone.

GHADIR KHUMM AND THE ISSUE OF SUCCESSION

Mecca was the last city whose conquest led to the absolute domination of Islam over the Arabian Peninsula. It has the Haram (Sacred premises) of Allah and the site of Kaaba. This city fell in the hands of the army of Islam in the 8th year of Hijrah. Shortly afterwards, the city of Ta'if was also conquered.

In the 10th year of Hijrah, the Holy Prophet (SA) set out for Mecca to perform the Hijjatul Wada' (last Hajj). After performing the Hajj manasik (rituals) and giving necessary instructions to the people, the Holy Prophet (SA) headed for Madinah. In the course of his journey, he ordered to stop the caravan at a place called "Ghadir (Pond) Khumm." Among one hundred and twenty thousand Hujjaj (pilgrims) who had gathered for Hajj from all parts of the Arabian Peninsula, the Holy Prophet (SA) took 'Ali's hand in his own, lifted him up, and announced his Imamah (succession of Prophet Muhammad [SA]).

By this action, the matter of succession, which controls the affairs of the Muslims, guards the Book and Hadith, and protects the divine instructions and laws, was resolved. Thus the order given by Allah in the following Ayah was executed:

"O Messenger! deliver what has been revealed to you from your Lord; and if you do it not, then you have not delivered His message;...(5:67)"

Shortly, after returning to Madinah, the Holy Prophet (SA) passed away.

The Settlement of The Holy Prophet (SA) in Madinah and the Advancement of Islam

The invitation of the Holy Prophet (SA) to Islam was widely extended in Madinah and it had embraced every home, association, district, and quarter. The people embraced Islam in groups and multitudes in such a way that the people in Mecca, Madinah, and all the tribes in the surrounding areas submitted to Islam. During the ten years of the Holy Prophet's (SA) stay in Madinah, absolute domination of Islam established in the entire Arabian Peninsula. In these ten years, the Holy Prophet (SA) was preoccupied with carrying out his mission and never took rest.

He received wahy and taught the people the sublime teachings of Islam concerning education, ethics, and laws revealed to him by the Almighty Allah. The Holy Prophet (SA) gave people the necessary advice, answered their questions, discussed and debated with the opponents and scholars of various nations especially those of the Jews, and managed the affairs of the country, thus enabling the people to administer lives.

In spite of all these preoccupations, the Holy Prophet (SA) devoted a considerable part of his time for worshipping Allah. He observed Sawm on many days of the year, that is to say, he observed Sawm almost continuously during the three consecutive months of Rajab, Shaban, and Ramadan and also observed Sawm for about a month on different occasions during the year. Sometimes, the Holy Prophet (SA) observed the Sawmul Wisal (continuous fasting) which was one of his special characteristics, i.e., he did not take anything for several consecutive days and nights. He used to spend some of his time in the management of household affairs and necessities of life. Also, at times, he spent his time to earn his subsistence.

The Almighty Allah has briefly mentioned the events of these ten years in His words:

> *"They desire to put out the light of Allah with their mouths, but Allah will perfect His light, though the unbelievers may be averse (61:8)"*

Allah is the One who has sent His messenger with divine guidance and true religion to the people to make His religion dominant over all other religions and faiths, even if this is unpleasant for the polytheists.

As it is evident, this divine promise had been well realized during the lifetime of the Holy Prophet (SA) and after his passing away to the present day when more than one billion Muslims live all over the world.

He also states:

"You are the best of the ummahs (peoples) raised up for (the benefit of) men; you enjoin what is right and forbid the wrong and believe in Allah... (3:100)"

A Glance at the Intellectual and Spiritual Personality of The Holy Prophet (SA)

According to authentic historical documents, the Holy Prophet (SA) was brought up in an atmosphere which was the meanest environment for living and was the centre of ignorance, corruption, and moral vices. In such an environment and without academic education, the Holy Prophet (SA) spent the period of his infancy and youth. Although the Holy Prophet (SA) never worshipped an idol and was never involved with inhumane demeanours; nevertheless, he was among such people, and his ordinary life did not indicate such an eventful future; indeed it was unbelievable on the part of a poor, unschooled, and inexperienced orphan.

The Holy Prophet (SA) spent some time in this way until during one night, while worshipping Allah with usual peace of mind and freedom from worldly affairs, he suddenly gained a different personality.

His quiet inner personality converted into a divine one. The Holy Prophet (SA) regarded the thoughts and beliefs of thousands of years of human societies as superstitious. With his realistic views, he considered the customs and rites of the inhabitants of the world as cruel and unjust. He linked the past and the future of the world and fully recognized the path of man's prosperity. His observations and vision changed totally. He did not see or hear anything except the truth and reality. He began to speak of divine and heavenly words, wisdom, and guidance. His natural state of mind which was occupied with reforming daily routines in a poor atmosphere of trade and transaction grew stronger and, so he embarked on reforming the world and its inhabitants and subverting the thousands of years old organization of human aberration and cruelty. He rose to revive the truth and reality all by himself and challenged the terrifying and intense opposing forces of the world as if they were nothing. He talked about divine teachings and derived all the realities of existence from the Oneness of the Creator of the world.

The Holy Prophet (SA) described the sublime human ethics in the best possible manner and comprehended and clarified their relationships. He first believed what he said to anyone else. Also, he first carried out whatever he asked the people to do.

The religious laws and precepts brought forth by him consist of a series of worships and services which beautifully express the servitude of man towards the grandeur and power of the Almighty Allah. He brought other laws such as legal and penal laws which are completely interrelated and which are established on the basis of monotheism and respect for the sublime human ethics.

The set of laws brought by the Holy Prophet (SA) on worships and transactions is so comprehensive that it deals with every aspect of individual and social life that can be conceived of in the world of humanity, as well as various needs and requirements resulting from the lapse of time and issues instructions to fulfil them.

The Holy Prophet (SA) considered the laws of his religion as universal and everlasting, i.e. he believed that his religion is capable of eliminating the worldly and heavenly needs of all human societies for ever. He thought that the people must adopt the same stance in order to secure their prosperity. He frequently stated:

> *"The religion that I have brought guarantees your worldly and heavenly prosperity and happiness."*

Surely, the Holy Prophet's (SA) statement was not in vain and groundless, rather he arrived at this conclusion after studying the creation and foreseeing the future of the human world. In other words, firstly, after he recognized the complete harmony and coordination between his laws and the physical and mental creation of man and secondly, after he generally considered the changes that would take place in the future and the harms that would be done to the Muslim society, he passed a judgement on the durability and perpetuity of his religious precepts. The prophecies of the Holy Prophet (SA), that have reached us through authentic documents, have described the general circumstances and conditions after his passing away up to the remote future.

The Prophet (SA) performed all these tasks in a period of twenty three years, out of which, he spent thirteen years under severe torture and harassment of the unbelievers of Mecca. He spent the remaining ten years in battles, campaigns, and external struggles against overt enemies; in domestic campaign against the munafiqin and trouble-makers; and the management of the affairs of the Muslims, the reformation of their beliefs, ethics, and deeds, and thousands of other involvements.

The Holy Prophet (SA) achieved so much due to his firm resolution in pursuit of truth and its revival. His realistic views were only directed to truth. He did not follow what was contrary to truth even if it was in his own interest or in the interest of the public. He accepted wholeheartedly what was true and never refused it. On the other hand, he refused whatever was false and never accepted it.

The Spiritual Personality of The Holy Prophet (SA) was Extraordinary

If we impartially consider the subject already covered we will have no doubt that the appearance of such a personality in those conditions and circumstances was nothing but an extraordinary occurrence and miracle and had no reason other than the special support by Allah.

Therefore, the Almighty Allah repeatedly mentions in Quran about the earlier unschooledness, orphanage, and poverty of the Holy Prophet (SA). The Almighty Allah states:

"Did He not find you an orphan and give you shelter? And find you unable to see and show the way? And find you in want and make you to be free from want? (93:6-8)."

Allah also states:

"And you did not recite before it any book, nor did you transcribe one with your right hand...(29:48)."

Again the Almighty Allah states:

"And if you are in doubt as to that which We have revealed to Our servant, then produce a chapter like it...(2:23)."

The Character of The Holy Prophet (SA)

The only basis and principle upon which the Holy Prophet (SA) laid the foundation of his religion is the principle of Tawhid which he recognized as the source of the prosperity for the people of the world.

According to the principle of Tawhid only Allah is the Creator of the world and worthy of being worshipped. We must not bow down and pay homage to anyone except the Almighty Allah.

Thus the principle that must be practised in human societies is for all to act like brothers and be equal with one another and not to regard anyone as their unconditional sovereign except Allah.

As the Almighty Allah states:

"Say: O followers of the Book! come to an equitable proposition between us and you that we shall not serve any but Allah and (that) we shall not associate aught with Him, and (that) some of us shall not take others for lords besides Allah... (3:64)."

The Holy Prophet (SA) pursued no objective other than the propagation of the religion of Tawhid. He invited the people to Tawhid by the best morality, the most cheerful disposition, and the most convincing reasoning and proof. He also advised his friends to follow the same principle accordingly. As the Almighty Allah issued His order upon him:

"Say: 'This is my way I call to Allah, 1 and those who follow me being certain...(12:108)."

On the basis of his character, the Holy Prophet (SA) regarded all people as brothers and equal to one another. He never showed prejudice in carrying out the divine precepts and penance. He did not discriminate between his acquaintance and the stranger, the weak and the strong, the rich and the poor, the man and the woman, the black and the white. He provided the people with their rights on the basis of the precepts and laws of religion and states: "Even if my daughter Fatimah, who is the most beloved of all people for me, commits a theft, I will cut off her hand."

No one had the right of domineering, commanding, and oppressing others. The people enjoyed the utmost freedom outside the domain of the law (certainly freedom against law bears no meaning not only in Islam but also in any other social order).

This freedom and social justice is stated by the Almighty Allah in introducing His Holy Prophet (SA).

> *"Those who follow the Messenger Prophet, the Ummi, whom they find written down with them in the Tawrat and the Injl, (who) enjoins them good and forbids them evil, and makes lawful to them the good things and makes unlawful to them impure things, and removes from them their burden and the shackles which were upon them; so (as for) those who believe in him and honour him and help him, and follow the light which has been sent down with him, these it is that are successful. Say: 'O people! Surely I am the Messenger of Allah to you all'..(7:157-158)."*

This is why the Holy Prophet (SA) desired no privileges for himself in his life. One could never tell that the Holy Prophet (SA) differentiated from other people someone having a former acquaintance with him. The Holy Prophet (SA) managed the chores of the house, welcomed everyone in person, and listened to those who turned to him out of need. He did not sit in the position and seat of honour. He did not have any means of riding and official protocol for moving from one place to another. If he earned some money, he would give to the needy over and above his necessary expenses.

At times, he gave even his least available money to the needy and lived with hunger. He always lived like the needy and associated with them. He did not display the slightest procrastination in granting the rights of the people, but he used the maximum connivance and condonation for his personal rights. When the dignitaries of Quraysh were brought before him after the conquest of Mecca, he did not display the slightest harshness and pardoned them all, although they had treated him most cruelly before the Hijrah and had even provocated sedition after the Hijrah.

In his humane ethics and virtues, the Holy Prophet (SA) was conspicuously recognized among friends and foes. He was matchless in sociability, cheerfulness, forbearance, modesty, soberness, and dignity. As the Holy Quran has praised his munificent conduct by a statement:

> *"And most surely you conform (yourself) to sublime morality (68:4)."*

He took the lead in greeting those whom he met, even women, children, and subordinates. One of his friends asked his permission to bow down, i.e., to prostrate in front of him. The Holy Prophet (SA) stated: "What do you mean? These are the customs of Caesar and Casra. And I am for prophecy and servitude".

Ever since he was appointed to a mission by Allah to propagate the religion and to guide and lead the people, the Holy Prophet (SA) did not neglect his duty for a moment and did not refrain from his untiring efforts. Thirteen years before the Hijrah, when he was in Mecca although he faced unbearable difficulties caused by the Arab polytheists, the Holy Prophet (SA) was constantly engaged in the worship of Allah and the propagation of the religion of Allah. During the ten years after Hijrah, the Holy Prophet (SA) conveyed the teachings of religion and the laws of Islam with its amazing enormity to the people, despite the ever-increasing troubles made by the enemies of religion and the hindrances caused by the Jews and munafiqin pretending to be Muslims. The Holy Prophet (SA) also fought more than eighty battles with the enemies of Islam.

In addition to handling the affairs of the Islamic society which at that time included the whole Arabian Peninsula, the Holy Prophet (SA) personally looked into the complaints and minor requirements of people without a doorkeeper and chamberlain attending on him.

With regard to the bravery and courage of the Holy Prophet (SA), it suffices to say that with his rightful invitation, he rose all alone against the world of that time which ruled the people with nothing other than coercion and injustice. All the tortures and sufferings inflicted on him by the oppressors never produced weakness and disappointment in him. He never retreated in any battle.

The Holy Prophet (SA) kept himself very clean and neat. He considered cleanliness and neatness as a sign of faith.

"Cleanliness is a part of the belief."

In addition to the cleanliness and neatness of his clothes and body, the Holy Prophet (SA) was well-dressed and well-behaved also. Whenever he wanted to leave the house, he would set out in the best outward appearance. He particularly liked to use perfumes.

He never changed his disposition in the course of his life. His life came to an end with the same modesty and humbleness. Although he had such a valuable position, he never gave preference to himself to demonstrate his social value.

During his lifetime, the Holy Prophet (SA) never insulted anyone and never used empty remarks. He never laughed boisterously and never performed disrespectful and worthless deeds. He was highly interested in thinking and reflection. He listened to the remarks of every afflicted person and the complaints of every protestor and then replied. He never interrupted the speech of others and never marred the freedom of thought; however, he clarified their mistakes and eased their discomfort.

The Holy Prophet (SA) was very kind and tenderhearted and was always saddened by sufferings; nevertheless, he did not waver in punishing the criminals and the wicked and did not discriminate between the individuals in carrying out the divine laws.

Once a Jew and a Muslim were accused of a theft in the house of one of the Ansar. In this connection, a great crowd of Ansar went to the Holy Prophet (SA) and insisted that the Jew be punished for the sake of the prestige of the Muslims, specifically the Ansar and keeping in view the overt enmity of the Jews. Since the Holy Prophet (SA) discovered the truth contrary to what they had demanded, he openly supported the Jew and punished that Muslim man.

Amidst the throes of the Battle of Badr, when the Holy Prophet (SA) was personally organizing the arrays of the division, he saw a fighter standing a little bit ahead of the others. The Holy Prophet (SA) pressed his stick at the belly of the man to move him back a little and get him in line with others. The fighter said, "O, Messenger of Allah! I swear by Allah that my stomach is hurt and I should go for qisas (Islamic reprisal)". Giving the stick to the man, the Holy Prophet (SA) pushed his dress aside from his stomach and said, "Go for qisas". The man ran towards the Holy Prophet (SA), kissed his stomach, and said, "I know that 1 will be killed today and I wanted to touch your holy body". Then he attacked the enemy and stroke with his sword until he was martyred.

The Holy Prophet (SA) always patronized the weak and the oppressed and urged his friends to inform him of the exigency of the needy and of the complaints of the weak and not to procrastinate in this regard.

It is related that the Holy Prophet's (SA) last words were a recommendation to the people regarding the slaves and women, after which he ceased speaking and passed away.

Peace be upon him and his holy family.

Bibliography

Abbas Hashmi : *Rasul (PBUH)*, Adam Pub., New Delhi, 2001.

Abdali, M.R. : *Scientific Thought in Islam*, Pious Publications, Hyderabad, 2001.

Abdul Qadir : *Criminal Law of Islam*, Kitab Bhavan, New Delhi, 1999.

Abdul, H.S.: *The Life of Muhammad (PBUH)*, Islamic Pub., New Delhi, 1997.

Abdullah Enan : *Decisive Moments in the History of Islam*, Islamic Book Company, Delhi, 1996.

Adil, H. M. : *Letters of Hadrat Usman Ghani (R.A.A.)*, Kitab Bhavan, New Delhi, 1992

Ahmad, Ilyas : *Sovereignty, Islamic and Modern*, Allies Book Corporation, Karachi, 1965.

Ahmad, Imtiaz : *Ritual and Religion among Muslims in India*, Manohar Publishers, New Delhi, 1984.

Ahmed, Hasanuddin : *Islamic Economics*, Goodword Books Pvt. Ltd., New Delhi, 1991.

Ali, Ameer : *Muhammadan Law*, Kitab Bhavan, New Delhi, 1986.

Arnold, T. W. : *The Caliphate*, Routledge & Kegan Paul Ltd., London, 1965.

Asghar, Ali : *Islam : Women and Gender Justice*, Gyan Books Pvt. Ltd., New Delhi, 2001.

Ataur-Rahim : *Jesus a Prophet of Islam*, Idara Ishaat-e-Diniyat Pvt. Ltd, New Delhi, 1995.

Azam, Zaki : *The Ideas of Arab Nationalism*, Cornell University Press, New York, 1956.

Baral, Raj : *Regional Migrations : Ethnicity and Security*, Popular Prakashan, Bombay, 1995.

Beverly, Milton : *Islam and Politics in the Contemporary World*, Blackwell, New York, 1987.

Bosworth, C.E. : *The Legacy of Islam*, Oxford University Press, New York, 1979.

Carl, W. : *Teaching of Sufism*, Deep & Deep, New Delhi, 2000.

Charles Howard : *The Constitutionalism*, Great Seal Books, New York, 1947.

Chave F. : *Islamic Histroriography*, Cambridge University press, New York, 1990.

Daniel, N.A. : *Islam and the West : the Making of an Image*, University Press, Edinburgh, 1962.

De, Laet : *The Political Systems of Empire*, Oxford, New York, 1963.

Edwin, Elliot : *Worship in Islam*, University of Madras, Madras, 1925.

Fauzi M. : *The Islamic State : a Study in Traditional Politics*, Oxford, New York, 1967.

Gardet, Louis : *Mystique Musulmane*, Allen & Co., Paris, 1961.

Gellner, E. : *Post-Traditional Forms in Islam : the Turf and Trade*, Oxford, New York, 1982.

Ghulam Sarwar : *Muhammad (PBUH) the Holy Prophet*, Dar-ul Ishaat, Karachi, 1997.

Gibb, H.A.R : *Studies in the Civilization of Islam*, Beacon Press, Boston,1962.

Glubb : *The Story of Arab Legion*, Feroz Pub., Lahore, 2000.

Gulzar Ahmed : *The Prophets (PBUH) Concept of War*, Aziz Pub., Islamabad, 2000.

Herbert, Friedman : *The Amazing Universe*, National Geographic Society, Washington D.C., 1980.

Husaini, S.A.Q : *The Pantheistic Monism of Ibn al-Arabi*, Feroz Pub., Lahore, 1970.

Hussain, Ahanger : *Customary Succession among Muslims*, Uppal Publishibng House, New Delhi, 1997.

Hussain, M. : *Imam Abu Hanifah : Life and Work*, Kitab Bhavan, New Delhi, 2001.

Hussain, S. : *Human Rights in Islam*, Kitab Bhavan, New Delhi, 2001.

Ikbal Ali : *Islamic Sufism,* Idarah-I-Adbiyat-I-Delhi, Delhi, 1979.

Ikram, S.M. : *Muslim Civilization in India,* Oxford, New York, 1981.

Jafar Sharif : *Islam in India,* Atlantic Publishers, New Delhi, 1999.

Jafar, Sharif : *Islam in India,* Oxford, New Delhi, 1972.

James, Piscarton : *Islam in the World of National States,* Macmillan, New York, 1982.

Jean-Baptiste : *Travels in India,* W.Crooke, London, 1925.

Jha, V. : *Indian Society: Historical Probings,* Rawat Pub., Delhi, 1974.

John L. Esposite : *Islam in Transition,* Oxford, New York, 1969.

John Surowiecki : *The Pulse of the Planet,* Crown Publishers, U.S.A. 1972.

Kalim Bahadur : *Domestic Conflicts in South Asia,* South Asia Publishers, New Delhi, 1986.

Kalim, M. Siddiq : *Studies in Pakistan Culture : an International Perspective,* Manohar Publications, New Delhi, 1993.

Karnal, A. : *Islam : Today and Tomorrow,* Deep & Deep Pub., New Delhi, 1989.

Katharine, Scarfe : *Perception of the Islamic Word,* Cambridge University Press, New Delhi, 1992.

Kaur, R. : *Islamic Co-operation and Unity,* Deep & Deep Publications, New Delhi, 1993.

Kazim Munishi : *Alamgir-Nama,* A.B.C. & Co., Calcutta, 1865.

Khaduri, M. : *War and Peace in the Law of Islam,* Hopkins Press, Baltimore, 1955.

Landau, R. : *The Philosophy of the Ibn Arabi,* Century Pub., London, 1959.

Lewis, Richards : *Universe,* Harmony Books, New York, 1973.

Mac, Closky : *Pacts for Peace,* New Century Pub., London, 1980.

Margery Milne : *The Nature of Life,* Crown Publishers, New York, 1995.

Mathew, Thomas : *Political Economy of Etimic Conflict,* School of International Studies, Jawaharlal Nehru University, New Delhi, 2003.

Mayne, P. : *Saints of Sind,* New Century Pub., London, 1965.

Meer, Ali : *Observations on the Musulmauns of India,* Macmillan & Co., London, 1832.

Mohiuddin, Ahmad : *Saiyid Ahmad Shahid,* Modern Pub., Lucknow, 1975.

Moreland, W.H. : *From Akbar to Aurangzeb,* MacMillan & Co., London, 1923.

Mualana, Taqi : *Fundamentals of Ijtihad,* Idaara-I-Adabiyat, Delhi, 1986.

Muhammad, Asad : *Islam at the Crossroads,* Kitab Bhavan, New Delhi, 2003.

Murtaza, G. : *Judicial System of Islam,* Kitab Bhavan, New Delhi, 1994.

Muslehuddin, M. : *Islam : its Political System,* Kitab Bhavan, New Delhi, 1999.

Nabith, A. : *The Foundations of the Articles of Faith,* Feroz Pub., Lahore, 1963.

Nicholson, R.A. : *Studies in Islamic Mysticism,* Cambridge, New York, 1967.

Nikki, R. : *Saints and Sufis, Muslim Religious Institutions since 1500,* University of California Press, California, 1972.

Noomi, Kurtha : *Prisoners of War and War Crimes,* Deep Publications, Lacknow, 1980.

Padwick, C.E. : *Muslim Devotions,* MacMillan & Co., London, 1960.

Palamer, E.H. : *The Quran,* Atlantic Publishers, New Delhi, 1996.

Peter Lambron Wilson : *Traditional Modes of Contemplation and Action,* University Press, Tehran, 1977.

Qazi A. Qadir : *The Changing World of Islam,* Royal Pub., Lahore, 1992.

Richards, J.F. : *Mughal Administration in Golkonda,* Oxford, New York, 1975.

Robert, D. : *Exploring our Living Planet,* National Geographic Society, Washington, 1989.

Rodinson, Maxime : *Islam and Capitalism,* Penguin, London,1974.

Rosenthal, E.I.J. : *Islam in the Modern National State,* University Press, Cambridge,1965.

Sardar, Ziauddin : *The Future of Muslim Civilization,* Croom Helm, London, 1979.

Sarton, George : *Introduction to the History of Science,* Carnegie Institute, Washington, 1950

Saxena, K.P. : *Human Rights: Perspective and Challenges,* Lancers Books, New Delhi, 1996.

Saxena, V. K. : *Muslims and the Indian National Congress,* Discovery Publishing House, New Delhi, 1985.

Scarman, Leslie : *Law : the New Dimensions,* Stevens and Sons, London, 1974.

Schacht, J. : *The Origins of Muhammadan Jurisprudence,* Clarendon Press, Oxford, 1953.

Schwartz, E. : *Science and Civilization in Islam,* Cambridge, London, 1966.

Seervai, H. : *Constitutional Law of India,* N.M. Tripathi & Co., Bombay, 1967.

Setalvad : *War and Civil Liberties,* Feroz Pub., Lahore, 1992.

Sharif, M. : *Islamic Social Framework,* Islamic Book Foundation, Dacca, 1980.

Sharma, S.R. : *Women's Education in Ancient and Muslim Period,* Discovery Publishing House, New Delhi, 1996.

Siddiqi, M.Z. : *Hadith Literature,* Deepali Pub., Calcutta, 1961.

Singh, Nagendar : *Human Rights and International Cooperation,* S. Chand & Co., New Delhi, 1969.

Sir William : *The Caliphate, its Rise, Decline and Fall,* Oxford, Edinburgh, 1915.

Sir, Richard : *Sind and Races that Inhabit the Valley of the Indus,* Allen & Unwin, London, 1851.

Sir, Thomas : *The Caliphate,* MacMillan, London, 1965.

Smith, M. : *An Early Mystic of Baghdad,* Cambridge, New York, 1920.

Smith, M.: *The Mystic and her Fellow Saints in Islam,* Cambridge, London, 1929.

Smith, W. C. : *Modern Islam in India : a Social Analysis,* Manohar Publishers, New Delhi, 1985.

Suhrawardi, Umar : *Awarif al Maarif bin Muhammad*, Sheikh Ghulam Shahabuddin Ali & Sons, Lahore, 1964.

Syed Husain : *Three Muslim Sages*, Cambridge, New York, 1959.

Syed, Amir Ali : *The Spirit of Islam,* Royal Pub.,Lahore, 1979.

Taqi Muhammad : *An Introduction to Islamic Finance,* Idara Ishaat-e-Diniyat Pvt. Ltd., New Delhi, 1999.

Thompson, H.R. : *Sculptures and Inscriptions of Darius the Great on the Rock of Behistan,* Oxford, London, 1907.

Valliuddin, Mir : *The Quranic Sufism,* Motilal Banarsi Das Publishers, New Delhi, 1989.

Wahed, Husain : *Administration of Justice during the Muslim Rule in India,* Ashish Publishing House, New Delhi, 1977.

Waheed, Akhtar : *Sufi Approach to the Problem of Alienation,* Wilson & Co., New Delhi, 1975.

Waheed, Mirza : *The Life and Works of Amir Khusrau,* Kaveri Pub., Calcutta, 1935.

Walker, Benjamin : *Foundation of Islam : the Making of World Faith,* Rupa & Co., New Delhi, 2001.

Watt, M. : *The Faith and Practice of Al-Ghazzali,* MacMillan & Co., London, 1953.

Watt, W.M. : *Islam and the Integration of Society,* Routledge, London, 1961.

Yazbeck, Haddad : *Islamic Values in the United States,* Oxford, New York, 1997.

Yezbeck Haddad : *Islamic Values in the United States,* Oxford, New York, 1999.

Zafeeruddin, M.M. : *System of Modesty and Chastity in Islam,* Idara Ishaat-e-Diniyat Pvt. Ltd, New Delhi, 1995.

Zahid, Malik : *Subjects of Quran,* Kitab Bhavan, New Delhi, 1998.

Zahurul Hasan : *Tarikb-i-Sufiya-i-Gujarat,* Jamil Academy, Ahmadabad, 1981.

Zaydan, Jurji : *Umayyads and Abbasides,* Luzac & Co., London,1907.

Index

J

K

L

M

N

O

P

Q

R

□□□